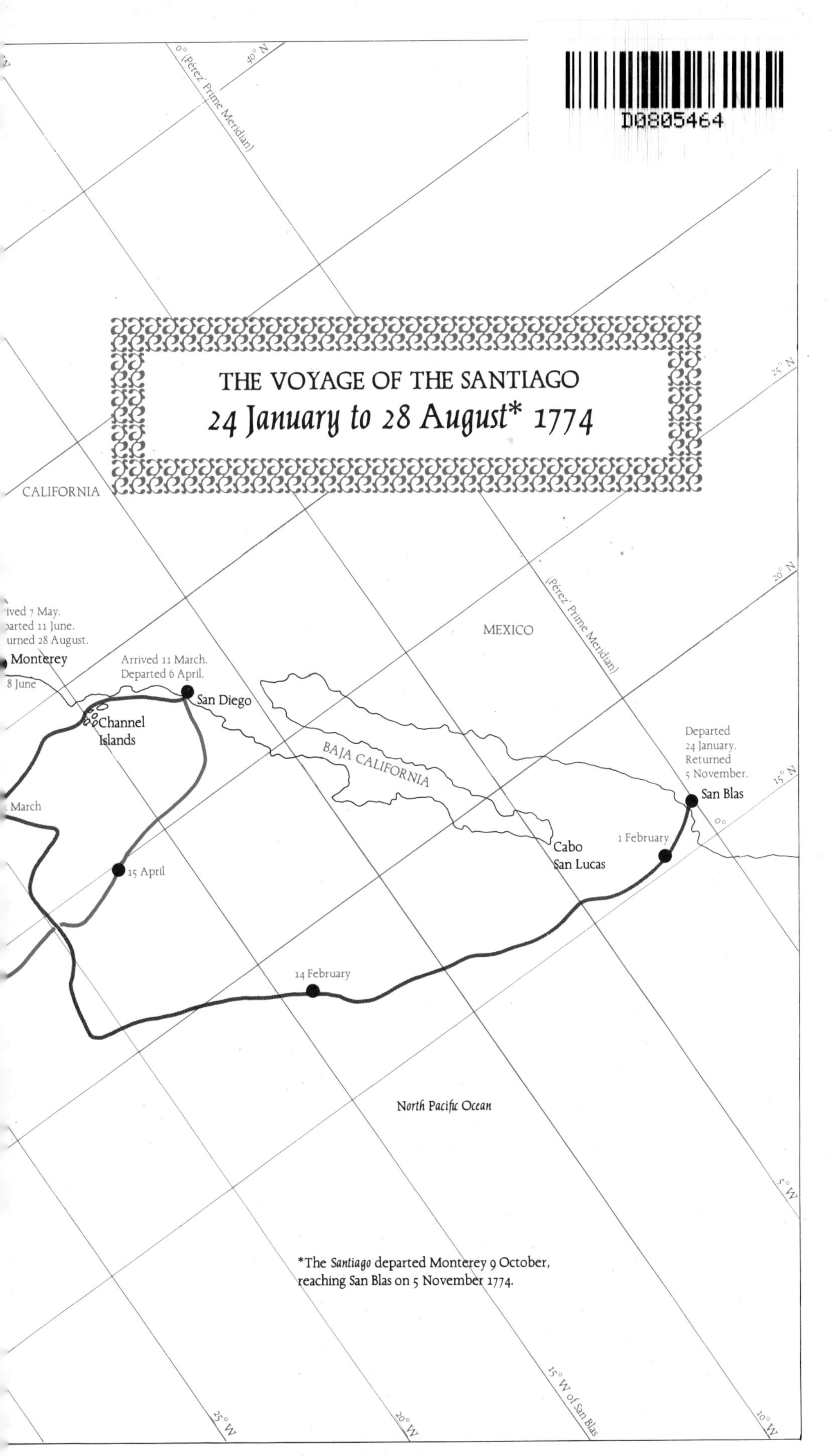
THE VOYAGE OF THE SANTIAGO
24 January to 28 August* 1774
CALIFORNIA
MEXICO
(Pérez' Prime Meridian)
0° (Pérez' Prime Meridian)
40° N
25° N
20° N
15° N
ived 7 May.
parted 11 June.
urned 28 August.
Monterey
8 June
Arrived 11 March.
Departed 6 April.
San Diego
Channel
Islands
BAJA CALIFORNIA
Departed
24 January.
Returned
5 November.
San Blas
0°
1 February
Cabo
San Lucas
March
15 April
14 February
North Pacific Ocean
5° W
*The Santiago departed Monterey 9 October, reaching San Blas on 5 November 1774.
25° W
20° W
15° W of San Blas
10° W

This copy of

JUAN PÉREZ ON THE NORTHWEST COAST

is for
William Mathers
with many thanks
for the Concepción Project
publications.

Herbert K. Beals

26 October 1994

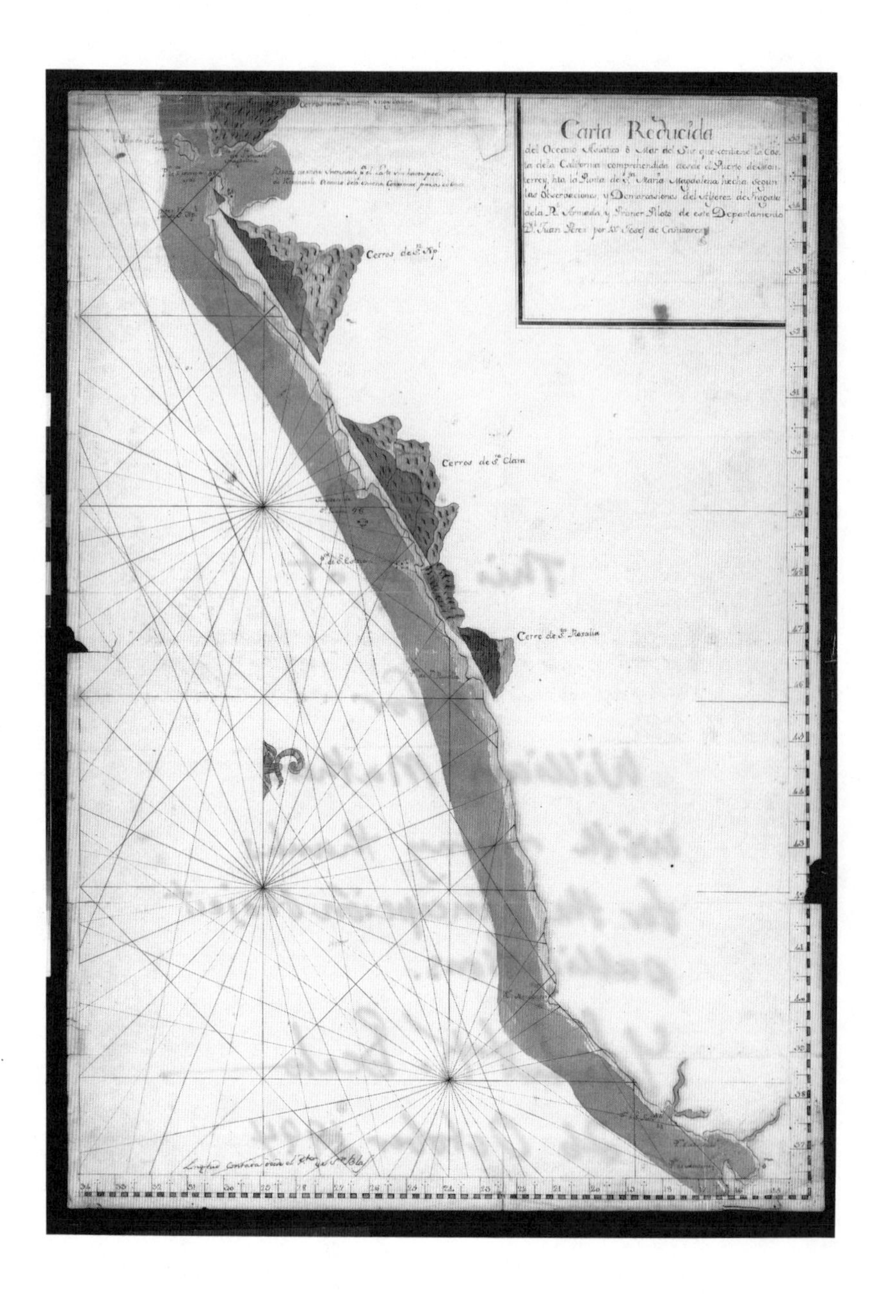

THIS MAP, recently discovered in the U.S. National Archives, depicts discoveries of the Pérez expedition of 1774. Its title reads: "*Small-scale Map* of the Asiatic Ocean or South Sea, which encompasses the entire coast of California from Puerto de Monterey up to Punta de Santa Magdalena, prepared in accordance with the observations and surveys of Ensign, Frigate Grade, and Pilot First Class of the Royal Navy, Department of San Blas, Don Juan Pérez, by Don Josef de Cañizarez." (*Courtesy, U.S. National Archives, Washington,* D.C.)

JUAN PÉREZ

ON THE NORTHWEST COAST

Six Documents of His Expedition in 1774

Translation & Annotation by

HERBERT K. BEALS

OREGON HISTORICAL SOCIETY PRESS

Designed and produced by the Oregon Historical Society Press.

The paper used in this publication meets the minimum requirements of American National Standard for Information Sciences—Permanence of Paper for Printed Library Materials, ANSI Z39.48–1984.

Library of Congress Cataloging-in-Publication Data

Juan Pérez on the Northwest coast: six documents of his expedition in 1774 / translation and annotation by Herbert K. Beals.

p. cm.—(North Pacific studies; no. 12)

Bibliography: p.

Includes index.

Contents: Two letters, Juan Pérez to Viceroy Bucareli—Juan Pérez's "Diario," 11 June to 28 August—

Extract from Esteban José Martínez's "Diario," 20–21 July 1774—Francisco Mourelle's narrative of the Pérez voyage, 25 January to 5 November 1774—"Tabla diaria," 24 January to 3 November 1774.

1. Northwest Coast of North America—Discovery and exploration. 2. Spaniards—Northwest Coast of North America—History—18th century. 3. Spain—Exploring expeditions. 4. Pérez, Juan, d. 1775—Journeys—Northwest Coast of North America. I. Beals, H.K. (Herbert Kyle), 1934- . II. Series.

F851.5.J83 1989 979.5-dc19 87–36883

ISBN 0–87595–189–9

1200 SW Park Avenue, Portland, Oregon 97205

Printed in the United States of America.

To the memory of my parents,
James H. & Mae A. Beals,
who set me on course

THE PRODUCTION OF THIS PUBLICATION was made possible by funds provided by the United States Information Agency, Division of Private Sector Programs.

In 1988 the importance of the Oregon Historical Society's North Pacific Studies program was recognized at the Federal level. With the support of Senators Mark O. Hatfield and Robert Packwood, Congressman Les AuCoin and then USIA Director Charles Z. Wick, legislation was signed by President Ronald Reagan establishing the North Pacific Studies Center in the Oregon Historical Center in Portland, as an integral department of the Oregon Historical Society.

The current funding support has been made possible through the good offices of USIA Director Mr. Bruce S. Gelb, and Dr. Raymond H. Harvey, Chief, Division of Private Sector Programs.

CONTENTS

SIX DOCUMENTS OF THE 1774 PÉREZ VOYAGE

APPENDICES

ILLUSTRATIONS

The fair breeze blew, the white foam flew,
The furrow followed free;
We were the first that ever burst
Into that silent sea.

Samuel Taylor Coleridge,
The Rime of the Ancient Mariner

. . . no es posible poder explicar
cuanto no[s] ha acaecido
con los malos tiempos.
Dios me conceda buenos temporales.

. . . it is impossible to be able to explain
all that has befallen [us]
due to the bad weather.
God grant me good weather.

Juan Pérez, *21 July 1774*

FOREWORD

Wind-filled sails, swaying masts and creaking timbers replaced cross and sword as symbols of Spanish expansion in the twilight era of colonization. During a score of years the Spanish Royal Navy in North America carried out the greatest series of maritime explorations of the colonial period. In 1769, Spain occupied California and five years later began planned expansion northward. In the succeeding two decades Spain's imperial colors were seen frequently along the North Pacific Coast. One motive for these exploratory efforts was to find the Northwest Passage, called by the Spaniards the Strait of Anian. Perhaps equally important was the desire to reconnoiter the entire coast and not find the fabled waterway. Lack of its existence might serve Spanish interests more than discovery followed by a contest for control.

Other motives for northward reconnaissance were fears of encroachment of rival European powers. Russian interests from not-far-distant Siberia were reported. England had earlier demonstrated a potential, though as yet unrealized, capacity to become a challenge. But no competitor had all the assets of late-eighteenth-century Spain, for it had a naval base and shipbuilding facility at San Blas in Nayarit near the mouth of the Rio Santiago (in present-day Mexico). Some experienced mariners had been assigned there and many more from the homeland were soon to follow.

These mariners were what made Spanish exploration of the Pacific Coast unique. Discoveries were carried out exclusively by Spain's navy. Thousands of man-hours of sailing, taking bearings, making celestial observations, contacting local Indians, and taking ceremonial possession were spent without evident economic motivation and almost without civilian participation. It was a last burst of expansion unparalleled not only in Spain's long history but also in the American experience of other European powers. Never before, and never again, would any area of the earth be under such close scrutiny by as many exploratory expeditions in such a brief period.

Not only did Spain focus on a remote coast, but it also sent some of its most promising mariners to carry out the dual naval mission of exploration and occupation. Veterans of the North Pacific campaigns lived to become some of Spain's most distinguished senior officers. Under normal circumstances this should have been enough to make events of those days live brightly in historic memory.

Unfortunately for the participants in the unfolding drama, Spain played a strong but losing hand. Victors are remembered much more than losers, with the result that even in Spain only minimal attention has been given to the last years of empire.

It is into this framework of international and regional events that Herbert Beals has woven the story of the first of many Spanish exploratory efforts. The initial expedition was atypical. Because it was the first sortie, and because naval academy graduates were not yet available, the expedition of 1774 was entrusted to a mariner who began his career in the pilotage corps. He was Juan Pérez, whose life is the least well documented of a bevy of contemporary naval officers. For Pérez, who was not trained at the academy, promotion came slowly, his naval commission being the culmination of a long career rather than the beginning. Beals has brought together the little available information concerning this pioneer Northwest Coast explorer. Scarce as references are to Juan Pérez in surviving documentation, Beals in his introduction and with his careful translation has permitted the reader a better look at the former pilot. The tone of the Pérez original narrative is preserved most satisfactorily, and from it one sees a prudent mariner who wrote a careful journal based on his log. There is no suggestion that he added any literary touches to make it more colorful. If anything, Pérez was more succinct than we would like, especially since he was keeping the official account. Two centuries later we might wish for fewer details of sailing, of weather conditions, and of course changes.

The importance of Pérez's account stems both from what he did and what he failed to do. He was ordered to go into unfamiliar northern waters. From what we know of his previous experience, he had been on the Acapulco-Manila-Acapulco galleon run, which on its return route sailed in North Pacific waters, but far out at sea. The 1774 expedition, coming from the opposite direction, was to follow the coast into the great unknown with only vague guidance from untrustworthy, fanciful maps. Pérez's selection was an honor and a great responsibility, and he acted circumspectly. To risk needless danger in a lone vessel would have been to court disaster and to sail into oblivion.

A major criticism was that during the cruise Pérez failed to go ashore and establish sovereignty by the oft-repeated and long-utilized symbolic act of possession. In retrospect, Pérez ought to have done so. However, his failure did not stop Spain from laying claim on the basis of prior discovery, nor did it at a much later time prevent the United States from asserting claim to the area up to 54°40′ as successors in interest to Spain's discoveries. Clearly United States pretensions were based on Pérez's 1774 exploration, translated documents of which are herein made available.

These are key documents of regional history, of international relations, and of geographical discovery. Although Pérez's account is properly the first important document in a series of key journals, it has been preceded in publication by *For Honor and Country: The Diary of Bruno de Hezeta*, also brought out by Beals and the Oregon Historical Society. The favorable reception of the Hezeta account is a stimulus for the present publication, the two being important contributions in bringing these earliest events of regional history to increasing public attention and interest.

Donald C. Cutter
Professor Emeritus of History
University of New Mexico
Albuquerque

PREFACE

In the summer of 1790, the British and Spanish nations hovered briefly and precariously on the brink of war. The two colonial powers had often found themselves on opposing sides since the early sixteenth century, when England's Henry VIII broke with the Roman Catholic church over his marriage to Anne Boleyn. This new crisis in the waning years of the eighteenth century could boast no such romantic cause, having grown out of a territorial dispute in July 1789 between two hitherto obscure naval officers named James Colnett and Esteban José Martínez. The subject of their confrontation was a harbor on the Pacific side of North America, known to the English as Nootka Sound, to the Spanish as Surgidero de San Lorenzo, or San Lorenzo de Nutka. At issue were the rights of both parties to its use.

Although it was on the west coast of Vancouver Island, half a world away from Europe, the harbor had already attained minor fame as a result of Captain James Cook's well-publicized, month-long sojourn there in the spring of 1778. Believing that Cook's visit there had been the first such by Europeans, Colnett and others of his countrymen (not to mention some of their recently rebellious Yankee brethren) had confidently used Nootka's commodious harbor as a base for their fur-trading activities. However, when ordered by Martínez, in the name of King Carlos IV of Spain, to leave Nootka Sound forthwith, Colnett soon learned that the Spanish had quite another perspective on the matter. On the basis of a treaty signed nearly three hundred years earlier and sanctioned by the papacy, dividing the so-called uncivilized and unchristianized world between Spain and Portugal, the Spanish believed they had exclusive rights to the place. Lest

Colnett should doubt this, Martínez was quick to point out that Spanish mariners had been at Nootka some four years before Cook—to the truth of which he, Martínez, could personally attest, for he had been the pilot and second officer in command of the very ship that had accomplished the feat.

Colnett's stubborn refusal to comply with the Spaniard's orders was met with equal tenacity on the part of Martínez, who thereupon ordered Colnett's ship, the snow *Argonaut*, seized, and its officers and men arrested as trespassers, clapped in irons and sent unceremoniously off as prisoners to the Spanish naval base at San Blas on the west coast of Mexico.

Their captivity, however, was not lengthy. On 14 July 1789, France was plunged into a revolutionary upheaval with the storming of the Bastille in Paris. Spain could therefore expect no French help in a war with Britain, and thus the crisis that arose unexpectedly over a harbor in a remote corner of the North Pacific subsided into diplomatic negotiations between London and Madrid. These succeeded in averting armed conflict. Furthermore, the Nootka Convention of 1790, being more or less favorable to the British position, effectively sounded the death knell for Spanish claims of exclusive sovereignty on America's Northwest Coast.

That Colnett knew nothing of an earlier Spanish presence at Nootka Sound was partly because of Madrid's reluctance to announce details of the explorations of its mariners in the area. The Spanish crown had thereby hoped to discourage the interest of other nations in the region; instead, it was largely successful in weakening the rights that might have ensued from well-publicized discoveries or possession-taking ceremonies by its explorers. The policy also failed to reckon with the enthusiasm—some might say avarice—with which other countries capitalized on the much-touted discovery by Cook's seamen that fortunes could be made selling Northwest Coast sea-otter pelts to the Chinese at Canton.

This book offers a selection of hitherto unpublished documents, annotated and translated into English, describing the voyage of 1774 in which Esteban José Martínez was a participant. More than two centuries have elapsed since the frigate *Santiago*, under the command of a Majorcan-born ensign of Spain's *Real Armada* (Royal Navy) named Juan Pérez,* left Mon-

*Sources, mostly secondary, give his full name as Juan Josef Pérez Hernández. The truth of this, however, has been challenged by historian Donald C. Cutter, who suggests that it was more likely Juan Pérez Millán.

terey Bay early in June 1774. Sailing without the benefit of a consort vessel, the expedition nevertheless succeeded in making the first documented European reconnaissance of the coasts of present-day British Columbia, Oregon and Washington, including the first direct contacts with native peoples of the region. Some two decades later, the English poet Samuel Taylor Coleridge, writing in his "Rime of the Ancient Mariner" of a fictional voyage elsewhere in the Pacific, would say of its seamen that they "were the first that ever burst/ Into that silent sea." Excepting Northwest Coast natives with their marvelous seagoing cedar canoes, as much can surely be said of the officers and men of the *Santiago* in 1774.

Adverse weather and bad luck, however, mixed with an unwillingness to expose his ship and crew to what he considered unacceptable risks, prevented Pérez from achieving many—if not most—of the detailed objectives the viceroy of New Spain had expected of him. Nevertheless, the voyage remains a pioneering venture that paved the way for other Hispanic mariners, perhaps more daring, zealous or lucky, who came later and enjoyed greater success. As Pérez himself wrote to the viceroy in Mexico City, reflecting on the voyage's outcome: ". . . whether or not it is the will of God or that such success is reserved for someone else, the fact is that the way is opened and recorded for others who may be worthy of sailing it with better fortune."

ACKNOWLEDGMENTS

In my endeavor to bring these documents of Pérez's voyage of 1774 to print in English-language versions, certain persons and institutions have been most helpful. I begin by acknowledging my continuing debt to Thomas Vaughan, Oregon Historical Society executive director, and his wife, E.A.P. Crownhart-Vaughan, whose encouragement and inspiration have been unfailing. Without their earlier efforts to assemble a microfilm collection of archival materials concerning Spanish exploration of the Northwest Coast, my task would have been several times greater, if not impossible. The many documents they uncovered in those repositories of history, the Archivo General de la Nación (Mexico City) and the Archivo General de Indias (Seville), are all of interest and importance, some of them shedding significant new light on old problems.

Permission to use materials housed in the aforesaid archives in this publication has been generously granted by both. I am most appreciative of this, and of the assistance of Directora Rosario Parra Cala (Archivo General de Indias); and Dir.-Gen. Lic. Leonor Ortiz Monasterio and Lic. Doris Perlo Cohen (Archivo General de la Nación).

Initially, I planned to translate and annotate only Pérez's 1774 *Diario*, as I had Bruno de Hezeta's 1775 *Diario* in *For Honor and Country* (Volume 7 in the Oregon Historical Society's North Pacific Studies Series). But further probing of the archival materials suggested that additional documents might be properly included. In the summer of 1985, I traveled to The Bancroft Library at the University of California in Berkeley, where, with the kind assistance of its staff, I was able to find documents that had been acquired by Hubert Howe Bancroft and used by his specialist on the history of Hispanic exploration, Henry Lebbeus Oak, in writing their *History of the Northwest Coast*. My thanks are extended to The Bancroft Library, and in particular to Bonnie Hardwick and Peter E. Hanff, for their help in obtaining copies of these materials for use in the preparation of this book.

This is the second time I have had the pleasure of working with Bruce Taylor Hamilton, assistant director for publications of the Oregon Historical Society Press. He and his capable staff have been responsible for the design, editorial styling and production of this book. Their skills and talents, as well as their cheerful patience with my notorious proclivity for revision, are hereby recognized. The final text editing has been in the hands of Philippa Brunsman, whose good judgment and suggestions have helped ensure a more felicitous text.

In recent months the Oregon Historical Society Research Library has almost become my second home. And so, to Louis Flannery, assistant director for libraries, and his capable staff, many thanks for providing surroundings so favorable for the conduct of historical research and writing.

My interest in Pérez's account of his voyage in 1774 stemmed originally from a remark by Donald C. Cutter in his book *The California Coast*. Writing in the book's Preface, Professor Cutter discusses the obscurity that has befallen Juan Pérez, noting also that his "navigational diary . . . awaits detailed study." Perceiving that, after almost two decades, the challenge implicit in that remark had (as far as I was aware) not been acted upon, it seemed to me an appropriate and long overdue thing to be done. I am indebted to Professor Cutter for providing this scholarly prod, to say nothing of his other writings concerning the early Spanish presence on the Northwest Coast. His willingness to review the text of this work—during which he offered a number of helpful suggestions—and write a foreword for it is also hereby gratefully acknowledged.

I was eventually to learn of an unpublished English translation of Pérez's 1774 *Diario*, made in 1911 by a University of California graduate student named Margaret Olive Johnson. Her work, a Master of Letters thesis entitled "Spanish Exploration of the Pacific Coast by Juan Pérez in 1774," is preserved in that institution's General Library, and includes an unannotated translation of the Pérez *Diario*, with an introductory essay too brief to qualify as a detailed study. But having an independent translation against which I could compare my own was of no small value, particularly where the Spanish text was ambiguous or otherwise murky. Although I have differed with a number of Ms. Johnson's interpretations, her pioneering scholarship deserves recognition. I am grateful for the University of California General Library's willingness to provide me with a copy of the Johnson thesis.

As this work was going to press, I learned that two staff members of the Library of Congress, James Flatness and John Hebert of the Geography and Maps Division, had discovered a map in the U.S. National Archives stated to be "prepared in accordance with the observations and surveys of . . . Don Juan Pérez, by Don Josef Cañizarez." I am much indebted to these institutions and to Messrs. Flatness and Hebert for their help in bringing this map to my attention and for the opportunity to use it as the frontis of this book.

The sands of time have long since run out for the officers and men who joined Juan Pérez in sailing the frigate *Santiago* on its first important mission. So they have, also, for the expedition's nineteenth- and early-twentieth-century students and interpreters. Among them are Robert Greenhow, Hubert Howe Bancroft, Henry Oak, Henry Wagner, and Herbert Bolton, about whom the reader will encounter more. Whether supportive or critical of Pérez, their efforts laid the foundation for a work such as this volume, a fact this writer readily and thankfully acknowledges.

EDITORIAL PRINCIPLES

The several documents presented in this volume are important for their historical rather than their literary value. They are written in unembellished, often pedestrian styles, sometimes liberally laced with nautical terminology, and only sparingly salted with metaphor, simile or dramatic rhetorical flourishes. So, too, their respective renderings into English must be. Except for idiomatic expressions, or where strict adherence to the Spanish text would produce stilted, awkward or ungrammatical English, the translations are intended to be as literal as possible. Occasionally, a sentence may require the insertion of a word or phrase implied by the context, in which case it is enclosed in brackets.

Punctuation of the original Spanish texts is altogether unlike that of today, and thus no attempt has been made to follow it in the translations. Modern rules of accentuation and use of the diacritical mark called a tilde (~) have been applied to all Spanish words or proper names where appropriate. Ships' names are italicized, in keeping with current usage.

Certain terms of measurement, such as *braza* and *vara*, have been left untranslated because their comparable English terms, "fathom" and "yard," are known to have had specifically different values. For example, when Pérez writes "10 *brazas*," it is misleading to read "10 fathoms," because ten *brazas* are equivalent to nine and two-tenths English fathoms. Other such terms, however—*legua* or *milla*, for example—are translated into English ("league" and "mile") because they are less likely to mislead the reader. Although it is not certain what precise value Pérez assigned these terms, it is likely that his *leguas* and *millas* were sufficiently close to their usage in English as to warrant their translation. The reader is referred to the Glossary (p. 219) for additional details.

Pérez kept his *Diario* by making daily entries in navigational tables, which are mostly quantitative in nature, followed by a usually brief narration of the day's events. For readers unfamiliar with navigational terminology, these tables are likely to be more cryptic than informative, serving only to interrupt such flow as there is in the narrative. But the data they contain are of considerable usefulness insofar as they interpret nautical aspects of the voyage. To avoid impeding the narrative, while retaining their valuable information (as well as offering a better understanding of them for the general reader), the tables have been grouped in Appendix 3, preceded by an explanation of their contents (pp. 159–213).

In the treatment of Spanish place names, I have continued to use an approach similar to that in *For Honor and Country*. Such names are neither italicized nor translated into English (Punta de Pinos, for example, not *Punta de Pinos* or Point of Pines), except when given by Pérez to newly discovered landmarks. In these cases, the names are italicized and followed by their English equivalents in brackets (such as *Surgidero de San Lorenzo* [St. Lawrence's Roadstead]) when they first occur in the text. In subsequent instances only the italicized Spanish names are used. As far as possible, every effort has been made in the annotations to identify the correspondence between English or anglicized modern toponyms and their Hispanic antecedents.

Juan Pérez must have taken some delight in his command of nautical terminology—or jargon, as less admiring landsmen might put it. Compared with Bruno de Hezeta's *Diario* of the *Santiago*'s voyage in 1775, Pérez's writings are far more replete with nautical detail, with a proportionately greater resort to such vocabulary. Typically, on a routine day at sea, his narration of events is dominated by descriptions of wind and weather conditions, together with changes made in the ship's rigging or sail configuration. These are necessarily described in the words best understood by seamen of that era of sailing vessels. Today's reader will find some help (if not comfort) in consulting the following: Appendix 3 and its brief explanation of Pérez's Navigation Tables (pp. 159–61); a diagrammatic illustration of eighteenth-century Spanish compass directions (p. 221); the Glossary (p. 219); and a drawing illustrating the *Santiago*'s various sails and their names (p. 220).

Spelling of personal names in these documents (as elsewhere in the secondary literature) falls far short of satisfying the twentieth century's penchant for orthographic consistency. Pilot Martínez's two given names are cases in point, with at least five variations of his first name and three of his second, as follows:

Esteban José
Estevan Josef
Estéban Joseph
Estévan
Estephan

The accents on the penultimate syllables of "Estéban" and "Estévan" are unnecessary under present Spanish rules of accentuation, and thus have been discarded. Interchangeability of the letters "b" and "v" in Spanish usage is a somewhat different matter. In modern usage, "Esteban" is the preferred spelling, and in most cases is adhered to in this work. However, in some instances, such as in "Estevan Point" or in the documentary texts, Martínez is sometimes referred to as "Estevan" or "Estephan." These variant spellings have been allowed to stand. As for his second given name, its preferred form is "José" in modern Spanish usage. But where the variants "Josef" and "Joseph" occur in the documentary texts, they have also been allowed to remain. This principle is extended to all personal names in the documentary texts, with one exception explained below.

The spelling of Francisco Antonio Mourelle's surname is another troublesome matter. Its preferred form today is generally considered to be "Mourelle," which was usually—though by no means always—the way he spelled it. A variant spelling in which an "a" is substituted for the "o" is sometimes encountered in both the primary and secondary literature. Whether spelled with an "o" or an "a," in the Gallego language of Spain's northwesternmost province of Galicia, the two versions would be pronounced the same way. In any event, the currently preferred form has been adhered to in this work.

In the translated documentary texts, numbers have been spelled out or given as numerals, according to the Spanish texts.

As for the English-language documentary text in Appendix 4, "Extract from Joseph Ingraham's Letter to Martínez," a number of silent emendations have been made in punctuation to improve the text's readability. Minor grammatical or spelling errors, however, have been neither emended nor noted, since the author's intentions are substantially clear.

Finally, a few words are offered about the annotation of this work. For brief, essentially parenthetical comments, asterisks are used that refer the reader to a footnote on the same page of the text. Numbered notes, on the other hand, provide source references and more substantive or lengthy commentary, and are located near the end of this volume.

JUAN PÉREZ ON THE NORTHWEST COAST

EXPLORING THAT CHILLY, FOG-BOUND COAST

EXPLORING THAT CHILLY, FOG-BOUND COAST

The native people of British Columbia's Queen Charlotte Islands* met their first Europeans at 4:30 in the afternoon of 19 July 1774. Three Haida canoes, their occupants singing and spreading feathers on the water, approached a Spanish sailing vessel, its decks lined with curious and bemused sailors. Some of the natives stood up, extending their arms in the form of a cross and beckoning the Spaniards to come ashore. But the invitation could not then be accepted, and the occupants of the canoes, having been informed by signs that the strangers would try to visit them ashore next day, paddled away at 5 o'clock.

Thus, in the brief span of half an hour, the history of the Haida people changed abruptly and irrevocably. They were now "discovered" by men who had ventured forth from places so remote and foreign as to be scarcely imaginable. The reasons impelling those strangers to set out upon the mysterious ocean were, if anything, even less comprehensible. But the event, however little its import may have been understood, unfolded inexorably, propelling its participants into a veritable new age.

Scant attention has been given this and other similar events concerning early contacts between Europeans and natives on the Northwest Coast of North America. The region's remoteness from the centers of eighteenth-century European civilization was no doubt partly responsible. What is more, both Spain and Russia, the nations most active in first exploring that scenic, chilly and often fog-bound coast, did little to publicize the earliest activities and encounters of their respective countrymen there.

*As they are known today.

The story of the Spaniards who appeared off the Queen Charlotte Islands that July day in 1774 is of particular interest, since they were apparently the first Europeans to make direct contact and engage in trade with Northwest Coast Indians. Although, during the voyage of Aleksei Chirikov in 1741, Russian explorers may have fleetingly observed Tlingit Indians, that instance involved neither direct contact nor trade.[1] Whatever honors such a "first" may confer probably belong to Juan Pérez and the men who sailed under his command aboard the frigate *Santiago* in 1774.

Pérez's own account of these events and the navigational record of the *Santiago*'s voyage from Monterey northward to the Queen Charlotte Islands and back are contained in the *Diario*, or Diary, he kept. For all practical purposes, it begins the documentary history of the Pacific Northwest, containing as it does the earliest eyewitness descriptions of the Oregon Country and its native inhabitants.[2] Despite its significance, no English translation of Pérez's account has hitherto appeared in print, and only one such translation is known to have been made.[3]

The expedition's second officer, Esteban José Martínez, and its two chaplains, Fray Tomás de la Peña and Fray Juan Crespi, also kept accounts of the voyage. The chaplains' diaries have been published in English translations,[4] but to some extent depend on information obtained from the captain, especially for their nautical data. Thus Pérez's *Diario* (supplemented by Martínez's) is the primary source for navigational aspects of the voyage, and for this reason alone deserves more attention than it has received in the two centuries since it was originally committed to paper. Moreover, it is, after all, a record of the expedition from its commander's perspective—an especially important consideration because Pérez was later the subject of harsh criticism for his seeming timidity as an explorer. No informed judgment on this question is possible without careful examination of the account left by the central figure in these events, which effectively initiated European penetration of the Oregon Country.

THE NORTHWEST COAST BEFORE PÉREZ

If Pérez's voyage in 1774 was pivotal in Northwest Coast history, it was not without antecedents. Other navigators from Spain, Russia and Britain had been nibbling at this remote corner of the northeastern Pacific since at least the middle of the sixteenth century. In 1542 the viceroy of New Spain (Mexico), Antonio de Mendoza, ordered Juan Rodríguez Cabrillo to lead an expedition northward along what later Spanish explorers routinely called *la costa septentrional de Californias* (the northern coast of the Californias).

Also termed Alta or Nueva California (to distinguish it from Baja or Antigua California), its coastline, as then conceived by the Spanish, extended northward vaguely for an indefinite distance to wherever the North American West Coast eventually led—to Asia, to the North Atlantic, or even, by some great river or strait, into the heart of the continent.

The purposes of Cabrillo's expedition are clouded with a degree of uncertainty. Presumably the viceroy hoped that such a probe might reveal a waterway providing access to the interior of North America, where a fabulously wealthy place called Quivira was rumored to exist. Neither Quivira nor its wealth, however, had sufficient roots in reality to be found by even the most intrepid explorer. But Cabrillo (who did not survive the expedition) and his chief pilot, Bartolomé Ferrelo, did succeed in uncovering something of the truth about California's coastal geography as far north as the fortieth parallel (near today's Cape Mendocino). Moreover, Ferrelo and the crewmen of the expedition may well have been the first Europeans to glimpse sections of the southern Oregon coastline.[5]

With no fabulous cities discovered, and only vague hints of a great river on the coast, the viceroy had little inducement to renew such explorations from Mexico northward. Instead, twenty-two years later (in 1564), a trans-Pacific expedition was mounted, under the command of Miguel López de Legazpi, to secure a foothold in the Philippines, where access to China's riches seemed a better gamble. Trading between those islands and the nearby Asian mainland and New Spain hinged on establishing a reliable means of crossing the Pacific Ocean with large cargo vessels.

Although the westward passage, using the equitorial trade winds, had been more or less known since the time of Magellan's circumnavigation in 1521, the question of an eastward or return route was still unsolved when López de Legazpi set out. The expedition's *capitana* (flagship), the *San Pedro* (and apparently a smaller ship, the *San Lucas*, independently), provided the solution by returning to New Spain in 1565, following the westerlies across the North Pacific to Alta California and thence down the coast to Mexico. Discovery of the route—as momentous as anything in Iberian maritime annals—inaugurated a trans-Pacific trade, between the Spaniards' Philippine outpost at Manila and the splendid harbor at Acapulco on the Mexican coast, that was to continue for some two hundred and fifty years. The last of the Manila galleons, or *naos de China*, as they were called, did not put into port until 1815.[6]

The connection of the Manila–Acapulco trade with the Northwest Coast might seem only slight at best. But the courses the pilots set in crossing the North Pacific sometimes took them as high as the forty-second parallel (the latitude of the present California-Oregon border). There are even indications that at least one of the giant, lumbering vessels was blown off course and shipwrecked on the northern Oregon coast.[7] The need for harbors where Manila galleons in distress could be succored on the Alta California coast was thus a major reason for renewed exploration northward along the American West Coast. Other considerations, however, opposed such investigations.

Under a treaty signed in the Castilian town of Tordesillas on 7 June 1494, Spain had agreed with Portugal to confine its colonizing activities to lands west of a meridian three hundred and seventy leagues (one thousand one hundred and ten nautical miles) west of the Atlantic Ocean's Cape Verde Islands, while the Portuguese agreed to stay east of the line.[8] López de Legazpi's incursion in the Philippines might have been construed as violating the treaty, had the longitude of the Pacific extension of the Tordesillas meridian been known with more exactitude. Whatever the uncertainties when Spaniard and Portuguese met in the western Pacific, the treaty left no doubt as to who held sway in the remaining watery expanse of the Mar del Sur (or South Sea, as it was called in the sixteenth century). There, the Pacific seemed a virtual Spanish lake, whose waters washed shores (including those of the Northwest Coast) presumed to be reserved eventually and exclusively for Spanish colonies or exploitation. With the world thus comfortably divided between two of sixteenth-century Europe's principal maritime powers, the Spanish crown and its viceregal agents in New Spain were under no urgent compulsion to expand their knowledge of *la costa septentrional de Californias.*

Any complacency the Treaty of Tordesillas may have fostered in Spain's official circles was rudely shaken late in 1578, when a stocky, red-haired, English navigator named Francis Drake sailed defiantly into the Pacific. Passing from the South Atlantic through the strait Magellan had discovered more than half a century earlier, he moved north along the South and Central American west coasts, systematically raiding Spain's largely undefended settlements there, almost with impunity. His efforts were crowned with the capture of several Spanish ships, laden with silks, porcelains and other luxuries from the Orient and with gold and silver from American mines, intended for the purchase of more such goods. Drake's forays in the *Golden Hind* along North America's West Coast during the late spring and early summer of 1579 were to make Spain's claims of exclusivity in the area decidedly less secure than they had hitherto been.[9]

Accounts of Drake's sojourn on the Northwest and California coasts—or Nova Albion, as he called them collectively—and the voyage that took him there from Mexico have been endlessly studied and analyzed for clues as to exactly where the *Golden Hind* sailed. Unfortunately, the original journals and navigation logs have not survived, thereby rendering definitive conclusions about the voyage difficult to reach, and perpetuating one of maritime history's more durable mysteries.[10]

What is known with some certainty is that the *Golden Hind*, accompanied by a captured Spanish frigate, left the Mexican port of Guatulco on 16 April 1579,*[11] sailing directly into the Pacific some five hundred to six hundred leagues westward until a northing was gained. The ships then ascended to a point off the Northwest Coast between 42° and 48°N (latitudes that bracket the coasts of today's Oregon and Washington). Encountering unseasonably chilly weather, Drake perfunctorily searched for a rumored passage, known variously as the Strait of Anian or the Northwest Passage. Had it been found, it would have enabled him to return to England by way of the North Atlantic. However, heavy weather forced the two ships to seek shelter, and they cast anchor in "a bad bay, the best roade we could for the present meet with."[12] After a brief stay there, they steered southward along the coast until, on 17 June "a conuenient and fit harborough"[13] was found at a bay in the vicinity of latitude 38°N, where the *Golden Hind* was careened and repaired. Abandoning the frigate, on 23 July Drake and his men embarked upon a westward crossing of the Pacific, which eventually took them home to England.

Considerable evidence favors the view that Drake's second anchorage was at modern-day Drakes Bay, in the lee of Point Reyes (latitude 38°00′N), some twenty-five nautical miles northwest of today's Golden Gate. But identification of his earlier anchorage somewhere on the Northwest Coast has proven especially elusive. Opinions about its location have varied widely over the years; they now seem mainly to fall into three categories: South Cove, at Cape Arago (latitude 43°20′N), on the south-central Oregon coast; a cove or bay somewhere on the Washington or northern Oregon coasts between latitudes 44° and 48°30′N; a cove or bay somewhere on the southwestern coast of Vancouver Island between latitudes 48°30′ and 49°N.[14] The issue may never be settled conclusively, although partisans of various localities will no doubt continue to comb the meager

*Dates referring to Drake's expedition, and those of the Russians in the ensuing pages in this work, are reckoned by the Julian (Old Style) calendar.

evidence for clues supporting their respective theses. What can be reasonably affirmed is that Drake's *Golden Hind* (and its accompanying frigate) were, in early June 1579, the first European ships to drop anchor on the North American West Coast above the forty-second parallel.

For more than two decades after Drake's exploits, no documented instances of European ships visiting the Northwest Coast have come to light. Yet there are reasons—however tenuous—to suspect that some such visits may have occurred, and that documentation of them has either been lost or has not yet been uncovered.[15]

One such example concerns the voyage of the English privateer Thomas Cavendish, who sailed into the Pacific much as Drake had, eight years earlier. In November 1587, two vessels of the Cavendish expedition—its flagship *Desire* and a consort named *Content*—successfully intercepted and captured a seven-hundred-ton Manila galleon, the *Santa Ana*, off Cabo San Lucas, the southernmost point of Baja California. Soon afterward, heavily laden with the galleon's valuable cargo, the ships set sail to cross the Pacific westward, but in so doing the flagship lost contact with the *Content*, which was never seen again. When the *Desire* reached the Philippines, a Spanish pilot named Thomas de Ersola, who was aboard as a captive from the *Santa Ana*, is reported to have remarked that "the other ship [*Content*], as he supposed, was gone for the North-west passage, standing in 55 degrees."[16] There had previously been disagreement over a division of the spoils, and the officers of the *Content* may have decided to part company with the flagship in hopes of finding the passage Drake had sought. Success in the endeavor would have enabled them to reach England without having to circumnavigate the globe. The realities of geography assure us that they found no such passage; they may have reached the Northwest Coast, only to be shipwrecked on some lonely, windswept beach.

Incursions such as those of Drake and Cavendish were clearly a threat to Spain's economic interests in the Pacific, to say nothing of its territorial claims under the Treaty of Tordesillas. Not only had the loss of the *Santa Ana* and its immensely valuable cargo triggered a depression in the markets of New Spain,[17] but Drake had taken possession of Nova Albion in the name of England's Protestant monarch, Elizabeth I. Spain could ill afford to ignore such challenges.

Spanish exploration of the California coast was resumed with some earnestness, if not with urgency. Only a few days before the *Santa Ana* had been captured, a much smaller vessel, a fifty-ton frigate named *Nuestra Señora de Esperanza*, under the command of Pedro de Unamuno, had safely slipped into the harbor at Acapulco after crossing the North Pacific from the Philippines. It had orders to search for locations that might serve as havens for Manila galleons in distress.[18] However, neither that expedition nor another eight years later, in 1595, commanded by Sebastián Rodríguez Cermeño on the *San Agustín*, learned much about Alta California's coastal geography.[19]

At least two other expeditions are alleged to have been launched northward from New Spain early in the 1590s, one of which may have reached the Northwest Coast in 1592. The only information concerning this reputed voyage and its explorations above the forty-second parallel is attributed to an obscure Greek pilot named Apostolos Valerianos, or, as he is better known, Juan de Fuca. His story was recounted second-hand by an Englishman named Michael Lok the Elder, in a publication that first appeared in London in 1625.[20] According to Lok, Fuca claimed that he had participated in two expeditions ordered by the viceroy in Mexico City, Luis de Velasco. The first was aborted well before it was able to accomplish anything; but the second succeeded in finding "a broad Inlet of Sea, betweene 47 and 48 degrees of Latitude,"[21] into which Fuca sailed for twenty days. No corroboration of such a voyage has yet turned up in official Spanish documents, and the voyage has therefore long been considered apocryphal.[22] But, imaginary or not, the story served to spur later explorers, especially in the late eighteenth century, who hoped to rediscover Fuca's passage.

A better-documented expedition was launched in 1602 from Mexico, on more or less the same track Cabrillo had followed northward a half century earlier. Under command of Sebastián Vizcaíno, it included three ships: the two-hundred-ton flagship *San Diego*, and two smaller vessels, the *Santo Tomás* and the *Tres Reyes*. Despite the hardships they endured beating windward up the coast, they were successful in finding and charting a number of the more important harbors and anchorages between the thirty-second and forty-second parallels, including San Diego, Monterey and Drakes bays. (San Francisco Bay, the most commodious of them all, however, eluded them.) Accounts of the expedition also assert that two of the ships, the *San Diego* and the *Tres Reyes*, reached latitudes above the forty-second parallel, where their officers and men seem to have glimpsed at least two promontories on the southern Oregon coast: Cape Blanco, at 42°50′N, and Cape Sebastian, at 42°19′N.[23]

Vizcaíno urged his superiors in New Spain to launch a second expedition to establish a colony at Monterey Bay, but the newly appointed viceroy, the Marqués de Montesclaros, was not convinced the advantages were worth the cost. He forbade any further Spanish maritime exploration of the Northwest Coast, in the belief that allowing the region to remain a vast wilderness, unpopulated by Hispanic settlers, would be the most effective and least expensive way to combat foreign intrusion there. However unrealistic the viceroy's thinking may have been, it was to govern Spanish policy for the next century and a half. No vessels flying the Spanish flag were to ply Northwest coastal waters again until 1774.

Some unintended Hispanic visits to *la costa septentrional de Californias* may have occurred during the seventeenth or early eighteenth centuries, as a result of one or more Manila galleons' being driven off course and wrecked there. In particular, the disappearance of the one-thousand-ton *San Francisco Xavier* in 1705 has led to speculation that it suffered such a fate on the Oregon coast.[24] But, except for castaways who may have survived such a tragedy, there is little indication that Europeans—whether Spanish or otherwise—reached the Alaskan or Northwest coasts during the four decades after Vizcaíno's voyage in 1602–03. When Europeans did reappear in that remote corner of the globe, they would not be Spaniards sailing out of New Spain or the Philippines, but Russians pressing eastward from Siberia.

The honor of discovering the nearest thing to the legendary Strait of Anian, which had been sought so long and unsuccessfully by sixteenth- and seventeenth-century English and Spanish navigators, is now credited to a little-known Russian cossack, fur-hunter and mariner named Semen Dezhnev. Embarking in the summer of 1648 from the mouth of the Kolyma River on the Arctic coast of Siberia, he led a fur-hunting expedition of seven small, shallow-draft vessels called *kochi* eastward until they reached what is now known as the Bering Strait.[25] Four vessels of the flotilla were lost on that leg of the journey, and a fifth was wrecked as the others attempted to sail through the strait from north to south. The two surviving *kochi* were separated in the process, and only Dezhnev and the men aboard his vessel survived to tell of their experiences in reaching the mouth of the Anadyr River on Siberia's Pacific coast.[26]

Dezhnev's voyage demonstrated conclusively that Asia and North America were not connected by an isthmus. However, its main purpose was not to explore, but to hunt for furs. Members of the venture, including Dezhnev himself, were largely if not entirely illiterate, and kept no daily logs or journals. Oral accounts by the survivors were recorded later, but for nearly a century they were neither published nor given the credence that they now appear to have deserved. The authenticity of Dezhnev's voyage was consequently doubted, and relegated to the same limbo in which Juan de Fuca's purported voyage has languished. Recent scholarship, however, seems to confirm this as the earliest known Russian expedition to have sailed through the Bering Strait.[27]

Eighty years elapsed between Dezhnev's voyage and the next European venture into the waters between Siberia and Alaska. In July 1728, Vitus Bering, a Danish-born officer of the Russian Imperial Navy, set sail in the *Sviatoi Gavriil* (named for the archangel Gabriel) from the east coast of the Kamchatka Peninsula to explore northeastward along the Siberian Pacific coast above the sixtieth parallel. By mid-August he had succeeded in entering from the south the strait that Dezhnev had discovered from the north.[28]

Unlike Dezhnev's, Bering's voyage in 1728 was carried out under the auspices of the Russian government in St. Petersburg. Plans and directives for the expedition were initiated by Tsar Peter the Great himself, although they were not executed until after his death in January 1725.[29] It has long been thought that the expedition's primary mission was to gather scientific and geographic information, especially to learn whether Asia and America were joined, and, if not, whether a Northeast Passage would link European Russia with Siberia or other parts of the Far East.[30] A recent reinterpretation, however, suggests that the main purpose of Bering's first voyage was to reach the North American coast, in the hopes of opening trade with its inhabitants and establishing a basis for subsequent Russian claims there.[31]

Whatever his mission was, Bering did not go far enough north or west of Siberia's easternmost point (once called East Cape, now Cape Dezhneva) to convince later detractors conclusively that no land connection existed between the two continents. Moreover, if reaching the American mainland was his objective, he failed in his attempt.[32] A second expedition was thus deemed necessary, and when it set out in 1741, there is little doubt that its intention was primarily to reach America's Northwest Coast, for the same political and economic reasons the 1728 voyage appears to have been launched.[33]

Known to history as the Second Kamchatka Expedition, it was a more complex and ambitious undertaking than its predecessor. It included, for instance, a veritable international corps of naturalists and geographers, several of whom were German or French.[34] Gathering information was clearly on the agenda, and the expedition earned the distinction of being the first to explore northeastern Siberia, Kamchatka, the Aleutian Islands, and sections of the Alaskan coast with something of the scientific spirit that animated the European Enlightenment. That the expedition had been dispatched across the North Pacific for territorial reasons, however, seems not to have been fully understood by the scientists among its number.[35]

The voyage of the Second Kamchatka Expedition was commanded jointly by Bering and a Russian naval captain named Aleksei Chirikov, who had also participated in the 1728 voyage. Two ships, built under Bering's supervision at Petropavlovsk (Peter and Paul Harbor) in Avacha Bay on the southeast coast of the Kamchatka Peninsula, were used. Like the harbor where they were built, they were named for two of the apostles: the *Sv. Petr* (St. Peter), captained by Bering, and the *Sv. Pavel* (St. Paul), under Chirikov's command.

The expedition set out early in June 1741, on a course more or less southeasterly from Avacha Bay, directly into a section of the North Pacific. There, it was theorized by two Frenchmen—a geographer, Joseph Delisle, and his half-brother, Louis Delisle de La Croyère (an astronomer aboard the *Sv. Pavel*)—that a land mass of some sort would be found. They called it Juan de Gama Land.[36] Bering and Chirikov, however, satisfied themselves that no such land existed when they reached the forty-sixth parallel at approximately longitude 174°, a position some seven hundred nautical miles southeast of Avacha Bay, and about twenty-four hundred nautical miles due west of the Columbia River's mouth. Over the vigorous objections of Georg Steller, a German-born naturalist aboard the *Sv. Petr*, the naval officers agreed to abandon the search for Gama Land, altering course to the northeast in hopes of finding the American coast.[37]

Within a week of this decision, the two ships lost sight of each other in bad weather, after which they completed their respective voyages independently. Chirikov and the *Sv. Pavel's* crew were the first to sight North America. In the early morning hours of 15 July 1741, they came upon some small offshore islands clustered along the west coast of the much larger Prince of Wales Island, in the southernmost part of the Alaskan Panhandle. Their landfall, which the ship's records place at latitude 55°21′N,[38] was within view of capes Addington and Bartolome, a position no more than forty nautical miles northwesterly of Forrester Island (latitude 54°48′N), which was the northernmost landmark Pérez would sight in 1774, and which he would name *Isla Santa Christina*.

The *Sv. Pavel* next turned northwestward, following the coast in search of a suitable place to anchor and go ashore. Three days later, on 18 July, a boat with an eleven-member landing party was sent ashore in the vicinity

EARLY APPROACHES

Chirikov—1741 Pérez—1774

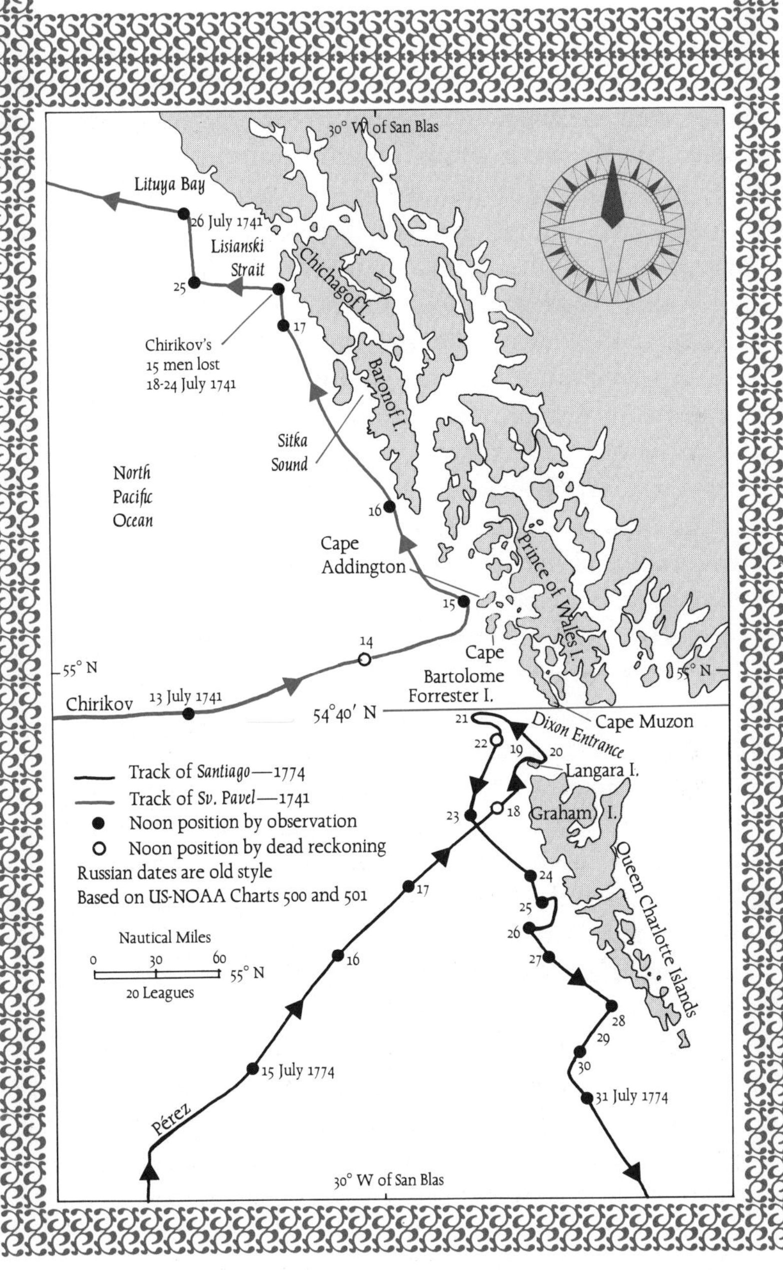

of what is today called Lisianski Strait. The party's failure to return after almost five days prompted Chirikov to send out the ship's second and only remaining boat with four men aboard, hoping that their missing shipmates might yet be found. But this only multiplied the tragedy, for the four men vanished as mysteriously as the crew they had been hoping to rescue.[39]

Toward the end of this unhappy episode, on 25 July 1741, Chirikov's men sighted two boats approaching the *Sv. Pavel*, one noticeably larger than the other. At a distance, they appeared to be the ship's missing boats and their fifteen crewmen. But, as the smaller craft came closer, its sharply pointed bow, and the fact that its four occupants were paddling rather than rowing with oars, indicated that they were not Russians but native Americans. In all likelihood, they were Northwest Coast Indians of the Tlingit branch, and this was doubtless their first encounter with Europeans. Despite the Russians' efforts to coax them to come alongside the *Sv. Pavel* by waving white kerchiefs, the natives abruptly departed. Chirikov says that "they stood up and shouted twice 'Agai, Agai,' waved their hands, and turned back to shore."[40] There was no direct contact or exchange of trade articles, but this remains the earliest recorded European sighting of Northwest Coast Indians. While equipment or trade articles carried on either of the missing boats may have fallen into native hands, no evidence confirms this conclusively.[41]

Loss of the *Sv. Pavel's* only two boats ended any further attempts to go ashore. All Chirikov could do was to put the ship's bow on a westward course, hoping to find his way back across some two thousand, two hundred nautical miles of uncharted North Pacific waters before he and his men perished from scurvy, starvation, thirst, or shipwreck. Within a week, on 1 August 1741, after sailing westward nearly five hundred nautical miles, the *Sv. Pavel* succeeded in crossing the Gulf of Alaska at roughly the fifty-ninth parallel. There, it made landfall on the southeastern coast of Alaska's Kenai Peninsula. Surmising correctly that the land would bar further westward progress at latitude 59°N, Chirikov turned south and southwesterly, skirting Kodiak Island and the Alaska Peninsula, to the fifty-third parallel, the approximate latitude of his home port at Avacha Bay. The *Sv. Pavel* then resumed a westward course, which took it along the Aleutian Islands, more than a half-dozen of which the ship's company sighted.[42] Although the Russians had lost their means of going ashore, in at least one instance (at Adak), the Aleutian islanders paddled their kayaks out to the ship and engaged in a brief exchange with Chirikov and his men. Desperately short of food and water, scurvy-ridden, and without a boat to remedy their plight, the Russians welcomed the natives' offer to sell them fresh water (in animal bladders rather than wooden casks) in exchange for knives.[43]

The *Sv. Pavel* eventually reached the haven of Avacha Bay early in October 1741, just before the onset of the autumn storms. But it was not before seven members of the crew, including the astronomer, had perished from scurvy. These losses were in addition to the fifteen sailors who had been left to an unknown fate on the American coast. Thus, of the *Sv. Pavel*'s original company of seventy-six officers and men, fifty-four survived the voyage.[44]

Meanwhile, aboard the *Sv. Petr*, Bering had come upon the North American coast at a considerably higher latitude—between 59° and 60°N—than Chirikov's initial landfall at 55°21′N. On 16 July 1741, the summit of a massive, snow-covered mountain loomed above the northern horizon, in full view of the ship's company. Modern charts label it Mount St. Elias, an eighteen-thousand-foot-high peak at latitude 60°17′N and longitude 140°55′W. On 20 July, the *Sv. Petr* approached the coast, where it anchored off a long, narrow island Bering's party named *Sv. Elias*. Today it is known as Kayak Island, although its southernmost point (at latitude 59°48′N and longitude 144°36′W) retains in anglicized form the name Bering originally gave it, namely Cape St. Elias. Avoiding whatever tragedy may have befallen Chirikov's landing parties, the two boats Bering sent ashore—one of which had the naturalist Steller on board—returned safely with casks of fresh water, together with the first European impressions of Kayak Island's terrain, flora and fauna.

Although the American mainland lay nearby, readily visible and inviting exploration, Bering ordered the *Sv. Petr* to put to sea the next day, 21 July. Writing disapprovingly of this decision in his journal, Steller observed that "two hours before daybreak, the Captain Commander, much against his usual practice, got up and came on deck and, without consulting anyone, gave orders to weigh anchor."[45] The ship's water supply had not been fully replenished, nor had Steller's thirst for scientific investigation ashore been nearly satisfied. But these considerations did nothing to change the captain-commander's mind or lessen his evident apprehension about the return voyage. The *Sv. Petr* stood briefly to the west, then southwesterly, through more or less the same waters the *Sv. Pavel* would pass about a week later off the southeastern coasts of the Kenai Peninsula, Kodiak Island and the Alaska Peninsula. When he was near the fifty-third parallel, Bering set his course to the west, as would Chirikov also, hoping to run down that latitude to reach Avacha Bay.

Unlike Chirikov, however, Bering still had boats with which to go ashore. He took advantage of this to finish replenishing the water supply between 29 August and 6 September, amidst an archipelago off the Alaska Peninsula, still known today as the Shumagin Islands, after one of the *Sv. Petr's* sailors, Nikita Shumagin, who died and was buried there.[46] The week-long stay among the bleak, treeless islands, however refreshing it may have been, delayed the *Sv. Petr's* westward passage significantly—and, as events would soon prove, tragically. Chirikov's ship, until then a week behind Bering's, forged ahead in what was becoming a race to reach Avacha Bay before the autumn storms and contrary west winds set in. By the time the *Sv. Petr* began threading its way through the Aleutian Islands, it was already past the middle of September. Entries in the ship's log bear witness to the extremely adverse weather encountered in October: "frightful storm, heavy squalls, waves washing over the deck" (1 October); "terrific storm, heavy squalls and high seas" (2 October); "waves from both sides washing over the deck" (6 October); "terrific storm . . . frightful squalls" (10 October).[47]

Neither Bering nor some thirty-two members of the *Sv. Petr's* crew lived to see Avacha Bay again. Storm-battered and blown off course, the ship was beached on 6 November 1741, on an island now named for Bering in the Komandorskie archipelago, roughly midway between Attu Island, the westernmost of the Aleutian Islands, and the Kamchatka Peninsula. More than half the *Sv. Petr's* crew (including Bering) who lost their lives in the course of the expedition did so while wintering on this desolate, uninhabited island. Survivors of the ordeal (among whom were Second Officer Sven Waxel and Steller) succeeded in rebuilding the *Sv. Petr* into a makeshift, thirty-six-foot-long, single-masted vessel. Launched on 10 August 1742, it enabled them to escape, although its poorly constructed, leaky hull nearly put them all on the ocean's bottom. Nevertheless, within ten days of leaving their temporary island refuge, they managed to sail safely into the harbor of Petropavlovsk at Avacha Bay.

There are probably no more notable voyages in the annals of North Pacific maritime exploration than those of Bering and Chirikov in 1741. Within two years, the Aleutian Island chain they had discovered was luring other Russian vessels—privately financed, and more commercial than exploratory—eastward in search of furs.[48] As far as foreigners were concerned, the St. Petersburg government regarded the expedition's results as closely guarded state secrets.[49] Yet, almost within a decade, French maps of the North Pacific began depicting quite accurately the routes of the *Sv.*

Petr and *Sv. Pavel* in 1741.[50] Evidently, papers that Louis Delisle de La Croyère, the deceased astronomer, had kept while aboard the *Sv. Pavel* had fallen into the hands of his half-brother, Joseph Delisle, who was then a member of the Imperial Academy of St. Petersburg. After his return to Paris, Delisle published the contents of the papers in 1750, and they became the basis for a number of French maps of the North Pacific. Warren Cook asserts that an edition of the maps, issued in 1758, first roused the Spanish crown's concern about Russian activities in North America.[51]

A second government-sponsored Russian expedition to chart and explore the Aleutian Islands in greater detail was mounted in 1768. It consisted of two vessels built in Kamchatka, the *Sv. Ekaterina*, captained by Petr Krenitsyn, and the *Sv. Pavel*, under Mikhail Levashev. The St. Petersburg government went to considerable pains to keep the expedition's purposes and results secret, presumably for fear they might provoke countermeasures by other European nations—Spain in particular—that had interests in the region.[52] It was probably no coincidence that 1768 was also the year in which the Spanish crown's *visitador-general* to New Spain, José de Gálvez, initiated the efforts that led to Spanish colonization of San Diego and Monterey in Alta California, and eventually to the voyage Pérez would lead in 1774 to find out, among other things, whether—or where—the Russians really were on *la costa septentrional de Californias*.

JUAN PÉREZ: MAJORCAN MARINER

Even before his voyage to the Pacific Northwest in 1774, Juan Pérez had established a secure place for himself in history. By commanding one of the two ships to reach the harbor of San Diego in 1769, he helped begin Spanish colonization of what is today the state of California. In succeeding years, his nautical skills ensured that the fledgling missions at both San Diego and Monterey were kept supplied as they struggled to attain some degree of self-sufficiency. Pérez was warmly praised for his efforts by Fray Junípero Serra, the Franciscan missionary whose own dedication contributed so much to the founding of those and other missions in Alta California.

Few particulars of Pérez's early life survive, and what is known must be sorted from scattered references offering only an incomplete biographical outline.[53] The day and month he was born, for example, are known because Fray Tomás de la Peña (one of the chaplains aboard the *Santiago* in 1774) refers by chance to a celebration of the captain's birthday on 24

June.[54] But the year of his birth remains a mystery. A similarly incidental remark by Serra, in which he refers to Pérez as a "countryman from the shores of Palma,"[55] suggests that his birthplace was somewhere on the island of Majorca (whose principal city is Palma), in the Mediterranean islands called the Balearics, east of the Iberian Peninsula.

Pérez's experience aboard ships of the Manila-Acapulco trade is confirmed by Fray Juan Crespi (the other chaplain on the *Santiago's* 1774 voyage), who remarked that "the captain . . . has spent a great deal of time in China and the Philippines."[56] His service on the arduous and risky trans-Pacific voyages of the Manila galleons was probably in the capacity of a *piloto* (roughly equivalent to the English "pilot"), whose primary responsibility was for navigation. In any event, when Pérez was assigned to duty at the newly established naval base at San Blas, Mexico, some time in 1767, he held the rank of *primer piloto graduado de alférez de fragata* (pilot first class, acting frigate ensign).[57]

The education Pérez received as a mariner was probably more practical than academic. Although he may have been a graduate, as Warren Cook asserts, of a school "preparing petty officers for lower ranks in the navy,"[58] most of the San Blas pilots were primarily schooled by experience, and Pérez was no doubt no exception. He and his fellow pilots at San Blas were likely to have been as knowledgeable as anyone in the eighteenth century about sailing the eastern Pacific and the coastal waters of the Californias.

However, this did not entitle the pilots to the same precedence or promotional prospects as commissioned officers of the line. Pérez never rose above the rank of ensign, and was destined to remain a San Blas pilot until the day he died. When the Spanish government began increasing the naval personnel at San Blas in 1773 and 1774, it sent officers of the line, all of whom outranked the veteran Majorcan, together with two new pilots who were graduates of the Colegio de San Telmo, the renowned pilots' school at Seville.[59] It is impossible to know whether Pérez resented being overshadowed in this way, but it could scarcely have failed to rankle him, and may have dampened his ardor, particularly during his final year of service.

Seamen in the eighteenth century were no strangers to illness aboard ship, but Juan Pérez seems to have had more than the usual number of maladies. Both chaplains on the 1774 voyage to the Northwest Coast remarked that the captain fell suddenly ill with a stomach disorder overnight on the 17th and 18th of June, soon after their departure northward from Monterey.[60] The captain's own *Diario* mentions nothing of this; evidently he recovered sufficiently to complete the voyage without complaint.

When the *Santiago* returned to Monterey in late August 1774, Pérez indicated to Serra that he planned to stay at Monterey until the middle of October, which would have enabled the ship to explore the bay at San Francisco for possible mission sites. Serra was much pleased with this, but then, suddenly and with almost no explanation, Pérez changed his mind, deciding to return to San Blas immediately. At least one writer, James G. Caster, has speculated that this "could well have been dictated by his [Pérez's] realization that he was ill and needed medical attention of a kind not available at frontier Monterey."[61]

Whatever Pérez's state of health may have been in September 1774, there is little doubt that when he accompanied the Hezeta expedition northward in the following year he was ailing. His *Diario* of that voyage has gaps suggesting that he was sometimes prevented from making his daily entries, conceivably by illness. This and his always cautious advice to Hezeta hint that his grip on life was slipping.[62] It was to be his last arduous sea venture, for on 2 November 1775, soon after the *Santiago* left Monterey for San Blas, Juan Pérez died of what one of the chaplains described as "typhus."[63]

Despite his disappointments and his untimely death, Pérez had become something of a legend in his time for his role in the expedition that had ushered in Spanish colonization of Alta California. His exploration of the Northwest Coast would also add luster to his name, even if his performance in that venture would not be without its critics.

PÉREZ AND THE "SACRED EXPEDITION"

Spain's occupation of Alta California in 1769 was, as Herbert Bolton has written, "one of the dramatic episodes of American colonial history."[64] Sometimes referred to—mostly in the secondary literature—as the "Sacred Expedition" (*la santa expedición*), its purposes were, broadly, to evangelize the California natives and to bring the lands they inhabited firmly within the realm of the Spanish king, Carlos III. But other, more complicated, motives lay behind it.

It was nearly a century and three-quarters since Sebastián Vizcaíno had first suggested, in 1603, that a permanent settlement should be established at Monterey Bay to assist Manila galleons in their eastbound voyages across the North Pacific.[65] That consideration alone had not been sufficiently persuasive to justify the expense of such an enterprise. In 1768, after years of debating the merits of colonizing California, Spanish officials seem finally to have been prompted to act by reports that Russians had reached the Northwest Coast from Siberia. If California were to be protected from foreign encroachment, they reasoned, it must be permanently occupied by military garrisons (presidios) and Franciscan missions.

José de Gálvez, the crown's energetic, impatient and sometimes eccentric appointee as *visitador-general* to New Spain, was the key figure in launching the expedition to occupy Alta California. In May 1768, while on his way from Guadalajara to the Pacific coast, he received an urgent message from Francisco de Croix, the viceroy in Mexico City. In it, Gálvez later wrote, "was enclosed a copy of another order communicated by His Honor, the Marqués de Grimaldi, first Secretary of State, in which His Majesty [Carlos III] ordered me to take the necessary steps for safeguarding that peninsula [California] from the repeated probings of the Russians."[66] The *visitador*, acting with the determination and speed for which he was known, moved to establish a naval base on the Nayarit coast to support whatever operations would be necessary to carry out the crown's orders. Although the place he chose, an obscure village called San Blas, was surrounded by mangrove swamps and possessed a harbor that was less than ideal, it offered the most direct sailing track northward to Alta California and the Northwest Coast.[67]

On 16 May 1768, a special council was convened in which Gálvez appointed the various civilian and military officials of the newly created Naval Department of San Blas. They were told their responsibilities and duties, including the great importance the crown attached to their mission. Juan Pérez was doubtless in attendance.[68]

The new naval base was immediately assigned six ships, including four packetboats (*paquebotes*) and two schooners (*goletas*).[69] Two of the packetboats, the *Concepción* and the *Lauretana*, were older, relatively small vessels (with displacements of only sixty-two and fifty-four tons respectively), confiscated from the Jesuits when they had been expelled from New Spain in 1767 by Carlos III.[70] The schooners, named the *Sonora* (also called *Nuestra Señora de la Soledad*) and the *Sinaloa*, and the other packetboats, the *San Carlos* (or *El Toisón*, "the Golden Fleece") and the *San Antonio* (or *El Príncipe*, "the Prince"), had just been built the previous year on the banks of the Río Santiago, some twenty-six miles from San Blas. While the schooners were tiny craft (with a displacement of about thirty tons each), intended mostly for mail or supply runs to Baja California or shallow-draft exploration, the two packetboats were considerably larger, each with a displacement of one hundred and ninety-five tons, and Gálvez envisioned using them in the Sacred Expedition. He was soon to have at his disposal another new packetboat, the *San José* (also called *El Descubridor*, "the Discoverer"), which was under construction in the harbor at San Blas and due to be launched some time in July 1768.[71]

Gálvez's plans called for an overland as well as a maritime advance into Alta California. Fray Junípero Serra, *padre presidente* of the missions already established on the peninsula of Baja California, would go northward with an overland party to be led by Captain Gaspar de Portolá, military governor of the Californias. Meanwhile, a seagoing contingent consisting of the packetboats *San Carlos* and *San Antonio*, loaded with supplies and additional personnel, would sail up the peninsula's outer coast to San Diego, where the sea and land parties would aim to rendezvous. Once this was accomplished, "they resolved to found," in the words of Fray Francisco Palóu, "three missions, one at the port of San Diego, another at that of Monterey with the title of San Carlos, and the remaining one with that of San Buenaventura, halfway between the two ports."[72]

While these ambitious plans were being formulated, Juan Pérez could only watch, unsure of how he might participate in the events about to unfold. The *San Carlos* was already captained by Vicente Vila, who, as senior pilot at San Blas, was assured overall command of the sea expedition. As for the *San Antonio*, it, too, already had a captain, Antonio Faveau y Quesada, a former mathematics professor well-versed in Pacific coast and Philippines navigation.[73] What part the *San José* might have in the expedition—or, for that matter, who would command the ship—remained to be decided.

Then, some time in October 1768, for reasons that were apparently never disclosed, Gálvez unexpectedly removed Faveau y Quesada from command of the *San Antonio*, supplanting him with Pérez.[74] The appointment would give the Majorcan a momentous place in California's history, to say nothing of paving the way for his later role in exploring the Northwest Coast. Pérez would be joining the Sacred Expedition in command of his own ship.

It was nearly November 1768 when he sailed the *San Antonio* out of San Blas, bound for La Paz on the southeastern coast of Baja California, to rendezvous with the *San Carlos* (which had already left San Blas late in September).[75] The *visitador*, having completed a whirlwind tour that summer of the king's Sonoran and Baja Californian possessions, impatiently awaited the arrival of both ships to give them their final orders before they sailed north for San Diego.

In the face of stiff winds and high seas, the *San Carlos* (under Vila) barely survived its crossing of the Gulf of California. Reaching La Paz on Christmas Day, it limped into port with its tackle and rigging in shreds, leaking and requiring an extensive overhaul.[76] Having foreseen such trouble, however, Gálvez was ready with a gang of skilled workers, who labored furiously to put the *San Carlos* in condition to renew its northward voyage. That task being completed on 9 January 1769, the *visitador* gave Vila a rousing send-off, "accompanying [in the *Concepción*] the flagship [*San Carlos*] as far as . . . Cabo San Lucas, where," according to Palóu, "he had the pleasure of seeing it sail with a wind astern on 11 January of the said year, 1769."[77] When Pérez's *San Antonio* finally hove into view off the Baja California coast it was 15 January, and the *San Carlos* had already left for San Diego.

Adverse winds prevented the *San Antonio* from putting in at La Paz; instead, Pérez met Gálvez at the same harbor in the lee of Cabo San Lucas, from which the *San Carlos* had just sailed. Although Pérez's ship had apparently not suffered much damage in crossing the Gulf, it was decided to give it a thorough overhaul. When all was ready, religious services were held for the crewmen, following which Gálvez made an address exhorting them to be "peaceful and harmonious, to do their duty and obey their superiors and officers, and to respect the missionary Fathers Juan Vizcaíno and Francisco Gómez who were going with them for their [spiritual] comfort."[78] It was 15 February 1769.

The voyage of the *San Antonio* to San Diego was evidently both uneventful and without serious mishap. Pérez sailed a considerable distance north of his objective before making landfall at an island in the Santa Barbara Channel archipelago.[79] After taking on water there and bestowing the name *Santa Cruz* on the island,[80] he proceeded to San Diego, where he arrived safely on 11 April. The harbor was empty, however, and there was no sign of the *San Carlos*.

Whichever ship reached San Diego first had been ordered to remain there for twenty days. If within that time neither the other ship nor the land expedition had appeared, "they were to set sail in search of the port of Monterey."[81] Finding nothing to indicate that Vila's flagship or the land party had already been there, Pérez began to wait out the required time. Just as it was about to elapse, sails were seen on the western horizon. On

30 April 1769, only a day short of Pérez's impending departure, the *San Carlos* cast anchor in San Diego Bay.

It was a less joyous occasion than it should have been, for nearly everyone aboard the flagship was gravely ill with a mysterious malady. According to Palóu, the theory prevailed that the cause was bad water taken on at Isla de Cedros, off the Baja California coast.[82] The disease was highly contagious, and was far more lethal than scurvy—although at least one account uses that name to describe it.[83] The advance party of the overland expedition finally reached San Diego on 14 May. One of its members, Fray Juan Crespi, described the dismal scene in a letter of 9 June 1769 to Palóu:

> *We found the crews of both ships and the soldiers from the* San Carlos *filling a [tent] hospital on shore, recovering from the disease of loanda or scurvy. Up to the present twenty-two have died from the crews of both ships, besides one or two of the soldiers on the* San Carlos. *At this time the sailors on* El Príncipe [San Antonio] *are very few, since those who are somewhat stronger, and able to walk and do a little work, are only about six or seven, while of the soldiers only three are well . . . many dying, the majority with cramps in the legs or all over the body.*[84]

Conditions had grown even worse by the time the overland contingent's main party reached San Diego on 1 July. Gaspar de Portolá, who had overall command of that expedition, relates in his *Diario* that "of the naval force there remained only a few sailors, and in particular on the *San Carlos* nearly all the men had died."[85]

In the first few days of July, the expedition's commanders, Portolá and Vila, after considering their precarious situation, decided that the *San Antonio* should return to San Blas to seek aid. The few remaining able-bodied sailors were assembled, and on 9 July the vessel set sail with Pérez in command. According to Palóu, it took only twenty days to arrive. Nine more men succumbed on the voyage, leaving a crew scarcely able to manage the ship, but Pérez's dash to New Spain, and subsequent return in March 1770 with supplies and reinforcements for his beleaguered comrades, would forever number his name among the heroes of Spanish California. Meanwhile, a third packetboat, the *San José*, was being readied for the relief of the colonists; as fate would have it, it vanished at sea before reaching San Diego.[86] Instead, it was Pérez in the *San Antonio* who managed to make his way successfully back up the coast.

Although he had been instructed to sail directly to Monterey Bay (where part of the land expedition was expected to be), he chose instead to put in at San Diego, improvising as the situation seemed to warrant. Palóu explains:

> *The* San Antonio . . . *continued its voyage for* Monterey *as far as* Point Concepción *on the channel of Santa Barbara, where it learned from the heathen . . . by clear and unmistakable signs, that the land expedition had retreated and returned to San* Diego. *On this account, and because he had accidentally lost an anchor in that channel,* Don *Juan Pérez . . . decided to retrace the voyage to the port of* San Diego. He *was in sight of it on the 19th of* March [1770] *in the afternoon.*[87]

It was not the last time Pérez would adjust his actions contrary to orders, nor was it the only time he was concerned over a lost anchor. Such traits were evidently ingrained in his character, which some critics have seen as overcautiousness and a certain lack of "intrepid qualities."[88] In this instance, however, events proved Pérez correct, for when he entered San Diego Bay on 24 March 1770, it was "to the joy of everybody, who gave a thousand thanks to God."[89]

A new effort to reach Monterey Bay by land and sea was soon mounted, and on 31 May Pérez and the *San Antonio* hove into view off that harbor's southern cape, Punta de Pinos. When he entered the bay later in the day, he attained the distinction of being the first Spanish navigator since Vizcaíno, one hundred and seventy-one years earlier, to enter both San Diego and Monterey bays.

In the next three years, Pérez would establish himself, in James Caster's words, "as a dependable and competent sailing master,"[90] helping to maintain the supply line so vital to the Alta California missions. His seamanship by that time was certainly equal, if not superior, to that of any of the other San Blas pilots, and his crucial role in the success of the Sacred Expedition distinguished him from all of them. When the viceroy of New Spain, Antonio María de Bucareli y Ursúa (newly appointed in 1771), conceived of an expedition to probe the geographic darkness of the coast, away to the north of Monterey, it was therefore not surprising that he settled on Juan Pérez to lead it.

VICEROY BUCARELI'S INSTRUCTIONS

By 1773, the missions and presidios at San Diego and Monterey, to whose establishment Pérez had contributed so much, were modestly secure, if not thriving. Viceroy Bucareli began concerning himself with what lay beyond those outposts, particularly with how far south the Russians might have penetrated on the coast. In July, Pérez appears to have received his first intimations that a voyage to the far north was being contemplated and that he was likely to lead it. At the time, Bucareli, emphasizing the crown's concern over possible foreign encroachment on the northern coasts, requested that Pérez draw up plans for such an expedition.[91]

Pérez's tentative proposal, which reached the viceroy in September 1773, was to employ a two-hundred-and-twenty-five-ton frigate, the *Santiago* (nicknamed *Nueva Galicia*), which had just slid down the ways at San Blas.[92] With a "year's supply of provisions . . . requisitioned from the presidios of Alta California . . . and crew members . . . recruited, in part, from the California presidios,"[93] he envisioned the ship's leaving San Blas some time during December, January or February. Once the plans had been approved in outline, viceregal instructions for the expedition were drafted and issued, placing Pérez in command of the *Santiago*, and specifying other details governing the conduct of the voyage. Article I of these instructions avows that the reason for the endeavor was to enlarge the king's territories "through new discoveries in unknown areas, so that their numerous Indian inhabitants . . . may receive by means of the spiritual conquest the light of the Gospel which will free them from the darkness of idolatry."[94] Concern over Russian encroachment on the coast is never explicitly stated, although that motive almost certainly underlies the instructions Pérez received to search for foreign settlements. The exhaustively detailed document bears the date 24 December 1773.

According to Article III of Bucareli's instructions, the personnel of the *Santiago* comprised, besides Pérez, a second pilot, a chaplain, a surgeon, a boatswain, two boatswain's mates, two caulkers, two stewards, a gunner, fourteen helmsmen (*timoneles*),* twenty seamen, thirty apprentice seamen, six cabin boys, and four cooks. The ship's regular complement was thus to number eighty-six officers and men, although the instructions give the total as eighty-eight—possibly a slip of the pen, or poor arithmetic.[95] Also aboard would be a number of passengers, en route for Monterey, about whom the instructions say nothing. They included *padre presidente* Serra, his Indian servant, and several families or individuals who planned to settle there.[96]

The *Santiago*'s departure from San Blas, say the viceroy's instructions, was to be set by Pérez whenever "he considered it suitable, according to his

*The *Santiago*'s roster, dated January 1774, lists fourteen gunners (*artilleros*), but says nothing of this many helmsmen.

judgment and experience . . . acquired in the numerous voyages made to Monterey."[97] The ship left San Blas on 24 January 1774.

In addition to its regular complement and passengers, the ship had on board sufficient provisions to feed the crew for a year, with "four boxes of beads containing 468 bundles" to distribute among any natives who might be encountered.[98] It also carried supplies for the settlement at Monterey, for which reason Article VI authorized Pérez to stop there to off-load them. The viceroy specifically warned him against lingering any longer than necessary—a warning to which little heed was paid.[99] On 28 February, in the Santa Barbara Channel, the *Santiago* experienced structural troubles, and Pérez elected to return south, putting in at San Diego. This was essentially contrary to his instructions, but the settlers there, who were on half rations, were delighted at the ship's appearance, as they had been when Pérez made his unauthorized stop there in 1770. Compounding the delay this caused, when the *Santiago* finally reached Monterey on 8 May, it took nearly a month to discharge the cargo and prepare for its voyage to the north.[100]

Once it had departed northward from Monterey, when the voyage became one of discovery and exploration, the viceroy's instructions provided twenty-six additional articles, specifying in minute detail what was to be accomplished and how the operation should be conducted. The orders in Article VII seemed simple enough: "[Pérez] is to ascend to the latitude which he considers suitable, keeping in mind that the landing is to be made at sixty degrees of latitude. After the landfall has been made, he will follow the coast looking for Monterey."[101] However, considering that no less than fourteen hundred nautical miles separated Monterey from latitude 60°N, and that the viceroy and the ship's officers were not sure whether such a high latitude could even be reached by sea in that part of the Pacific, it was a challenging assignment, to say the least.

Nevertheless, Bucareli, supposing that the voyage was perfectly feasible, went on to pile up orders and directions governing nearly every imaginable aspect of the expedition. On his southward return, Pérez was to follow the coast, "never losing sight of it . . . , and make the most minute exploration and to land at those places where it can be done without obvious risk."[102] While ordered to make no settlements himself, he was to mark with a wooden cross, and formally take possession of, sites deemed suitable for such purposes. If foreign settlements were encountered, he was to avoid them and instead go farther north, where he was to perform possession-taking rituals prescribed in a formulary attached to the instructions.[103] Should foreign ships be encountered, nothing was to be done to divulge the purpose of the voyage; if compelled to respond by a ship more powerful than the *Santiago*, Pérez should only "state that he sailed from San Blas with provisions for the new settlement of San Diego and Monterey, provided he is within a reasonable latitude; but if he is beyond this, it will be necessary to add to the above-said that the weather has driven him further, etc."[104]

Beginning with Article XV, the native peoples and natural resources of whatever lands Pérez might discover were the subject of the viceroy's wide-ranging instructions. If Indian settlements were found, their inhabitants were to be treated "affectionately and given . . . the articles which he carried for this purpose."[105] The customs, characteristics, religion, political organization, and other aspects of such natives were to be recorded. Bucareli was anxious to know whether the Indians were visited by other ships, and, if so, "what taxes and tributes they pay and render, in what way, to what persons."[106] Under no circumstances, except in self-defense, was Pérez to use force against natives, and he was strictly warned not to "antagonize the Indians or forcibly take possession of land."[107] This was mainly to ensure that subsequent voyagers or settlers would not be faced with natives seeking revenge.

As for natural resources the viceroy's instructions were equally insistent: Pérez must strive to learn whether those regions had metallic ores, precious stones, or "spices, drugs or aromatics, wheat, barley, corn, beans, chickpeas [*garbanzos*]."[108] The orders also specified that spices such as pepper, cloves, cinnamon, and nutmeg were to be carried, so that the natives could be shown them as examples of what the Spaniards were looking for. (Pérez and his men would learn soon enough the futility of seeking tropical spices on the chilly and rain-drenched Northwest Coast.) While the viceroy's instructions allude to collecting information about flora and fauna, they do so only perfunctorily, suggesting that Bucareli assigned little or no importance to animal pelts as an exploitable natural resource.

Lastly, Pérez was given careful instructions about how to record both the information collected and the events of the voyage. Because it sheds light on the nature of the documents translated elsewhere in this book, the principal article governing record-keeping deserves to be quoted in full:

> *From the very moment that he* [Pérez] *sets sail from San Blas, he will keep an exact logbook of all the navigational details, noting down the winds, courses, shoals, landmarks,*

etc., and determining the position of the sun whenever possible. Thus, nothing should be missing from the logbook that may be instructive or may furnish information and data for the voyage. Every day that he is able to do so, he will read the daily entry which is written to the ranking officers of the packet boat; and at the end of what has been read, a certified statement should be made, attesting to the truth of the events entered. If anyone should make any observations, he is to make note of it and have it signed by everyone, so that the account of the events may be more authentically attested to.[109]

The ship's second officer was similarly ordered to keep a record.

Nowhere do the viceroy's instructions suggest that Pérez or his officers record their observations on maps or charts; moreover, there is only one—essentially negative—mention of cartographic import. In the penultimate article, Bucareli writes: "Notwithstanding that the charts published in St. Petersburg in the years 1758 and 1773, concerning the alleged voyages of the Russians, may be of little use to him, copies are included so that he may not be without this information."[110]

With these painstakingly elaborate instructions, so curiously neglectful of mapping, Juan Pérez set out first from San Blas, then from Monterey, to discharge those responsibilities of explorer and discoverer with which the viceroy had charged him. For all their detail, and however well-intended they may have been, the instructions did not always prove useful or even applicable in the harsh realities of the northern Pacific. Besides failing to stress the importance of cartography, as events would show, they were also optimistic in the extreme in setting the expedition's goals.

PARTICIPANTS IN THE VOYAGE

The names of eighty-eight officers and men and twenty-four passengers appear on the *Santiago*'s rosters when it left San Blas in January 1774.[111] Biographical details survive of only a few of the ship's company, and the identities of some have been obscured by various changes that inevitably left some confusion in their wake.

Of the two principal officers there is the least uncertainty. Aside from Pérez himself, whose biographical background has already been sketched, its second officer, Esteban José Martínez, was later to achieve sufficient notoriety—if not fame—in Northwest Coast exploration to ensure that his name and deeds would be as well remembered as those of the captain.

A thirty-two-year-old native of Seville in southwestern Spain, Martínez was a graduate of the Colegio de San Telmo.[112] When the *Santiago* sailed, he held the rank of *piloto segundo*, or pilot second class. Before his assign-

SPANISH STAMP (issued 1967) commemorating Esteban José Martínez, who was second-in-command and pilot of the *Santiago* during its voyage to the Northwest Coast in 1774. He then held the rank of pilot second class. In 1788, he commanded an expedition that successfully reached Prince William Sound in Alaska, where he encountered Russian fur hunters. When the Nootka Controversy erupted between Spain and Britain in 1789, Martínez was among its central figures.

ment to San Blas the previous year, he had served aboard various ships plying the eastern Pacific between Mexico and South America. Unlike that of Pérez, much of his career as a naval officer still lay ahead of him in 1774. He was to command an expedition from San Blas in 1788 that—despite serious dissension among its officers—succeeded in reaching latitude 60°N, making contact with Russians in the vicinity of Alaska's Prince William Sound.[113] In 1789 his impulsive arrest of the English fur trader James Colnett at Nootka Sound not only sparked an international controversy but guaranteed him a place in Pacific Northwest maritime history.[114]

As Viceroy Bucareli's instructions had specified, Pérez's expedition in 1774 was to have a chaplain. The man to whom this honor was supposed to have fallen was Fray Pablo de Mugártegui,[115] who boarded the *Santiago* in that capacity at San Blas. However, when the ship put in at San Diego in March, he was too ill to continue, and no one was available to replace him. Serra, who was also aboard the *Santiago* from San Blas to San Diego, determined to make the final leg of his journey overland on the *Camino*

Real. He reached Monterey on 11 May 1774, three days after the *Santiago* arrived, after which he selected Mugártegui's replacement.[116]

The task of ministering to the expedition's religious needs fell to two Franciscans stationed at Mission San Carlos Borromeo, just south of the Monterey Presidio. Serra decided that Fray Juan Crespi, whose exploits as missionary-explorer on the overland expeditions to Alta California had already earned him a place in the province's history, was the man for the job. But the *padre presidente* also concluded—evidently at Crespi's urging—that a second chaplain should be assigned to the voyage. Thus Fray Tomás de la Peña y Saravia became one of the expedition's number.

Like Serra and Pérez, Crespi was a native of Majorca.[117] He had been born on 1 March 1721 in Palma, where seventeen years later he entered the Franciscan Order. Their common island origins no doubt contributed to ties among the Majorcans that otherwise might not have existed. At the age of fifty-three, Crespi may well have been one of the oldest on board the *Santiago*, and there are indications that he did not especially relish the prospects of the hardships that a voyage into the unknown would entail. "Notwithstanding my great fatigue after so many expeditions by land," he wrote in his diary, "I sacrificed self in order to take part in this enterprise, in conformity with my vows of obedience, trusting in God for all happiness during the voyage and bearing with me the consolation that, by dint of entreaty, . . . the favor that Father Predicator Fray Tomás de la Peña y Saravia should go with me as a companion."[118] Apparently a confirmed landsman, he was nevertheless embarking on a sea venture about which many younger men would have thought twice.

Fray Tomás, at the age of thirty-one, seems to have had better sea legs than his colleague, and probably looked forward to the voyage with somewhat more enthusiasm. He was born in 1743 in northern Spain, at Brizuela, near the Cantabrian coast, and entered the Franciscan Order nineteen years later.[119] Although he had done less exploring than Crespi, he was a keen observer, and we sometimes learn from his account small details the other diarists fail to mention. He alone, for example, notes that not all the participants in the voyage of discovery were human. "The crew," he wrote just before leaving Monterey, "put on board ship four young bulls and some pigs which the Captain Commanding of the Presidio presented to the cabin mess."[120]

Of all the ship's company, the one about whom the most confusion has arisen is its surgeon—with some curious consequences. When the *Santiago* left San Blas in January 1774, a certain José (or Joseph) Dávila went on board, accompanied by his wife and son, bound for Monterey. Relying on a manuscript letter that Serra wrote to Bucareli from Monterey on 21 June 1774, Herbert Bolton recounts the brief and inglorious career of this person aboard the *Santiago*:

> *Dr. Joseph Dávila . . . was one of those many congenital landlubbers for whom the ocean has unconquerable terrors. . . . On the voyage to San Diego the doctor lay prone in his berth, "not from illness, but from fear," says Serra. "It would take long to tell what was done to encourage him, but all in vain. And as soon as he set foot on land [at San Diego] he armed himself with a firm determination not to embark again. His wife begged and I urged, but we could not budge him. And there he is remaining till he has an opportunity to come [to Monterey] by land."*[121]

Although Dávila was evidently a medical doctor, he was not the ship's surgeon. That title belonged to one Pedro Castán y Hoyos, whose name appears in that capacity on the roster drawn up at San Blas in January 1774.[122] Unlike his "congenital landlubber" colleague, Castán remained steadfastly aboard ship throughout the *Santiago*'s arduous northern voyage of discovery. How effective his services were in treating illness or injury among the crew is difficult to say, but only two lives were lost.

Whatever honor or glory is due the ship's surgeon, it was unquestionably Pedro Castán, not José Dávila, who had earned it. Yet, by an unkind and whimsical twist of fate, it was the latter who was so credited by Hubert Howe Bancroft in the 1880s, as well as, later, by the eminent authority on Spanish exploration on the Northwest Coast, Henry Raup Wagner. This mistaken identity seems to have arisen when Bancroft's writer, Henry Lebbeus Oak, wrote in the *History of the Northwest Coast* that "surgeon Dávila took the place of the regular surgeon."[123] Oak further inflated Dávila's undeserved reputation as surgeon-explorer by assuming that he had also sailed on the *Santiago* on its second voyage in 1775.[124] This may be only a ripple on history's grandly flowing tides, but Pedro Castán surely deserves better at the hands of posterity—and José Dávila equivalently less.

The name of Manuel López, the ship's boatswain (*contramaestre*), has suffered no such mistreatment by historians, but fate denied him the role he had expected to play in the voyage. On the morning of 7 June, the *Santiago* was warped into position off Monterey's Punta de Pinos, where its officers hoped to catch a favorable breeze. Fray Tomás, with his usual attention to detail, describes "the ceremony of hoisting the Spanish flag and firing a gun,"[125] but a persistent northwesterly wind prevented any progress. To make matters worse, boatswain López fell ill that night.

Whatever ailed him was serious. Three days later, while the ship still awaited a favorable wind, Peña wrote in his diary:

> *I received the confession of the boatswain,* Manuel López; *soon afterward* Father Fray Juan Crespi *administered the rite of extreme unction to him, and he expired at about half past four. The corpse was sent to the church at the* Presidio, *that it might be given sepulture by the fathers ministers of the* Mission *of* San Carlos.[126]

At noon the next day, June 11, the wind enabled the ship to get under way, but it sailed without its unfortunate boatswain. Who assumed López's duties is not immediately clear, nor does anything in the record shed light on the matter, until the end of the voyage.

When the *Santiago* returned to Monterey on 28 August, Pérez requested the ship's officers to sign a statement affirming that he had "read to us daily the events of this voyage, telling us the main happenings of each day; and that the . . . diary is a literal copy of the original . . . [and] that whatever is in it is true."[127] The first signatory to this statement is "As boatswain, Juan Pérez." Two members of the crew had the same Christian and surnames as the captain's, gunner Juan Melión Pérez and cabin boy Juan Acencio Pérez. Presumably it was the former to whom the boatswain's duties were assigned.

The statement attesting to the Diary's authenticity includes the names of four other members of the crew, namely Carlos Ortega, second [boatswain]; Francisco Fernández, first boatswain's mate; Manuel de Rojas, first carpenter; and Francisco Alvarez y Rua, first caulker. Both pilot Martínez and surgeon Castán signed similar but separate statements.[128]

There was evidently only one death on the voyage besides that of López. The demise of the young man named Salvador Antonio from an unspecified illness is recorded by Pérez on 24 July 1774.[129] The captain says he was "without a surname," describing him as a *grumetillo*—a young apprentice seaman. In a touching note, Pérez adds that he was married to one María Juliana, and that both of them were from the town of Guaynamota (in Nayarit, some fifty miles from San Blas). That Pérez knew and recorded such details about one of the lower-ranking members of the crew seems a little unusual. Both chaplains also mention the name and birthplace of the deceased sailor,[130] but it is the captain's account that adds the wife's name. Perhaps Pérez made a point of knowing those who served under him. The small tragedy reveals him as a man of some compassion, a quality not always evident in sea captains in the eighteenth century.

In few other instances are the names of crewmen mentioned. On 14 June, Pérez noted that a dozen men "most capable of handling a musket, were selected and placed under the command of Simón Fernández to train them in military procedure and perfect their knowledge of it in order to have them in readiness for any emergency."[131] Whoever Fernández was, his name does not appear on the ship's roster drawn up at San Blas, so he presumably came aboard at San Diego or Monterey.

The names of three crewmen not mentioned in the San Blas rosters were added to the record when Pérez wrote a cover letter transmitting his diary of the voyage to Viceroy Bucareli.[132] Writing at San Blas on 3 November 1774, he explains that the commander of the Monterey Presidio had requested him to leave a few crew members at the outpost to augment its personnel. Five soldiers who had been aboard during the expedition volunteered for the duty, one of whom was named Miguel Perigues. The names of the other four went unrecorded. In addition to the five, Pérez says he left "a muleteer who served since the first expedition named Manuel Badiola, and a discharged leather-jacket soldier named Juan Manuel Casillas."[133] Three other members of the crew, at the request of *padre presidente* Serra, were also left to assist at the Mission, but their names are not mentioned.

THE VOYAGE AND ITS CRITICS

When Viceroy Bucareli's instructions to Pérez are compared with the actual accomplishments of the 1774 voyage, there is no gainsaying that in many respects the Majorcan commander failed to fulfill the viceroy's purposes. The *Santiago* came no closer than within five degrees of the latitude (60°N) it was ordered to reach; at no point did Pérez make landings or perform possession-taking ceremonies; his sightings of the Northwest Coast were little more than glimpses. Measuring his achievements solely against his sailing instructions, one is hard pressed to grant him much glory.

The attention of historians writing about Pérez and his voyage of 1774 has inevitably been drawn to this gap between expectations and performance. As a result, he has been accused of lacking the courage considered vital to geographical search and discovery. Some have portrayed him as an enigmatic, irresolute figure, whose persistent and seemingly inexplicable reluctance to take risks robbed him of the achievements a more daring commander might have attained. It is a portrait that can leave one wondering how such a mariner ever held command on the quarterdeck of a vessel of exploration.

Robert Greenhow, a librarian and translator at the Library of Congress who researched early voyages of discovery to the Northwest Coast for the U.S. State Department in the 1840s, was particularly severe in his criticism of Pérez's competence as an explorer. Mincing no words, he wrote:

> *In this voyage [of 1774] . . . very little was learned, except that there was land, on the eastern side of the Pacific, as far north as the latitude of 54 degrees. The government of Spain, perhaps, acted wisely in concealing the accounts of the expedition, which reflected little honor on the courage or the science of its navigators.*[134]

More recent writers have similarly—and only slightly less harshly—recorded their low estimation of Pérez. Henry Wagner, in the 1930s, averred that "Pérez was entirely too timid for work in these northern waters. No good reason existed for not going up to 60° as ordered, and for not landing and taking possession, which was the real object in sending him."[135] And Warren Cook, writing almost on the voyage's bicentenary, observed that "Pérez seems to have lacked in full measure the intrepid qualities requisite for meeting the challenges of his mission."[136]

At least one of Pérez's fellow-officers, Pilot Francisco Antonio Mourelle, seems to have shared in the low opinion of him espoused by later historians. Based on remarks found in a 1791 compendium of documents, Henry Oak asserted that Mourelle accused Pérez of being

> *a commander who was driven back by thirst when he might easily have carried water for six months; who complained of scurvy, when only one man was lost; who could find no anchorage on a coast where many good ports existed; and who with his associates could write so many diaries with so little information.*[137]

Yet Oak hastened to point out that these stinging remarks, as well as those of Greenhow, might not be altogether fair. He went on:

> *It seems to me, however, that the criticisms are severe, since the diaries contain a tolerably good account of all that was learned in the voyage; and Pérez, a bold and experienced pilot, was a better judge than I, possibly better than the writers named, of the difficulties in the way of learning more.*[138]

Michael Thurman, who in 1967 published an exhaustive study of the Naval Department of San Blas, has also shown a willingness to interpret Pérez's actions more charitably. "It behooves the historian," he writes, "to consider Bucareli's evaluation of this expedition, and here there is less cause, apparently, for harsh criticism."[139] On 26 November 1774 the viceroy had written to Julián de Arriaga, Spain's minister of the Indies, that even if the expedition had not been "able to complete entirely the instructions . . . I always hold experience very useful, not that so much is accomplished in the first attempt as that it facilitates the outcome of those that follow and it affirms that in the 19 degrees to which we have advanced there is no fear of foreign settlement."[140] He had even recommended Pérez for a promotion.[141] Evidently, as Thurman suggests, the viceroy was not nearly as dissatisfied with him as subsequent historians have been.

Had Pérez really failed as miserably as his critics allege? A reasonable answer begins with recognizing that many of the things Bucareli's instructions sought were unlikely, if not impossible, for a vessel of the *Santiago*'s design, unaccompanied by a shallow-draft consort, to accomplish on a single voyage. The vastness and complexity of the unknown coastline Pérez had been sent to explore—to say nothing of its unpredictable weather—virtually guaranteed that few of the viceroy's ambitious aims could have been fulfilled in 1774. No one, least of all Bucareli himself, had a clear idea of how formidable the *Santiago*'s assigned task was.

Could Pérez have reached latitude 60°N as easily as Wagner thought? An examination of the ship's probable northward track as plotted on a modern map shows that, if it had continued to sail more or less due north, it would have eventually made landfall close to 60°N, in the vicinity of Yakutat Bay, Alaska. Instead, on 15 July at 8 o'clock in the morning, the captain called a meeting of the ship's officers, explaining "to them how I determined to fall in with the coast, considering the short water supply we had."[142] Whereupon he immediately set the *Santiago*'s bow on a course NE. From the point at which this decision was made, it was a little over five hundred nautical miles due north to Yakutat Bay, and some two hundred sixty nautical miles northeast to the landfall they would actually make in the Queen Charlotte Islands.

With hindsight and modern charts, one can easily fault Pérez for abandoning a course that could have put him on the coast almost precisely as ordered. But he was forced to make his decision on the *Santiago*'s rolling quarterdeck, essentially without knowledge of what lay ahead. At the conclusion of the voyage, he explained his dilemma in a letter he wrote to the viceroy dated 31 August:

> *The reasons attending this decision seemed reasonable to me, being as follows (not doubting Your Excellency's eminent consideration will judge them suitable):*

THE COURSE OF THE SANTIAGO

14 July to 17 July 1774

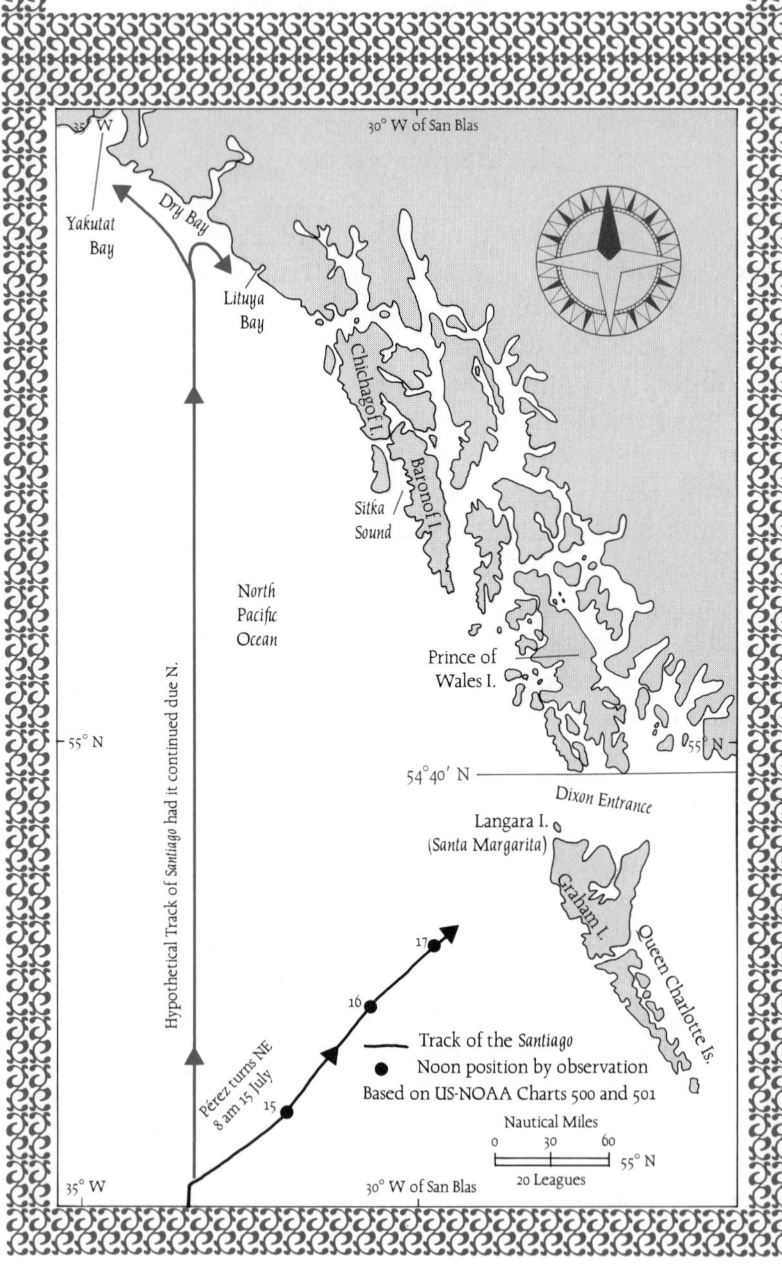

> *In the first place, the winds experienced were so consistently from the south, southeast and southwest, which are adverse for returning. Secondly, to see the men already weakening from the cold and various ailments which had attacked them. And thirdly, considering the small water supply we had and no certainty of a port to replenish it; and at the same time finding only two full water casks, others partly and some entirely empty.*[143]

While there is little doubt that this decision prevented Pérez from complying with the letter of his instructions (and possibly deprived him of the honor of discovering Yakutat Bay), it may just as plausibly have saved the lives of all aboard the *Santiago*. If he erred on the side of caution, in retrospect it was a reasonable error for which he cannot be entirely faulted.

As for his failure to go ashore once he reached the coast, that may have been more the result of unfavorable circumstances, or just plain bad luck, than excessive cautiousness. Even if the two-hundred-twenty-five-ton *Santiago* had been well suited to shallow-draft coastal exploration, the section of coast where Pérez made his first landfall (northwestern Graham Island, in the Queen Charlotte group) is not noted for its inviting harbors. And when he reached an area with the prospects of a better anchorage, the weather took a turn for the worse; uncooperative winds and powerful tidal currents (probably in Dixon Entrance) soon extinguished all hopes of anchoring and going ashore. His *Diario* records his frustration:

> *It was afternoon [20 July] and everyone was cheerful; but less so I, who wanted to anchor but was unable to get help from the wind. It made me ill-tempered, and even more so seeing that without a wind the furious flow of the current was separating me from the coast. I had thought about anchoring in an inlet formed by the coast, sheltered from all the winds, but since the wind and current prevented me from it, I had to submit to the will of God.*[144]

Eighteen days later, on 7 August, when the *Santiago* anchored in the outer harbor of Vancouver Island's Nootka Sound (which Pérez called *Surgidero de San Lorenzo*), the ship's launch was "put in the water fitted out with sails and masts, with the purpose of locating a good anchorage, this one being unsheltered from the wind."[145] But before the launch could leave, his luck ran out again, and the *Santiago* narrowly escaped being driven onto a rocky shore by a sudden and unexpected west wind. Thus the opportunity to go ashore and take possession of the coast in the name of Carlos III was missed again—but certainly not because Pérez had not tried.

Elsewhere on the coast, especially along what today are Oregon and Washington, he showed a marked reluctance to put in near the shore.

The close call at Nootka may have shaken his nerve, but he avers that he encountered frequent rain squalls, hazy conditions and outright fog, making a close inspection of the coast hazardous. That conditions were often unfavorable for exploration is corroborated by the ship's chaplains, and the commander's judgment to stay a respectable distance offshore can scarcely be second-guessed.

Perhaps the least supportable charge leveled at Pérez and his colleagues is the notion (espoused by Mourelle and echoed by others) that they had written diaries containing little useful information. Wagner was particularly critical of the commander's abilities to measure latitude accurately, generally regarding the expedition's nautical data with a skeptical, if not jaundiced, eye.[146] The diarists of 1774, however, strove as diligently as any of their successors to record what they witnessed, and Pérez's navigational data can hardly be judged fairly by twentieth-century standards of accuracy. Some of his latitudes are admittedly unreliable, but when conditions were favorable (such as at Nootka Sound), he could determine the sun's position with as much accuracy as any mariner of the times. Moreover, Pérez and his colleagues wrote some richly detailed descriptions of the events in which they participated and of the native peoples and geographic features they encountered. If there was anything in Bucareli's instructions that was followed to the letter, it was Article XXV, which enjoined the commander to "keep an exact logbook of all the navigational details." [147]

The expedition's failure to record data in the form of charts was unquestionably a serious oversight. Nothing in the viceroy's instructions had required that maps be drawn, but Pérez seems nevertheless to have given some thought to the matter. In his letter to Bucareli of 3 November 1774 at San Blas, he remarks somewhat apologetically that "It has not been possible to construct a map of the coast discovered because the rolling aboard ship rendered it impossible, as well as the inconveniences suffered in these quarters of which Your Excellency is not unaware."[148] This does seem a lame excuse, because other navigators (for example, Hezeta in 1775) managed to prepare maps despite the *Santiago*'s rolling or the inconvenience of its quarters. One can only lament that, for whatever reasons, Pérez did not see fit to make a cartographic record of his voyage.

There is no denying that he was inclined toward a certain pragmatism in which caution overrode heroics. With his genuine concern for the well-being of his men—and possibly for his own fragile health—he was destined for something less than olympian stature in history's view. Yet he and his crew surely sailed the *Santiago* northward into the Pacific's unexplored expanse with much the same fear and courage as that of countless more famous Iberian explorers since the time of Columbus. Even though the results were less splendid than Viceroy Bucareli had hoped, that did not diminish the fortitude of those who participated.

SIGNIFICANCE OF THE VOYAGE

An expedition that sailed into unexplored waters and returned with verifiable accounts of the venture can scarcely be dismissed as unimportant. Whatever his shortcomings, Pérez had carried out the first reconnaissance of a coast hitherto known to Europeans mostly from vague or secondhand accounts, some of them of dubious veracity. To claim that he "discovered" the Northwest Coast may be an exaggeration, because other European navigators—Drake (in 1579), Vizcaíno (in 1602–03) and Chirikov (in 1741)—had seen parts of the coast earlier. But Pérez is certainly the first to have examined the islands off British Columbia and the coastal mainlands of what are now Washington and Oregon, leaving accounts sufficiently detailed and accurate to identify their locations more or less conclusively. It was, by any measure, a notable accomplishment.

Based on Pérez's own *Diario*, we can say with confidence that his 1774 expedition saw and described at least five localities. These were: Dixon Entrance, including the nearby capes and islands; much of the west coast of the Queen Charlotte Islands; a small section of the west coast of Vancouver Island, including the outer harbor at Nootka Sound; the Olympic coast of Washington State; and the central Oregon coast, especially in the vicinity of Yaquina Head. Pérez's failure was in making no geographic discoveries sufficiently sensational as to capture the imagination of his contemporaries, or—perhaps more important—of later evaluators.

When the *Santiago* reached Dixon Entrance, somewhat above latitude 54°N, Pérez realized he had come upon something unusual, describing it as "a great enclosure, the waters within it flowing with more violence than even in a narrower strait."[149] Speculating that it was a large enclosed body of water and not a strait, he persuaded himself that some "rivers discharged inside, which caused the current experienced to be so rapid."[150] His reasoning may have seemed plausible, but was quite wrong, leading him to underestimate the significance of his discovery. Far to the south, he may later have glimpsed the opening in the coast, at 48°30′N, that was eventually named for the semi-legendary Juan de Fuca; if so, he

THIS TWO-REAL COIN, bearing the portrait of King Carlos III of Spain, was issued at the Mexico City mint in 1774, the same year Pérez undertook his voyage to the Northwest Coast. It is in the Tillamook County (Oregon) Pioneer Museum. The hole piercing it suggests that it was worn as personal adornment by Tillamook Indians or members of some other indigenous population. How it reached Tillamook County and any direct connection it might have with the Pérez voyage are unknown. (*Tillamook County Pioneer Museum*)

seems neither to have realized its import nor pursued the matter further.[151] While Pérez made the first recorded sighting of snow-covered peaks that were probably the Olympic mountains, he failed altogether to note the mouth of the Columbia River.[152]

The voyage was further obscured by the Spanish government's reluctance to publish details of the expedition.[153] Not until many years later, in the early 1790s, as Spain and Great Britain quarreled over the possession of Nootka Sound, was serious attention focused on Pérez's brief stop there in 1774. The strength of Spain's claim to that harbor depended in part on evidence that its navigators had visited it before James Cook's well-known stay there in 1778. Curiously enough, Cook's men had purchased from the Nootka natives evidence that seemed to confirm Spain's assertions—namely, two silver spoons that were generally supposed to be of Spanish origin.[154] Whether they were actually obtained from the *Santiago* or were even of Spanish provenance remains something of a mystery to this day, but the report of such articles among the Nootka natives added some credence to Spain's case. It also underscored the priority of Pérez's voyage, even if it did not necessarily confirm his presence at Nootka.

Perhaps the least foreseeable consequence of the *Santiago*'s voyage in 1774 was the role it would indirectly play decades later in the conflicting claims of the United States, Great Britain and Russia to the Northwest Coast. When John Quincy Adams, as secretary of state, negotiated the 1819 Transcontinental Treaty with Spain's foreign minister, Luis de Onís y Gonzales, one result was that the United States fell heir to Spanish claims on the Pacific coast, north of the forty-second parallel.[155] These claims (espoused by Viceroy Bucareli, among others) had once extended as high as the sixtieth parallel, but the rights ensuing from prior discovery more realistically extended only to the fifty-fifth parallel. This was Pérez's rough estimate for the latitude of the point he discovered and named *Santa Margarita* (probably today's St. Margaret Point, on the northernmost of the Queen Charlotte Islands).[156] On the strength of this, Adams pressed the Russian foreign minister, Count Charles Nesselrode, to accept this parallel as the southernmost limit of Russian claims in North America. Nesselrode readily agreed, provided that the line was set at 54°40′N, to ensure that the southern tip of Prince of Wales Island remained in the Russian sphere. The two nations reached formal agreement on the line in April 1824; within a year Great Britain (in a separate treaty with Russia) had also accepted this demarcation as the northern limits of the Oregon Country, which had been held by it and the United States in so-called "joint occupancy" since 1818.[157] The latitude that would later be made famous in the American electioneering slogan "Fifty-four forty, or fight!" thus divided Alaska and the Oregon Country; although its connection with Pérez's voyage half a century earlier has seldom, if ever, been mentioned, it nevertheless exists.

A major contribution of the 1774 expedition has suffered what may be the most undeserved neglect of all. Pérez and his fellow diarists wrote detailed descriptions of the Haida Indians at Langara Island in the Queen Charlottes, and other—though less complete—observations of the natives at Nootka Sound. These ethnographic notes may be the most valuable legacy of the entire voyage.

The accounts by the ship's chaplains have been available for some years in published English versions,[158] but it is regrettable that those of neither Pérez nor Martínez have hitherto been published in English translation. Their writings are as rich in information as those of Peña and Crespi, and in a number of instances they supply material not found in the chaplains' diaries. Added to Cook's exhaustive observations recorded four years later at Nootka, the documents provide us with a remarkably complete picture of native life unchanged by European contact in two parts of the Northwest Coast.

It is no small irony that, for all Pérez and his men did on behalf of Spanish imperial claims, the ultimate beneficiary of their exertions was a nation yet to be born in 1774. It may be even more ironic that their most lasting contribution was to provide us a glimpse of a way of life that has long since all but vanished.

SIX DOCUMENTS OF THE 1774 PÉREZ VOYAGE

INTRODUCTION TO THE DOCUMENTS

When the *Santiago* returned to Monterey late in August 1774, its historic voyage of discovery had been meticulously chronicled in the *diarios* of Pérez, Martínez, Crespi and Peña. Other accounts, written some time after the voyage had been completed, also exist.[1] No sooner had the ship put in at Monterey than Pérez—who knew he had some explaining to do for failing (among other things) to reach the sixtieth parallel—set about composing a letter to Bucareli on 31 August, essentially a summary narrative of the voyage. When he reached San Blas, he wrote a second letter, on 3 November, transmitting the diaries he and Martínez had kept to the viceroy in Mexico City. Moreover, at least two inventories from December 1774 list the articles obtained by the expedition in trade with Northwest Coast natives.[2] The Spanish crown, however, did not see fit to publish any of these records.

The *diarios* of the two Franciscan chaplains were turned over to *padre presidente* Serra at Monterey, who then sent them on to Bucareli in Mexico City. Peñas's Diary (in duplicate) was dispatched by overland messenger, while Crespi's was sent by ship a month later.[3] Through these documents, details of the voyage were gradually made public, and for two centuries they have remained the only available eyewitness accounts in either Spanish or English.[4]

A rather different fate awaited the writings of the ship's two principal officers. Their diaries remained on board the *Santiago* until it reached San Blas in November 1774. The authors had probably made clean copies of the diaries they had kept on the voyage, and it is likely that these fair versions were remitted to the viceroy. If that is so, it is not clear what became of the originals. The diaries sent to the viceroy went into the custody of one Melchor de Peramas, in the secretary's office of the viceregency, who was directed by the viceroy to make a copy of Pérez's Diary (for the period 11 June–28 August 1774), and of an extract from Martínez's Diary (for 20–21 July 1774), which were both certified on 23 November and sent on to Madrid. At the same time, certified copies of Pérez's two letters accompanying the diaries were also made and similarly remitted to Spain.

The Pérez and Martínez documents retained by Peramas were eventually housed in what is today the Archivo General de la Nación in Mexico City. The copies made from them and dispatched to Madrid found their way into the Archivo General de Indias at Seville. Since neither the documents on this side of the Atlantic nor those on the other have hitherto been published in two centuries, they are unlikely to have been read by more than a handful of persons. Microfilm versions of the manuscripts were obtained from these archival sources by the Oregon Historical Society in 1977; the translations of the first four documents herewith published have been made from them.

The only previous English translation of these materials known to this author is that made by Margaret Olive Johnson in a thesis she presented to the Faculty of the College of Social Sciences at the University of California in 1911 for a Master of Letters degree. Entitled "Spanish Exploration of the Pacific Coast by Juan Pérez in 1774," it opens with a brief introduction, followed by unannotated English translations of Bucareli's transmittal letter to Minister of the Indies Julián de Arriaga and the four documents of Pérez and Martínez that Peramas had had copied and certified for dispatch to Madrid. Ms. Johnson evidently made her translations from transcripts of these in The Bancroft Library.[5]

In discussing the importance of Pérez's Diary, she observes that it "contains a much fuller account than those of Father Crespi and Peña."[6] This may overstate its virtues a little, but Pérez's account unquestionably offers much more concerning the voyage's nautical aspects, and may have an edge in describing the newly discovered lands and native peoples the expedition had encountered. As a mariner, he was much more conversant with nautical technology and terminology than the chaplains, and as captain he was certainly in a good position to know about the workings of the ship under his command. His sailing instructions, moreover, impelled him to record an abundance of geographic and ethnographic details whenever new lands or natives were encountered. And no one aboard the *Santiago* was more diligent in this regard than the captain himself while constantly looking for any signs of foreign encroachment.

As for the extract from Martínez's Diary that Bucareli had copied and sent to Spain, we can only wonder why he chose merely the entry for 20–21 July (from noon to noon). His letter of 26 November 1774 to Arriaga explains only that the Pérez Diary "agrees with that of his second mate [Martínez] (with the exception of the latter's mentioning the events of the 20th and 21st of July which Your Excellency will see from the enclosed copy).[7] Whatever caught the viceroy's eye in Martínez's entry for 20–21 July can only be guessed. One likely possibility is the opinion Martínez advanced to account for the presence of "half of a bayonet and . . . a piece of a sword made into a knife" among the Indians at *Santa Margarita*.[8] It was the second officer's belief that these objects "may be relics from the unfortunate men" lost by the Russian explorer Aleksei Chirikov in 1741.[9] As this was the nearest thing to Russians the expedition had seen on the coast, the viceroy may have wanted Madrid to have all the particulars, including Martínez's speculations—which do not appear in Pérez's Diary.

The order in which these four documents are arranged here is the same as that in the microfilm versions obtained by the Oregon Historical Society: the two Pérez letters first, followed by his Diary and the Martínez extract.

In addition to these eyewitness accounts, documents written after the voyage was concluded also record the expedition's events and nautical data. In February 1791, Francisco Mourelle, pilot and second officer of the schooner *Sonora* in the expedition of 1775, compiled various papers relating to Pérez's 1774 voyage. This was done as part of his assignment as a special assistant to the viceroy, Conde de Revillagigedo, for the purposes of making a study of all maritime activity on the Pacific Coast. At the time, Mourelle was suffering from ill health.[10] Among these papers is a narrative chronicling the *Santiago*'s passages between San Blas and Monterey, as well as its exploratory phase on the Northwest Coast. Another of them, the "Tabla Diaria," takes the form of a ship's log book, with tables of nautical data interspersed with descriptions of events. Manuscripts of these two documents in The Bancroft Library have been used in preparing their translations.

These two accounts are essentially redactions of the Pérez and Martínez *diarios* made by Mourelle. In a brief preface to the collection, dated 15 February 1791, he explains his purposes to the viceroy, Conde de Revillagigedo:

SPANISH STAMP (issued 1967) commemorating Francisco Antonio Mourelle, who compiled and edited in 1791 a narrative and tabular summary of the Pérez voyage of 1774. Although he did not participate in the voyage, he was sharply critical of its commander's performance. Mourelle was pilot and second-in-command of the schooner *Sonora* during its epic voyage from Mexico to Alaska in 1775.

Considering that the information acquired by our explorations on the northern coasts of the Californias up to 61° of latitude is found scattered and jumbled in the voluminous diaries of their voyages, which only the learned professors can understand, I am arranging [them] with the utmost care to form a collection stripped of the useless repetitions that are common in said diaries; but which would nevertheless be instructive to mariners concerning the winds, [compass] variations, currents, harbors, rivers, and lastly, the character of the natural resources of their countries, and tendencies in trade, religion and government.[11]

In an editorial note appended to his narrative, Mourelle voices his displeasure about what he regards as the expedition's poor performance, remarking that "except for finding out that the coast continues to the northwest, we remained in almost the same ignorance after the voyage."[12] Whatever truth there may be in these allegations, the voyage effectively opened the coasts of what today we know as British Columbia, Washington and Oregon to European exploration. Although the expedition failed to meet the high hopes of its viceregal sponsor and to gain Mourelle's retrospective approval, it was by no means a debacle. Certainly the accounts written by its commander and second officer have not deserved the obscurity to which they have been assigned for so long. What follows only partially remedies that obscurity, but it does offer, for the first time in published form, English translations of Pérez's own detailed accounts (together with Mourelle's redactions) of this sometimes maligned yet epochal voyage to the Northwest Coast in 1774.

Juan Pérez's Letter to Viceroy Bucareli 31 August 1774

Most Excellent Sir:

On 31 August, I informed Your Excellency of my happy arrival at Puerto de Monterey, returned from the [voyage of] discovery that, by Your Excellency's order, I was to undertake. And, in case this may not have reached Your Excellency's hands, I have considered it advisable to insert its text in that which follows:

Most Excellent Sir:

On the 5th of June I communicated to Your Excellency my departure from this port in order to carry out the worthy orders that Your Excellency deigned to put in my care. Now, returned from my voyage, I am taking time to report to Your Excellency (although briefly) what happened during my voyage to the north of Monterey, reserving for my arrival at San Blas the relating of a full account with the diary, and the course followed from my departure until my arrival at Puerto de San Blas, which, God willing, will be by the 15th of next November.

I set sail the 11th day of June. It was not possible to set a course until the 18th of the same month, as a result of having experienced during this time light and variable winds with some calms and fogs.

Having set a course, as I have mentioned, with the wind out of the northwest, I lost latitude until the 24th, when I observed the latitude at 30 degrees 44 minutes.[1] From this day, the winds were more favorable to

2

Exmo Señor = En 31. de Agosto participè à
V. E. mi feliz arribo al Puerto de Monterey,
buelta del descubrimiento que de orden de V. E.
fui à emprender, y por si esta no huviere lle-
gado alas manos de V. E. he tenido por conve-
niente insertar en esta su contexto que es
como se sigue:

Exmo Señor.

Con fecha de 5. de Junio participè à V. E. mi salida de este Puerto para poner en practica las apre-
ciables ordenes que V. E. se digno poner ami cuida-
do y ahora regresado de mi viage, paso à informar
à V. E. (aunque sucintamente) lo acaecido durante mi Navegacion al Norte de Monterey re-
servando para mi llegada al Puerto de Sn. Blas
decir sobre todo con el Diario, y derrota executado
desde mi salida, hasta mi llegada al Puerto de Sn.
Blas que mediante Dios sera para el 15. de
Noviembre proximo.

INITIAL PAGE of Pérez's letter to Viceroy Bucareli, 31 August 1774. (*Archivo General de Indias, Seville*)

proceed north (but, sir, I experienced spells of such thick fogs that they caused great fear and trepidation in navigating these unknown waters, although the winds were favorable). On 2 July, I observed the latitude at 39 degrees 56 minutes north,[2] after which day the winds continued increasingly favorable for ascending to the north, but more and more the sky and horizon were shrouded in fog. It seemed as if it rained continually, falling with such violence that it caused much surprise among the crew, for they were not accustomed to cold climates. Nevertheless, I continued ascending with conditions such that on 15 July I observed the latitude to be 51 degrees 42 minutes north, in which latitude I determined, with agreement of pilot Don Estevan José Martínez and other officers, to set a course in search of the coast in order to discover it.

The reasons attending this decision seemed reasonable to me, being as follows (not doubting Your Excellency's eminent consideration will judge them suitable):

In the first place, the winds experienced were so consistently from the south, southeast and southwest, which are adverse for returning. Secondly, to see the men already weakening from the cold and various ailments which had attacked them. And thirdly, considering the small water supply we had and no certainty of a port at which to replenish it; and at the same time finding only two full water casks, others partly and some entirely empty.

In fact, I implemented my decision, the weather continuing the same, gaining some latitude until on the 18th of the same month I discovered the coast (which was no small good fortune). Having observed the latitude in 53 degrees 43 minutes north,[3] I continued sailing along the coast with the purpose of finding some shelter in order to anchor and take on water, and to take possession as Your Excellency ordered me in my Instructions. But all in all I was unable to find a place to do as I had so much wanted.

I continued, as I have just mentioned, ascending to the north without observing the sun or stars, because they were seldom seen on the entire voyage, until arriving at a place, where we were for several days, tacking in the certain hope of finding what we sought.

This location or place is in latitude 55 degrees north.[4] Presently, I found a large multitude of Indians who came out to meet me in their canoes. They were a beautiful people indeed, the men and women alike, being white complexioned, [with] fair hair and eyes blue and brown.[5] They were very docile, judging by the appearance of those who came along side in 21 canoes. There were up to two hundred or more Indians, not counting two canoes filled with women and some small children. They traded with the crew, exchanging various trinkets. I also gave them presents and they gave me some blankets made by their own hands, which I will forward to Your Excellency on my return.

The encounter with these people made me want to anchor in order to trade with them and inform myself about the land and everything Your Excellency requested of me in my Instructions; but the weather deprived me of this pleasure, as Your Excellency will see in minute detail in the diaries. Already tired of preparing to put into a port and not finding any, I determined to continue exploring from the said 55 degrees toward the south, endeavoring to approach the coast as close as possible. But neither the wind nor the cloudy weather gave me the opportunity until the 28th of the same month, whereupon in latitude 52 degrees 20 minutes I sighted from off the coast a view of a lofty mountain range.[6] I was unable to get near it, however, because I was immediately becalmed; and when the wind resumed blowing it did not allow me to get near [the coast].

I continued with some hope that at 50 degrees I would perhaps encounter some change in the winds. Perforce, I thus descended to 48 degrees 35 minutes without seeing the land, although I made every effort to reach it; this latitude being observed on August 5.[7] After this I was gaining [latitude] until 49 degrees 30 minutes north, where I anchored on the 8th of the said month in a roadstead which appeared suitable to me for the purpose of taking possession, although it was unsheltered.[8] But being becalmed and seeing that I was in 25 *brazas* of water, I anchored close to shore with a kedge anchor, spending the rest of the night in a calm sea.

The 9th dawned with the same conditions. Seeing that the weather was giving me some hope, I ordered the launch into the water, which was done very quickly because everyone shared in my desire to land. However, sir, when I was preparing to head for land a wind suddenly sprang up to the west so furious that in an instant it raised the sea, causing alarm, as that anchorage is uneven and extended about 4 or 5 leagues to sea. The condition of the sea and wind were becoming threatening. Seeing this unexpected contingency, and that the frigate was dragging the stream anchor and going rapidly toward the coast, I saw the need to order the stream cable cut; and I set sail to escape the danger of all perishing. Finally, with God's help and under a full press of sail, I managed to get away from this bad place, in which only the desire to land and comply with Your Excellency's orders had obliged me to drop anchor. It was not to be God's will, or, what is more certain, I was not deserving of it.

In this place many Indian canoes came out to us, which stood guard by us off the bow and stern all night. They came alongside the next day, and gave us sardines, and the men picked up some sea otter and seal furs in exchange for Monterey shells. They are very docile and not so lively as the ones earlier, but just as white and handsome as the others. They are also poorer and, by their appearance, less talented.

As I have explained to Your Excellency, I set sail with the launch at the stern as soon as I retired from this bad harbor. I prepared to take it on board, which was accomplished with a great deal of trouble from the heavy sea running and because of the men's weakened condition—there were already many of them afflicted with the evils of scurvy.

We continued running with the foresail all day and night, descending to the south, always endeavoring to keep the land in sight if the weather permitted—although the fogs did not allow us this one pleasure. Believe me, Your Excellency, the days we were not plagued by fog were few, as were the days that we took observations. Following the confusion of fogs, heavy showers and other adversities, we descended to the latitude of 39 degrees 47 minutes north, making landfall at Cabo Mendocino, at a distance of 10 leagues, of which an observation and bearing were taken at noon on August 22, fixing the said cape in latitude 40 degrees 8 minutes north, and not in 41 degrees 45 minutes in which Cabrera Bueno and Sebastían Vizcaíno situate it.[9]

Off the aforesaid cape we experienced calm and light winds, with extremely heavy seas. Following along the coast, without being able to see the land because the horizons were very cloudy, we sighted the Farallones, which are named for San Francisco, on 26 August at 10 o'clock. It was so dark that they were not discernible until we were almost upon them. It was necessary for me to haul as much wind as possible to sail past them.

Most Excellent Sir:

Believe me, Your Excellency, I wanted to enter Puerto de San Francisco and explore it, and I would have sacrificed myself in order to fulfill completely the orders Your Excellency had entrusted to me. But, sir, how could good fortune offer me hope with the better part of my men sick with scurvy, and those who were not suffering from that evil afflicted with other troubles? This, combined with darkness, prevented me from entering it.

When I left Puerto de Monterey the crew was very busy unloading, besides the additional work of which Your Excellency knows; and I notified you that things were done here just as at Puerto de San Diego. This, together with the sicknesses with which God has afflicted them, exhausted them, making it impossible to carry out Your Excellency's orders. I have no doubt that from the winds we experienced we could have gone up to 60 degrees, but it was necessary to be sure we would have sufficient [time] in which to return.

Finally, Most Excellent Sir, I have thus endeavored, as the others who have accompanied me, to do as much as has been possible in order to attain success as Your Excellency commanded, remaining regretful for not fulfilling Your Excellency's desire as I might have wished. But as I have already said, whether or not it is the will of God or that such success is reserved for someone else, the fact is that the way is opened and recorded for others who may be worthy of sailing it with better fortune.

After having sighted the Farallones I anchored in this Puerto [de Monterey] at four in the afternoon of the 27th of the current month [August],[10] with the intention of wintering in it and San Francisco until past the equinox, and at the same time giving the crew some rest.

With God's favor, I will arrive in San Blas sooner than these letters. I did not send the diaries, although the chief reason for not sending them on this occasion is that while at sea it has not been possible to write down everything, so we contented ourselves with taking the noon observations, and sometimes with difficulty because of a heavy sea and severe rolling.

I have nothing else to report to Your Excellency except that I ask and implore Our Lord to keep you in perfect health for many years.

Puerto de San Carlos de Monterey, 31 August 1774.

Juan Pérez

Most Excellent Sir, Knight Commander of Malta,
Viceroy Don Antonio María Bucareli y Ursúa.

Juan Pérez's letter to Viceroy Bucareli 3 November 1774

Up to here, Most Excellent Sir, the contents have been of the cited letter, and now it only remains for me to report to Your Excellency that my departure from Puerto de Monterey was on the 9th of the past month [October] and my arrival at this [Puerto] de San Blas was today [3 November 1774]. During the short voyage from one port to the other we experienced a furious windstorm out of the southeast. Finding ourselves in the vicinity of Puerto de Monterey, laying to, we carried a sail so stiff that we sprang two rudder boards. At length, as always happens, a calm followed for 48 hours, and we continued thus until the 19th, whereupon with the wind out of the northeast we continued losing latitude without having had the least inconvenience.

Prior to my departure from the stated port I delivered to the commander of that presidio the provisions which I judged were not needed in order for me to return; and also 5 men of my crew whom its commander requested for service at that presidio. Those who were at last embarked were volunteers: Miguel Perigues, with four soldiers, and also a muleteer who served since the first expedition named Manuel Badiola, and a furloughed leather-jacket soldier* named Juan Manuel Casillas. To the reverend fathers of the Mission of Carmel I also left three men of my crew for the service of that Mission at the request of father president Fray Junípero Serra.

Attached are verbatim copies of the diary which I have kept during

*_Soldado de cuera_, terminology referring to the leather jackets worn by soldiers at Monterey as protection against Indian arrows.

my voyage, and that which likewise pilot second class Don Estevan José Martínez has kept, in which you will see noted, Your Excellency, everything concerning the voyage and the ship's course outbound and on its difficult return, not with that excellence we would have liked, but if everything contained in them is the pure truth there is no doubting that Your Excellency will excuse the defects found in them for they are not intentional.

It has not been possible to construct a map of the coast discovered because the rolling aboard ship rendered it impossible, as well as the inconveniences suffered in these quarters of which Your Excellency is not unaware. It has been left to my care to send to Your Excellency a rough draft of everything, although not [done] with the excellence to which drafting instructors are accustomed.[11]

And regarding the frigate, I have to tell Your Excellency that there is no defect with the afterpiece of the rudder that was added at Monterey. Overall, its qualities are good and it could make a voyage to Europe if that were necessary. May Our Lord preserve the important life of Your Excellency for many years.

San Blas, 3 November 1774.

Juan Pérez

I certify that this is a copy of the original which remains in my keeping in this secretary's office and vice-regency of the Northeast.

[City of] Mexico, twenty-sixth of November, seventeen hundred and seventy four.

Melchor de Peramas

Juan Pérez's "Diario" 11 June—28 August 1774

Continuation of the Diary kept by acting ensign, frigate grade, Don Juan Pérez, pilot first class of the Department of San Blas, with the so-called *Santiago*, also known as *Nueva Galicia*, under his command, which covers his departure from Monterey to explore the northern coast, and his return to this original port on 26 August of this year, 1774.

11th to Sunday 12 June 1774 At noon this day we cut the stream cable and set sail, giving orders to the second pilot of *El Príncipe*[1] that with its launch he might be able to recover the stream anchor and if so bring it aboard. Failing this, it would be left for the use of his ship. At the aforesaid hour *El Príncipe* saluted us by firing two cannons, and we responded with three in order to salute it and the presidio. We proceeded under full sail, the wind to the NW, variable from W to WSW, endeavoring to sail to the windward. At six-thirty in the evening the main topsail split, but it was repaired at once.

At sunset, Punta de Año Nuevo bore NW 5 degrees W,[2] a distance of 6 to 7 leagues, and El Carmelo to the SSW 6 degrees SW,*[3] a distance of 7 to 8 leagues.

The weather gives promise of tranquillity and being fair, judging by the position of the sun. The wind has been light and variable; the night has been clear and beautiful; the sky mirrorlike. It was the same at dawn. But as the sun came out, the fog came in so that one could not see any part

*Readers interested in a visual depiction of the direction these and successive bearings take are referred to the diagram on p. 221.

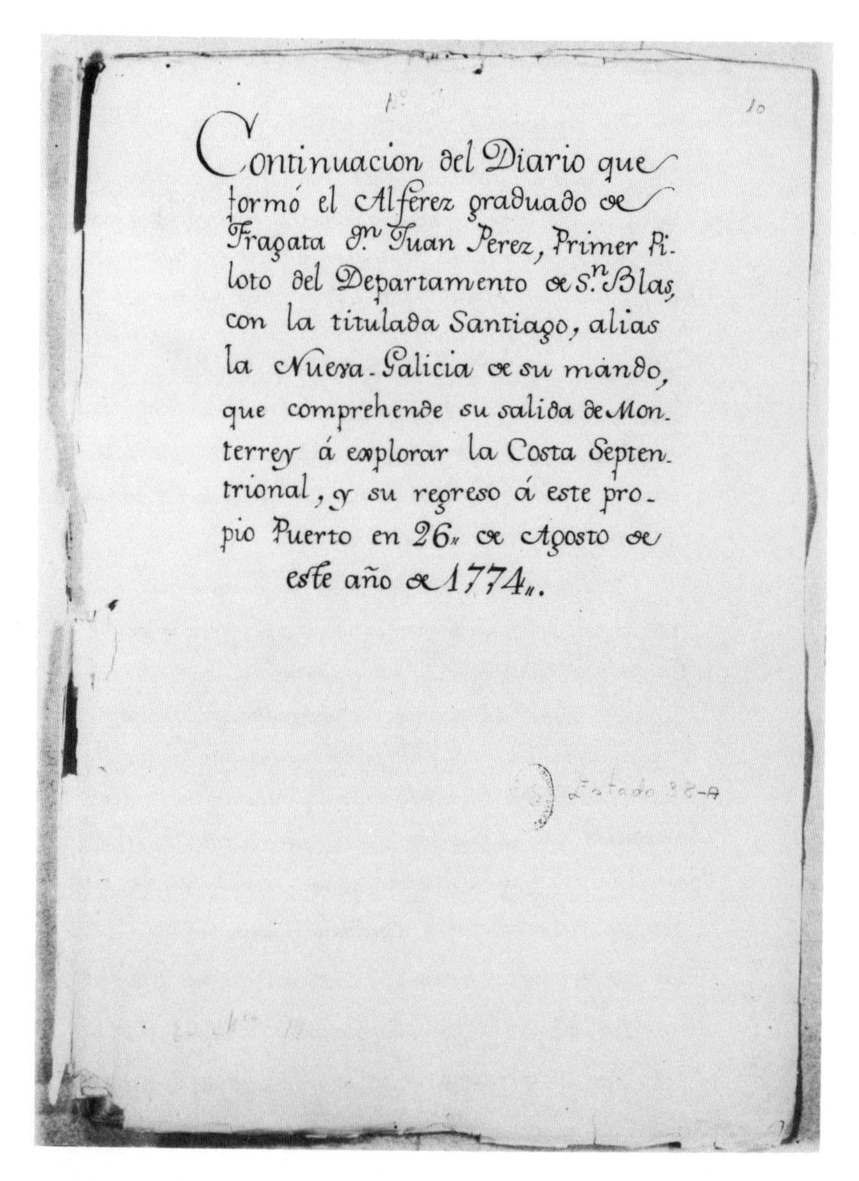

Continuacion del Diario que
formó el Alferez graduado de
Fragata Dn. Juan Perez, Primer Piloto del Departamento de Sn. Blas,
con la titulada Santiago, alias
la Nueva-Galicia de su mando,
que comprehende su salida de Monterrey á explorar la Costa Septentrional, y su regreso á este propio Puerto en 26 de Agosto de
este año de 1774.

TITLE PAGE of Pérez's "Continuación del Diario . . ." for the period 11 June to 28 August 1774. (*Archivo General de Indias, Seville*)

t.

Dia 11. al Domingo 12. de Junio de 1774.

A las doce de este dia picamos el Calabrote y nos pusimos a la Vela, dandole orden al segundo Piloto del Principe, para que con su Lancha recojiese el anclote, y si podia lo trajese abordo, y sino que lo dejase para el servicio de su Barco, a dha ora nos saludó el Principe con dos Cañonazos, y nosotros le respondimos con 3,, para saludarlo, a él, y al Presidio, y seguimos con todo el Aparejo largo el viento al NO: variable desde el O. al O.S.O: procurando salir para Barlovento. A las 6½ de la tarde nos faltó el Escotin de Gavia y luego inmediatamente se enmendó.

Al ponerse el Sol demoraba la Punta de año nuevo al NO. 5g.os O. Distancia de 6. a 7. leguas y la del Carmelo al SSO. 6g SO: Distancia de 7. a 8. Leguas.

El tiempo da esperanzas de serenidad, y bonanzas, segun la posicion del Sol, el viento ha sido lento, y variable, la noche ha estado clara, y hermosa, los cielos despejados y asi mismo amaneció, pero al salir el Sol, entró la neblina de suerte que no se pudo ver la tierra de una y otra parte y asi duró hasta las 10,, del dia que se avistó la tierra, y sondamos en 43. brazas de Agua, diligencia que continuamos toda la noche y de esta conformidad se concluyó la Singladura

INITIAL PAGE of Pérez's "Continuación del Diario . . ." for the period 11 June to 28 August 1774. (*Archivo General de Indias, Seville*)

of the land, and it stayed this way until 10 when the land was seen, and we sounded in 13 *brazas* of water. We continued on diligently all night, and in this way the day's run was concluded with nothing unusual happening.

12th to Monday 13 June 1774 We continued under full sail stretching our course to the W, hauling a rather fresh wind as much as we could. But this did not last long because presently it fell calm. At six in the evening one reef was taken in the main topsail.

At sunset Punta de Año Nuevo was observed at WNW 6 degrees NW, a distance of 4 to 5 leagues, and the extreme eastward part of [Monterey] Bay bore E1/4NE a distance of 2 to 3 leagues. As there was no steady wind, we maneuvered with the sails making use of the winds out of the E.

During the night there was much fog, such that no more water would have come down had it rained. At dawn the same conditions prevailed, and because of this the land was not seen.

Yesterday evening the novena to San Antonio of Padua was begun so that by his intercession we may have a happy and successful voyage.

The day ended with fog, and the weather was calm and variable. We found ourselves a distance of about 3 leagues from land and Punta de Año Nuevo.

13th to Tuesday 14 June 1774 With the wind WSW, varying as far as SW, we proceeded towards the south and SSE, until two in the afternoon, when we put about turning to a course NW1/4N; the wind, light out of the WSW.

When the sun set Punta de Año Nuevo bore to the NW 6 degrees W, a distance of 3 to 4 leagues, and at the aforesaid hour one reef was taken in the topsails.

At nine in the morning, finding ourselves close to the land, having sounded in 27 to 22 *brazas* of water, blackish sand, with Punta de Año Nuevo bearing to the NW a distance of 2 to 3 leagues, we prepared to anchor. A wind sprang up out of the WSW, so that we tacked toward the south, and in the aforesaid hour the reefings were let go in the main topsail in order to get away from the coast.

These entire 24 hours the wind has been light, the sea out of the NW, although it was not choppy. The skies and horizons were squally during the day as well as at night, with a very thick fog. And so it continued with nothing unusual happening.

Note: According to the map of the coast north of Monterey by Don Miguel Costanzó,[4] which Your Excellency (the Most Excellent Lord Viceroy of New Spain) transmitted to me, the Punta de Pinos is shown in latitude 36 degrees 36 minutes.[5] This is equivalent to the observation that I made in the first expedition, but on reflection that cannot be exact, considering that the horizons were covered with fog, as was evident to him since he accompanied me. Repeated voyages have convinced me that the said point is in 36 degrees 30 minutes, by observations made entirely to my satisfaction on clear and brilliant days.[6]

Today, 12 men, those most capable of handling a musket, were selected and placed under the command of Simón Fernández to train them in military procedure and perfect their knowledge of it in order to have them in readiness for any emergency.

14th to Wednesday 15 June 1774 At noon we remained becalmed, and at one a gust of wind came up from the WSW, and with full sails we steered to the south. At 6:30 in the evening a reef was taken in the main and fore topsails.

From 8:00 in the evening to 6:30 in the morning we have maintained one course or another with the purpose of keeping ourselves on a proportional mean, but at dawn we found ourselves a distance of 3 to 4 leagues from Punta de Pinos, bearing E1/4NE, and the Punta del Carmelo bearing SE1/4E a distance of 4 to 5 leagues, verifying that we had drifted with the current during the night.

At the last-mentioned hour a rather fresh wind came up out of the WNW; we tacked so as to head toward the SW and SW1/4S, but later it became calm.

During these 24 [hours] the horizons have been overcast, as have the skies, but fog has not been experienced as on previous days. For this reason it has been impossible to survey or make observations, although we have tried diligently.

15th to Thursday 16 June 1774 At noon we remained under full sail, the main and fore topsails with one reefing. At the said hour we tacked toward the NNW, the wind out of the W until 6:00 in the afternoon, when, with the wind having veered to the NW, we came about to the SW. At the said hour a reefing was taken in each top sail, but later they were loosened.

At sunset, the southern extreme of the Sierra de Santa Lucia bore SE1/4South,[7] a distance of 8 to 10 leagues; Punta de Pinos bore ESE, a distance of 6 leagues; and the northern extreme of Punta de Año Nuevo bore NW 1/4N, a distance of 6 to 7 leagues.

At sunrise, the southern extreme of the Sierra de Santa Lucia bore SE1/4E, a distance of 12 leagues. It was impossible to take a bearing on the other point because the horizons were overcast.

At the said hour, the reefings were loosened in the main and fore topsails, and we sailed on just as before.

All these 24 hours, the horizons have been overcast with the looks of a rain squall; the skies with clouds of varied hues; the wind fair; the sea from the SW, smooth.

Demarcation Point and Start of my Track I have learned from repeated voyages made to Monterey through repeated observations that Punta del Pinos is situated in 36 degrees 30 minutes of north latitude and in 15 degrees 55 minutes longitude. At noon today we found ourselves E1/4NE and W1/4SW a distance of 12 leagues from the said point, with the course W1/4SW and the distance 12 leagues. I found the difference in latitude 7 minutes south and the meridianal difference W35 minutes plane and 44 [minutes] spherical, which added to the longitude of 15 degrees 55 minutes makes 16 degrees 39 minutes of longitude, determined at noon; and subtracting the 7 minutes difference in latitude to the south from the latitude of 36 degrees 30 minutes leaves 36 degrees 23 minutes of latitude. These two points serve as the beginning of my track to the new discoveries that I am going to make in compliance with the orders you have communicated to me, Your Excellency, the Most Excellent Lord Viceroy of New Spain.[8]

Note: The longitude is determined by reference to the meridian of the Department of San Blas, the prime meridian being located in that port, which I note so as to serve as control.

16th to Friday 17 June 1774 We continued under full sail on a course NW1/4W and NW with not much wind. At six in the evening one reef was taken in the fore and main topsails.

All evening the wind has been weak, the clouds and horizon clear, and the sea smooth. [Our] having remained becalmed until five in the morning, the sun came up with the appearance of continued calm, which in fact happened.

At dawn the extreme [end] of the Sierra de Santa Lucia bore to the ENE, 18 leagues distant, by which bearing I consider I was in north latitude

36 degrees 9 minutes, and in longitude 16 degrees 56 minutes, not having been able to make observations because of the obscured condition of the horizons. Nothing has happened worth recounting.

[*17th to Saturday 18 June 1774*] We continued under full sail, the main and fore topsails on one reef, until one in the afternoon when they were loosened. At sunset Punta del Carmelo bore ENE a distance of 12 leagues. We took in a reef in the main and fore topsails at the said time.

As it grew dark the weather was calm, the sky and horizons were becoming foggy, and it remained so all night; it was the same at sunrise until 11 o'clock when it cleared up a little. At 6 in the morning the reefings in the main and fore topsails were loosened.

At noon we discovered the high land of Punta de Año Nuevo, which bore to the NNE a distance of 26 leagues, a bearing that agreed with the latitude observed today which is 35°44′, as mentioned above. Nothing in particular has happened.

[*18th to Sunday 19 June 1774*] We proceeded navigating with the fore topgallant sails, jibsail, and the main topmast staysail, turning to a course WSW with the wind from the NW rather fresh, the weather hazy. At four in the afternoon a reef was taken in the fore and main topsails; the jibsail was furled, as was the staysail, because of the freshening of the wind. At seven we experienced an increase in the wind's strength, and I ordered two reefs taken in. At nightfall the horizons were very hazy and obscure. At 10 in the evening we got powerful gusts that caused us to lower the topsails over the masthead caps until five in the morning. Owing to the wind's violence, whenever the sea got rougher we furled the [topsails] and remained with the two mainsails, enduring the northwester's bite, as well as the east wind which has caused us to experience a powerful rolling.

[*19th to Monday 20 June 1774*] At noon we remained laying to beneath the foresail as mentioned before in the events of the previous day. At three in the afternoon we hauled in the mainsail and loosened the foresail. At seven we noticed that the wind was returning to the same strength as when we were laying to. The foresail was hauled aloft, and we remained with the mainsail and the small foresail so as not to labor so hard as when making way under the foresail. It is, however, better to lay to with the foresail when there is some obvious danger from storm, which prevents heaving to broadside [and] is more expeditious for avoiding shipwreck or any other risk to which the unfortunate navigators who sail these waters are exposed.

At nightfall the horizons were bright, and at dawn they were the same. At 4:30 we hauled in the foresail and at 5:30 we set the topsails under two reefs. Nothing more especially new during these 24 hours. Thanks be to God.

[20th to Tuesday 21 June 1774] We proceeded navigating with the four principal sails, the topsails secured with two reefs, turning to a course West, with the wind out of the NNW, rather fresh and varying regularly within the fourth [NW] quadrant; the weather cloudless, the sea rather choppy from the N and NW. At one a reef was let out of the topsails, the jibsail, and the main topmast staysails. At 6 the jibsail was furled again, and with this we remained throughout the night with the other sails mentioned. At sundown the horizons were clear and beautiful, as they were at sunrise. At 5:30 in the morning the second reef was let out in the topsails and the jibsail in order to take advantage of the situation and not lose an instant of time.

Nothing more especially new during these 24 hours. Thanks be to God.

[21st to Wednesday 22 June 1774] We continued our voyage under full sail in order to keep up our vigilance, turning to a course W and WNW, with the wind fair out of the N, varying frequently from the NNW, depending on the courses previously ordered to be steered; the sea smooth, and the weather changeable, fair and gloomy. When the sun set the fore and main topsails were shortened by one reefing, and later at 8, noticing the obscurity and darkness of the horizons, a second row of reefs was taken in the topsails, and the jibsail was furled. Thus we remained all night. At 11:30 we had fog overhead, and it continued raining until the sun rose, which was at 6 in the morning, at which hour the reefings were loosened in the topsails and jibsails.

Nothing more especially new during these 24 hours. Thanks be to God.

[22nd to Thursday 23 June 1774] We proceeded navigating under full sail, turning to a course WSW. The wind fair out of the NW, and regularly varying from the N and NNW. The weather veiled the effects of the full moon, and the sea to the NW was rather quiet. At sunset a reef was taken in the fore and main topsails; at 8:30 we furled the jibsail and we remained with the said sails all night. At 6:30 in the morning the reefings were loosened in the

topsails and also the jibsail. Dawn broke with the same picturesque sky I have mentioned before.

Nothing more particularly new during these 24 hours. Thanks be to God.

[23rd to Friday 24 June 1774] We proceeded on our voyage under full sail, turning to a course WSW. The wind was from the NW, regularly varying from N to NNW. The weather was overcast, and the sea rather quiet as on the aforesaid courses. As the sun set we shortened both topsails with a reef, and furled the jibsail. At nightfall the horizons on the four quarters were squally, although they did not appear to offer any trouble, and at sunup they remained the same. At 5:30 we lowered the main topmast staysail, with the purpose of repairing it. Between the hours of 6 and 8, the two reverend fathers said mass,[9] and at 8:30 the reef of the topsails and the jibsail were loosened. At the same time the wind changed to NNE, fair, with frequent mist almost like fog. At 11 the sky became cloudless, but not for long; yet it gave me time to observe as much as I wanted. Nothing especially new during these 24 hours. Thanks be to God.

[24th to Saturday 25 June 1774] We proceeded on our voyage under full sail, except for the spritsail, turning to a course North. The wind NNE, rather fresh, as shown by the mileage tables. The weather was changeable, clear and squally, with frequent showers; the sea rather choppy from the NW. On account of the said weather, at sundown we shortened the topsails with two reefings, furled the jibsail and the main staysail. At nine they were loosened again; at 11 we noticed that the moon had cleared the horizon, and at the same time the wind changed to the ENE. A reefing was taken in the topsails, and with the sails thus set we passed the remainder of the night. It was the same at dawn; at 4:30 the reefings were loosened and the jibsail set, and at 5:30 the spritsail.

Nothing more especially new during these 24 hours. Thanks be to God.

[25th to Sunday 26 June 1774] We continued the voyage with all sails bent to the wind, turning to the NW. The wind NE1/4N, regularly varying from the East and ESE, with beautiful weather and a smooth sea. At 7 a reef was taken in the topsails and we furled the spritsail. Nightfall came with a delicate, picturesque sky from time to time, and at sunup it was the same. At 4:00 in the morning the reefings in the topsails were loosened and the spritsail

was unfurled. According to the observed difference in latitude sailed, and the course steered, it was found that the swells out of the NE have caused me to drift to the SW at the rate of 12°, with which the navigation of these 24 hours agrees.

Nothing more especially new during the said 24 hours. Thanks be to God.

[26th to Monday 27 June 1774] We proceeded on our voyage with all sails set, turning to a course NW1/4N. The wind was fair out of the SE, the weather beautiful, although occasionally light fog passed overhead, with rather small swells from the NE. At 6:30 we hauled the mainsail aloft, and we braced the yards all around. At 7 a reefing was taken in the topsails, and the jibsail and staysail furled, at which time the wind went calm. We remained throughout the night with the topsails above the masthead caps.

At nightfall the horizons were rather obscure and remained that way at sunup. At 5:30 we hauled the foresail aboard and the mainsail to the starboard; the topsails were set, as were the jibsail and staysail, [our] having observed the wind very slack NNE.

Nothing more especially new. Thanks be to God.

[27th to Tuesday 28 June 1774] We proceeded sailing on with the 4 principal sails, and the small sails, turning to a course WNW; wind calm from the North, varying frequently within the first [NE] quadrant; the weather beautiful; the sea from the N and NE did not fail, although it is nothing of much importance.

At nightfall the horizons were picturesque, and at sunup they were the same. At 5:30 in the morning we loosened the reefings in the topsails.

Nothing more especially new. Thanks be to God.

[28th to Wednesday 29 June 1774] We proceeded on our voyage under full sail, turning to a course NW. The wind fair out of the NNE, the weather clear and beautiful, and the sea favorable. At sundown a line of reefs was taken in the topsails, although I had little need to do it because it could be done when the moon rose. At nightfall the horizons were clear. At 10 in the evening we experienced a sudden lightning storm from the WSW direction, a rare occurrence in this part of the world. At sunrise the weather was the same as I have described. At 4 in the morning the reefings were loosened. At 9 the spritsail and the windward braces were secured over

the lines, the wind having changed to the NE. At 12 it swung around to ENE; the lines were loosened and we braced the rigging to the windward.

Nothing more especially new. Thanks be to God.

[29th to Thursday 30 June 1774] We proceeded on our voyage with all sails set, turning to a course NW1/4N. The wind ENE, varying frequently from the 2nd [SW] quadrant. The weather beautiful, although the skies covered with scudding, delicate clouds; the sea smooth. At 7 in the evening we furled the spritsail, and at 7:30 we took a line of reefings in the topsails, and night was passed with the rest of the sails that remained out. Sunup at 4, we loosened the reefings and put the jibsail on the yardarm of the spritsail in the same manner as a topgallant on the foresail, supplying lower studding sail. We had no opportunity to shoot the sun, neither at sunset nor at sunrise.

Nothing else in particular has happened during these 24 hours.

[30th to Friday 1 July 1774] We continued on our track with all sails set, turning to a course NW1/4N. The wind ESE, fair; the weather beautiful; the sea smooth. At sundown the jibsail was put in the place it had formerly been on the yardarm of the spritsail, replacing it. We hauled in the studding sail and its boom. At 7:30 we furled the spritsail, and we continued all night with the remaining sails. At nightfall the horizons were fine, and at dawn they were the same. At 11 at night the mainsail was hauled aloft because of the wind's having shifted to the SE, and in the said hour we furled the main staysail. At 1:30 the spritsail was set; at 4 the mainsail was hauled aloft, because of the wind's having calmed. At 6 it returned gently to the ESE, at which all the sails were set, including the studding sails.

Nothing more especially new. Thanks be to God.

[1st to Saturday 2 July 1774] We continued our voyage under full sail, including the upper and fore studding sails, turning to a course NW1/4N. The wind fair, SE; the sea favorable. At 12:30 we hauled the mainsail aloft and inserted the upper and fore studding sails inside, and at the same time we expanded the rigging on the port side because the fog had come in on us. The wind was moderate from the SW. At 4 in the afternoon we remained becalmed; the mainsail was hauled aloft, and the topsails lowered over the masthead caps. At 6:30 we took a reefing in them; at 7 we noticed the wind from the W. At this they were hoisted, and we hauled aboard the mainsail. The wind immediately went calm again. At nightfall the

horizons on the four quarters were clouded, and at sunrise they were the same. We spent this night continually working the sails because of the variable light winds. At 4 it began to rain and it continued until 6:30. For most of these 24 hours we have remained becalmed. Nothing more especially new. Thanks be to God.

[*2nd to Sunday 3 July 1774*] The calm I mentioned Saturday lasted until 3 in the afternoon, at which time we noticed the wind blowing fair out of the NNE, varying frequently between the 1st [NE] and 2nd [SE] quadrants. We continued hauling the little wind that was available with the 4 principal sails and the small sails, turning to a course NW1/4W. The weather was clear and beautiful; the sea exceedingly smooth. Nevertheless, at nightfall the horizons were obscured and thoroughly clouded over, as they also were at dawn, although they did not appear to offer trouble. At 3 in the morning we loosened the reefings in the topsails and studding sails, in view of the wind's having shifted to the East. At 10 we had fog overhead, although not enough to obstruct observation.

Nothing more especially new. Thanks be to God.

[*3rd to Monday 4 July 1774*] We proceeded on our voyage with all the sail that we considered could be used to our advantage, according to the wind, so as not to lose [the advantage of] a short duration that assists us in our enterprise, steering a course NW1/4N. The wind fair, ESE; the weather overcast; the sea favorable. At sundown we furled the spritsail, and took in the fore studding sail. The jibsail was furled, as was the main topmast staysail, because of the wind's having changed to SE. A reefing was taken in the fore topsail at 7:30. The horizons were obscured at nightfall, but threatened no trouble; they were in the same condition at dawn. At 9 we hauled a corner of the mainsail aloft, the wind being astern. At 4 the reefing in the fore topsail was loosened and the studding sails set. We descried at a distance some flocks of small birds. We do not know if they are land birds or live on the sea. Nothing more new. Thanks be to God.

[*4th to Tuesday 5 July 1774*] At noon we remained under full sail, following a course NW1/4N, with the wind out of the SE, small swells, and the weather ominous. At one it began to sprinkle and continued until 3 in the afternoon, at which time it stopped, although the skies remained overcast. At 6 we took the studding sail inside, and the fore topsail was lowered, because it was not filling [with wind]. At a quarter to 7 a reefing was taken in, and at 7:30 we brought the fore studding sail inside, and we furled the spritsail. The horizons on the four quarters were overcast at nightfall. At 8 we noticed very thick fog, and it persisted until 11 at night, at which time the sky became clear and bright. At dawn the horizons were the same as at nightfall. At 4 the spritsail and the studding sail were set.

Nothing more especially new. Thanks be to God.

[5th to Wednesday 6 July 1774] We proceeded on with all the sails filled, turning to a course of NW1/4N. The wind SE, fair; the sea smooth. We have experienced very changeable weather. Since doubling Puerto de San Francisco[10] and Cabo Mendocino, we have not been free of frequent, very heavy and confusing fogs that sprinkle where they pass like rain showers.

At 7 in the evening we furled the spritsail, and after half an hour we furled the fore studding sail. We hauled the mainsail aloft, finding the wind astern, and with the foresail, fore and main topsails lowered on the masthead, we passed the night. The horizons at nightfall were hazy, and at 10 at night they cleared up from the SE to SW. At dawn they were the same as at nightfall. At 4 in the morning the fore studding sail was set. At 11 the reefings in the fore topsail were loosened, and the jibsail and main top staysail set, because of the wind's having swung around to SSW. Nothing more new. Thanks be to God.

6th to Thursday 7 July 1774 We proceeded on our voyage under full sail, turning to a course NW1/4N, with the wind W1/4SW, very fair and variable. At 5 in the afternoon it became so calm that we scarcely moved, and in this condition we have passed the remainder of the 24 hours. The weather is very changeable and continually shrouded in fog, which has on occasion looked like rain showers. At 7:30 we furled the spritsail and the small sails, and a reefing was taken in the topsails. At the same time the mainsail was hauled aloft, and returned aboard at 8. The horizons at nightfall were obscure and foggy, and they were the same at dawn. At a quarter to 7 the mainsail was hauled aloft, and until now nothing else new. Thanks be to God.

7th to Friday 8 July 1774 At noon we remained in a dead calm, with the mainsail hauled aloft, and a reefing in both topsails; the small sails furled. At 4 in the afternoon we noticed a light and variable air out of the N, and the mainsail was hauled aboard.

At nightfall the horizons were shrouded in thick and damp fog that had the appearance of rain; and this condition persisted at dawn. At 11 we noticed a light air out of the SE. For most of these 24 hours we have experienced the aforesaid conditions, shrouded in pure fog. Nothing more especially new, except that we have encountered various bird feathers and much *aguas malas.* [11] The sea is rather muddy. This occurred after we doubled Cabo Mendocino. Nothing else in particular. Thanks be to God.

[*8th to Saturday 9 July 1774*] From noon we remained with foresail, fore and main topsails, jibsail and staysail, the rigging cross-braced, and the mainsail hauled up. Thus we remained until 7, at which time a reefing was taken in the topsails, and the small sails were furled. We passed the rest of the night in this condition, with the foresail and the topsails aloft.

At 7 in the morning we loosened the reefings because of a slight, very weak air having appeared out of the SE.

For most of these 24 hours we have been becalmed and covered by a very thick, continuous fog, which had the appearance of rain showers. At 9 we loosened the studding sails. Nothing more new. Thanks be to God.

[*9th to Sunday 10 July 1774*] We proceeded on with all the sails filled, turning to a course NW1/4N; the wind out of the SE, very fair. The weather was fraught with very thick fog, which was so damp that it looked like rain showers. At 7 in the evening we took in a reefing in the topsails, and brought in the studding sails. The horizons at nightfall were very hazy, because of the fog just mentioned, and they remained the same at dawn. We also experienced a rather quiet sea out of the W, which enabled us to drift on the course I ordered to the NW. From 5 to 10 in the morning the wind blew out of the SE, for which reason the reefings in the topsails and the studding sails were loosened.

Nothing more especially new. Thanks be to God.

[*10th to Monday 11 July 1774*] We proceeded on our voyage under full sail, turning to a course NW; the wind fair out of the SSE. The weather remains overcast in the same fashion as I have described on past days, rigorously covered with fog. The sea is quiet out of the West, maintaining the same appearance as yesterday. At 7:30 we furled the spritsail and studding sails, and we took a reefing in the topsails. At 8 the main top staysail was furled, and in this fashion we passed the rest of the night. At dawn the skies were clear and bright, except that the entire circle of the horizon was hazy and shrouded in fog. At 5 in the morning it returned to [being] overcast as usual. The reefings and upper and fore studding sails were loosened, and we hauled aft the starboard corner of the mainsail. According to the difference in latitude that was found from yesterday to today, and the course steered [ordered?], I consider that, with the [magnetic] variation, which can be 67 degrees from N by East, and the quiet sea out of the W, they [the helmsmen] have strayed from my course 16° in favor of the N.

Nothing more especially new. Thanks be to God.

[11th to Tuesday 12 July 1774] We proceeded on under full sail, including the studding sails, turning to a course NW. The wind out of the south, fair; the weather overcast with very heavy fog, from which water fell just as if it were raining; the sea was calm. At 7 we furled the spritsail and the other small sails, and a reefing was taken in the topsails. At 9 it began to hail, and it continued all night. At 5 the wind swung around to WSW, at which we hauled the mainsail aboard, and we made fast the lines. At dawn the weather was the same as I have described, overcast and raining. At 11 the wind veered to the West, fresh and very cold. The horizon also had a threatening appearance, and it was observed that the sea is turbulent on the said course. This morning various ducks and small birds were seen.[12] Nothing more new. Thanks be to God.

[12th to Wednesday 13 July 1774] We proceeded on with the 4 principal sails, the topsails secured with a reefing, and we steered in this fashion, turning to a course NNW. The wind out of the West, fresh, varying regularly within the 4th [NW] quadrant. The weather was just as in our country in winter, cold and heavy with dense dark clouds, although we have learned that they may not bring bad weather. The sea rather turbulent out of the W. At 4:30 we took in the 2nd line of reefs in the topsails.

The horizons were cloudy at nightfall, and thus it dawned, except that the 4th [NW] quadrant was rather clear. At 4 we loosened a reefing in the topsails, and at 7:30 the 2nd one was loosened, as well as the small sails. Nothing more especially new. Thanks be to God.

[13th to Thursday 14 July 1774] We proceeded on under full sail, turning to a course N. The wind out of the WNW, rather fresh, and regularly varying in the third [SW] and second [SE] quadrants; the weather unsettled. Nothing significant about the sea for the present, although its movement was South and West. At 5:15 a squall came up out of the SW, which brought nothing

except some raindrops. At 6 the wind swung around to the said course. At nightfall the horizons were very obscure with heavy fog. We took a reefing in both topsails, and we furled the jibsail.

At dawn the horizons were the same. At 7 in the morning the wind began to blow fresh, with thick fog which obliged us to secure the topsails with the second reefing, and furl the main top staysails, which were loosened again at 9:30. Nothing more especially new. Thanks be to God.

[14th to Friday 15 July 1774] We proceeded on our voyage, turning to a course N. The wind out of the W1/4SW, fresh and regularly varying within the third [SW] quadrant; the weather continually squally with frequent showers; the sea rough out of the South and SW. At 6 we furled the main top staysail, and at 7 we made fast the topsails with the second reefing, because the horizons were looking ominous. At 11 at night the wind changed to the South, for which reason we cross-braced the rigging, and the corner of the mainsail was hauled aloft. At dawn the horizons were the same. At 8 a reefing was loosened in the main topsail.

Note: At 8 on this day I called a meeting of my pilot and the ship's officers in order to propose to them how I determined to fall in with the coast, considering the short water supply we had, the uncertainty of a port in which to obtain it, and other reasons that are expressed in the instrument accompanying this diary;[13] and which was done so they could sign for my protection.

Nothing more new. Thanks be to God.

[15th to Saturday 16 July 1774] We proceeded on our voyage with the foresail, the main topsail, one reef taken in it, and the two fore topsails, lowered over the cap of the masthead because they were not filled, turning to a course NE. The wind SW fresh, somewhat variable and inclined to the South. At 7:30 I ordered the 2nd reefing taken in the main topsail, and in the said condition we passed the rest of the night. The horizons were overcast at nightfall, and at dawn they were the same. At 4 in the morning I ordered a course NE, on the lookout for the coast. The reefings were loosened in the main topsails, as were those in the fore topsails at 6. At the said hour, we set the fore studding sail and hauled aft the port corner of the mainsail.

Today I appointed my pilot as actuary of the expedition by virtue of the power the viceroy vested in me.[14] Nothing more new. Thanks be to God.

[16th to Sunday 17 July 1774] We proceeded on our voyage with all the sails filled, turning to a course NE. The wind out of the SSW, fair; the sea was found to be rather turbulent out of the W and SW. The weather squally, although we experienced no trouble except for some small showers we have seen during these 24 hours. At 6:30 we furled the spritsail, and at 7:30 the fore studding sail. At 8 we took a reef in the topsails. At 9 we hauled the mainsail aloft, the wind having changed to the SW. The horizons were squally at nightfall as I have described, and the same at dawn when the reefings were loosened. At 5 in the evening signs of land were seen which looked like onions because they had a large head and [long] tail. The Chinese commonly call them *porras*, and they flourish in the water, usually being found [between] 80 and 100 leagües from the coast.[15] Nothing more new. Thanks be to God.

[17th to Monday 18 July 1774] We proceeded on under full sail, turning to a course NE. The wind out of the SSW, frequently varying in the 2nd [SE], 3rd [SW], and 4th [NW] quadrants; the sea fair, the weather clear during the day. At 7:30 I ordered the spritsail furled, and we brought in the fore studding sail, at the same time they took a reefing in the topsails. The horizons were squally at nightfall when we experienced frequent small showers. It was the same at dawn. At 4 the reefings were loosened. At 9 we loosened the jibsail and spritsail.

At 11 we saw the coast.[16] Nothing more new.

Note: It being customary on approaching land that one ought to record the course and corrected distance of the voyage executed in one's ship, it seemed proper to me to keep the rule by means of a correction, and thus I state: from Puerto de Monterey to *Punta de Santa Margarita* [St. Margaret's Point][17] I made the course North 29°W, and for a distance of 423 leagues.

The said point was found to be in latitude 55°N and longitude 14°08′ West of Monterey.[18]

18th to Tuesday 19 July 1774 We proceeded on, coasting along the land a distance of 4 or 5 leagues, under full sail and with all studding sails, steering on a course NNW-SSW. The coast runs thus according to the surveys that we made after we saw land, which was on the 18th instant. The winds remained out of the SE, South and SW, and they have remained so for the past 20 days.

At 4:30 we brought in the studding sails because in the SE, from which direction the wind was blowing, the sky and horizons had become dark, and at the same time it was raining. At 6:30 two reefings were taken in the topsails, and the mainsail was hauled aloft. The fore topsail remained lowered over the masthead, because it held no wind. At 7 I noticed that the weather was growing worse, and I ordered the two topsails furled, and at this time we laid to with the bow to the SSW. We remained in this condition all night, with continuing heavy showers. At 4 in the morning we hauled the foresail aboard and the mainsail was carried aloft; and we changed direction from the land. At dawn the horizons were overcast and it was raining.

The survey that we made was before the coast became clouded over at 6 in the evening. The most distant point that was observed was in the northern sector, a distance to the North of 10 leagues, compared with the southern sector to the ESE a distance of 5 to 6 leagues, and at the closest 3 leagues to the ESE.[19] At 5 the weather cleared up over the land, and it was seen that we were approaching within a distance of 6 to 7 leagues of it. I ordered the mainsail hauled aboard, and I managed to determine that the other [distant point] bore from me SE5°S a distance of 12 leagues, and the others to the north at NE5°N a distance of 10 leagues. At 6 in the morning I gave orders to loosen the main topsail and the two reefings in the fore topsail. At 9 we loosened one of the jibsails and the main topmast staysail.

Note: According to the survey of this morning this section of land runs N-S. I have not been able to observe or do anything of benefit since we found the coast because the weather we experienced was so bad—overcast horizons and fog, with continuous showers as I have already said.

19th to Wednesday 20 July 1774 We proceeded on with the four principal sails, the jibsail, and the main top staysail with one reefing, turning to a course ENE, the wind SE fresh, heading for a point surrounded by the sea. It jutted out from an extended hill and was about 3 leagues long, appearing separated from the coast and looking like an island from a distance. I named it *Santa Margarita*.[20] A great deal of smoke came from the said hill, and at 3 in the afternoon we descried 3 canoes, which came toward us. At 4:30 they arrived alongside, and in the meanwhile we took the occasion to examine the character of these people and their things.[21] In the first place, the men were of good stature, well formed, a smiling face, beautiful eyes and good looking. Their hair was tied up and arranged in the manner of a wig with

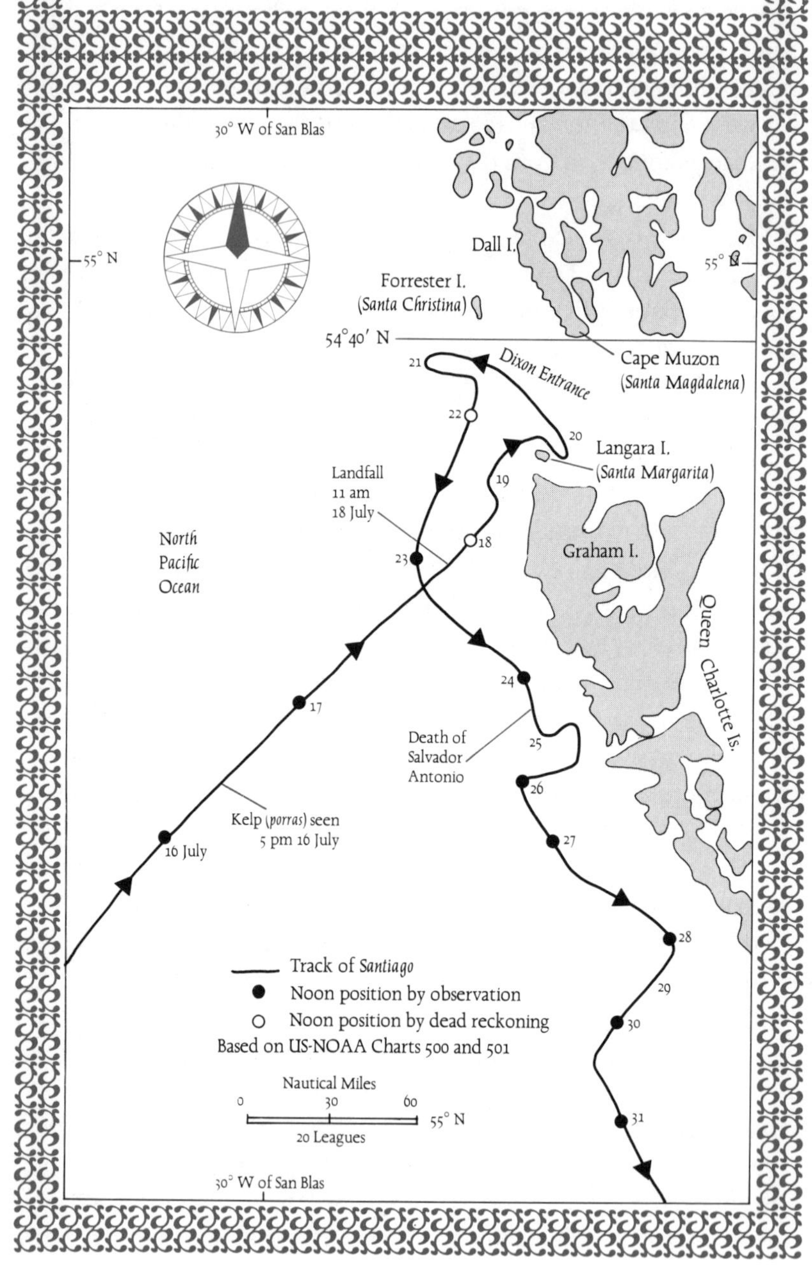
THE COURSE OF THE SANTIAGO
16 July to 31 July 1774
30° W of San Blas
55° N
Dall I.
Forrester I.
(Santa Christina)
54°40′ N
Cape Muzon
(Santa Magdalena)
Dixon Entrance
Langara I.
(Santa Margarita)
Landfall
11 am
18 July
North
Pacific
Ocean
Graham I.
Queen Charlotte Is.
Death of
Salvador
Antonio
Kelp (porras) seen
5 pm 16 July
16 July
Track of Santiago
Noon position by observation
Noon position by dead reckoning
Based on US-NOAA Charts 500 and 501
Nautical Miles
0
30
60
20 Leagues
55° N
30° W of San Blas

a tail. Some wore it tied in the back and had beards and mustaches in the manner of the Chinese people. The first thing they did when they approached within about a musket shot of the ship was to begin singing in unison their motet and to cast their feathers on the water, as the Indians do at the Santa Barbara Channel. But these [Indians] use a particular signal that is not used by the others of the Channel, nor those under our rule. They open their arms, forming themselves in a cross, and place their arms on the chest in the same fashion, an appropriate sign of their peacefulness.[22]

From what has been experienced with them, they are very adept at trading and commerce, judging by the briskness with which they dealt with us, and because before they would give any trifles they had to hold those things they wanted in their hands, examining them and satisfying their fancy with a look. If pleased with them they ask for more, making it clear that without giving more they will not pay. Noticing this, one may readily believe that there is frequent commerce between them. Their canoes are very well made and of one piece, except for a *farca* on the gunwale.[23] They are very swift. The Indians row with neatly-made oars or paddles that are one and one-half *varas* long. All their commerce amounts to giving animal pelts such as seals, sea otters and bears. They also have a kind of white wool, which they extract from an unknown species of animal that produces it.[24] They weave beautiful blankets, of which I acquired four. They are not large, but woven and wrought nicely. Of the three canoes referred to, the largest carried 9 men, and would measure about 24 *codos* long, and 4 wide.[25] The others carried 7 men. It was not noted that they had any weapons. They invited us by signs to come ashore, and we signalled that on the next day we would go there. With this they withdrew to the land at 5 in the afternoon.

The length of the hill I have mentioned runs North–South, for at 6:30 in the evening it bore from me E a distance of 5 leagues.

At nightfall the horizons were extremely overcast and it was raining. I ordered the second reefing taken in, and we remained in this condition, turning to a course SW1/4W. At 10 it went calm; at 11 the wind came up again, very fresh out of the SE, in such a way that at 12 I ordered the topsails furled. At dawn it calmed down somewhat, which gave occasion to use the topsails and to put about heading for the land. At 11:30 we drew near the *Punta de Santa Margarita*, with the intention of casting anchor if we found a fit place. Being advanced beyond the said point, we encountered a furious current, which had we not been careful would have halted the ship.[26] It had so much force that, moving along with the topsails and the foresail, and with a strong wind, we were barely able to keep the sails stiff, because of the greater flow of the current. And thus the day ended. Nothing more new. Thanks be to God.

20th to Thursday 21 July 1774 Considering that we were unable to accomplish anything against the swiftness of the current, we endeavored to withdraw ourselves somewhat, and being at a moderate distance [from shore], the wind slackened. Several canoes of Indians came into view, and seeing that we were not making any headway, they approached us and began trading with our crew.[27] But first, they sang and danced, and cast feathers in the air. All the rest of the afternoon 21 canoes of different sizes swarmed around. The largest of them, in which an old man came representing [himself] to be a king or captain, was from 25 to 30 *codos* long and about 10 wide.[28] It carried 24 to 30 Indians, and in the others some had 9, others 15 and others 7. All the people are stocky and good-looking, white in color as well as in their features. Most of them have blue eyes.[29] They tie their hair like the Spanish, and some wear a shoulder strap like soldiers. Those who wear mustaches also have beards. The king or captain referred to above carried his tambourine, jingling it. Before arriving they danced and sang; later they began to trade their pelts of sea otter, wolves and bears, of which the crew gathered in plenty in exchange for old clothes. They also collected some blankets beautifully woven and made, according to what I saw, on a loom. I also obtained some. I noticed among them some things made of iron in the canoes, such as instruments for cutting, like half of a bayonet and a piece of a sword.[30] Knives do not please them, and by signs they asked for long swords or *machetes*; but finally they settled for some knives that the sailors gave in exchange for pelts. They carried some small wooden boxes in which to store their things. I put a thousand questions to them, but they did not understand me, even by signs. Some of our crew jumped into their canoes, and two of them came aboard [the ship] to whom gifts of bread and cheese were given, as well as some glass beads to satisfy them. Meanwhile I held out hope that the weather would permit me to go ashore in their land. They embraced and kissed those who went in their canoes as a sign of friendship; and they invited them to go ashore to eat and sleep, telling them they had much to eat and drink.

Among the 21 canoes two were filled with women with babies at the breast and older children. They were all good looking, white and fair. Many of them wear bracelets of iron and copper, and some small rings of the same. They wear their clothes of pelts fitted to the body. They have a perforation in the middle of the lower lip, and in it they put a piece of painted shell, which strikes their noses when they speak, although they have normal movement.[31] Those who wear it apparently are married, because some of the young girls were not wearing it. They are of good build, like the men. Finally, they show evidence of docility and a good nature, because it was manifest in their actions. It was afternoon and everyone was cheerful; but less so I, who wanted to anchor but was unable to get help from the wind. It made me ill-tempered, and even more so seeing that without a wind the furious flow of the current was separating me from the coast. I had thought about anchoring in an inlet formed by the coast, sheltered from all the winds; but since the wind and current prevented me from it, I had to submit to the will of God. The referred-to inlet is sheltered from the winds of the South, SW, W and NW, because its entrance and outlet are NE, SW.[32]

The canoes retired at the close of evening with a great clamor. They were content having traded with us; while we were unhappy seeing that the current failed us. Though I was unable to go ashore, however, I had the pleasure of viewing the land up close and examining it as will be described below.

Note: A hill was found in latitude 55 degrees with a fairly high, steep point of land, which juts out seaward from the coast for about three leagues, forming a semicircle with the coast.[33] The hill stretched from N to S, very forested, and so situated that no more than the shore or edge of the coast was visible. It was so rocky that it appeared to be a cliff, judging by the large, sheer rocks that were seen; and above them, different species of trees flourished, such as beech, fir and poplar. There is a ravine in the aforesaid point and hill near where the coast is continuous, which looks from a distance of four to five leagues like an island (although it is not). At a distance of a cannon shot from the said ravine, a small island shows up which is about a league in circumference. Separated from the ravine by about a half league, I descried a rock that looked as if it was about 6 to 8 *varas* high. About a musket shot from the said isle 4 or 5 small rocks show up, which appear just above the water, so that one sees the waves breaking from a distance.[34] In front of the point there are 3 small islets, which are distant from it about a musket shot.[35] We passed within a distance of about a cannon shot of them at 4. I did not notice any danger in their vicinity, except for the rapid current that came out of there. As I have said, since it was hardly possible to carry a stiff sail with a strong wind, it stopped us, and if we had been careless, the force of the current would have turned us completely around.

The referred-to point is called *Santa Margarita* because of [our] having arrived off it on the day of her glorious name. From the said point the coast is divided into four angles: that of Monterey runs to the south until reaching a high snow-covered peak, from which peak it descends from greater to lesser until forming a point that resembles the tongue of a cow.[36] The coast runs from the said point to the SSE according to the surveys that were made. From the *Punta de Santa Margarita* the coast runs to the East a distance of 10 leagues, and the land is low and heavily forested. Without seeing a shore like the *Punta de Santa Margarita*, one sails along the coast steering E a distance of a league, and later to the SE one coasts along the hill remaining to the starboard. Later a low point is discovered that forms a small hill, below which there are two low rocks, yet still visible and out of the water.[37] From the said point to the continuous coast there is an expanse of about a league. In the SW part it has an inlet which was not possible to reconnoiter, because of having lost the wind.[38] When I was in front of the low point, which formed a mouth with the mainland of the referred-to inlet, and as I remained becalmed, the current gripped me and set me westward with so much velocity that it drifted me away from the coast some 6 or 7 leagues. I remained in the referred-to parallel for 4 days in order to succeed in anchoring, but it was not possible because of the powerful and contrary winds, heavy showers and excessive cold that gripped us all. Finally, it was not possible to return and get ourselves close in, due to the furious currents and the contrary weather, as I have related.

To the north of *Punta Santa Margarita* a distance of 6 to 8 leagues a rugged, precipitous cape was discovered which I named *Santa María Magdalena*.[39] The said cape makes a mouth with *Punta de Santa Margarita*, forming inside a great enclosure, the waters within it flowing with more violence than even in a narrower strait. For this reason, I was persuaded that some rivers discharged inside, which caused the current experienced to be so rapid, its direction being to the W. The coast turns from the said cape running to the NW a distance of 16 leagues, according to what was observed. To the west of the said cape is an island, averaging a distance of about 7 leagues.[40] It probably has a circumference of 5 to 6 leagues, and it runs with the *Punta de Santa Margarita* NW-SE the same distance. It appears there is a good passage between the cape and the island, [which was] named *Santa Christina*. It was discovered at 6 in the afternoon.

Also, the current flowed to the NW.

At 7 in the evening the coast bore from the S to SE a distance of 18 leagues, and from the N to NW1/4N the same distance; and the same for the *Isla de Santa Christina* to NW1/4W a distance of 6 to 7 leagues. At this hour a reefing was loosened in the topsails, and thus we remained all night, which stayed gloomy. The skies and horizons were shrouded in fog, with some heavy showers. At sunrise it was the same. At 5 in the morning we tacked to a course SSW, with the wind out of the SE.

I observed the sun at midday in latitude N 55 degrees,[41] the sighted land bearing S, as before.

Note: Having reflected on the inconstancy and confusion of the weather, and also the uncertainty of finding a place farther northward where one could anchor and take on water, [I realized that] by cutting the daily [water] ration I would scarcely be able to have [enough] for returning. I [therefore] determined not to press on farther, and from this latitude follow the coast to Monterey, fulfilling my orders and seeing if I can find a place to put into effect that which was ordered of me by Your Excellency—provided the wind and weather permit me, because it is impossible to be able to explain all that has befallen [us] due to the bad weather.

God grant me good weather.

[*21st to Friday 22 July 1774*] We proceeded on with the four principal sails, the jibsail, subject to one reefing. At 3 in the afternoon, seeing the sea was rough out of the South, I ordered a tack turning to the SW. At 5 in the afternoon the wind and a heavy shower forced us to take in the second line of reefings, and to furl the jibsail and the main topmast staysails. At 8 at night, we were in view of the *Cabo de Santa Magdalena*, from which I took the departure, being situated in latitude 55°24′N, a distance of 10 leagues.[42] At nightfall the horizons were very overcast, with heavy showers. It was the same way at dawn, as it has been for most of these 24 hours. With nothing more new. Thanks be to God.

[*22nd to Saturday 23 July 1774*] We proceeded on with the 4 principal sails, the topsails secured by two reefings, and we continued on sailing in this fashion turning to a course S1/4SW; the wind SE1/4E, fresh and regularly varying within the 2nd [SE], 3rd [SW], and 4th [NW] quadrants; the sea rough out of the SSW and from the W. The weather was the same, with a continual heavy downpour, and in this manner nightfall came. At 9 it fell calm, and at 11 a wind was noticed from the W, fresh, and at the same time the course was to the SSE. The sky remained clear. At 3 in the morning we loosened one reefing in the topsails. At dawn the horizons were foggy, although they appeared to offer no trouble. At 5 I gave orders to loosen the 2nd reefing in the jibsail, and [to loosen] the main topmast staysails, the spritsail, and the lower studding sails. [I am] steering to the ESE in search of the coast. At 8 the wind swung around to the SSW, at which we tacked to starboard hauling the lines and furling the spritsail. Nothing more new. Thanks be to God.

23rd to Sunday 24 July 1774 We proceeded on under full sail, except for the spritsail, turning to a course ESE in search of the coast. The wind fair out of the S; the weather beautiful, with the sea quiet out of the SSW and W. At 6 in the afternoon we descried the snowy coast, which, being very high, I named *Los Cerros de San Cristóbal* [St. Christopher's Peaks].[43] These mountains begin in latitude 54°40'N and end in 53°08′, being 33 leagues from end to end, and running SSE–NNW, the same as the coast. At 7:30 we took in two reefings in the topsail and the main staysails. At nightfall the horizons were rather overcast; aside from this the skies were clear and beautiful. At 8 we remained almost becalmed, and said condition persisted until 6 in the morning, at which time we noticed a wind out of the E1/4SE. Thus, we loosened the reefings and the small sails.

At dawn the horizons were in the same condition as at nightfall. What was perceived to be the end of the coast on the N was surveyed as being a distance of 18 leagues, and the bearing to the S the same distance. At 8 the viaticum was said for a poor sick [crewman]. At noon I observed the latitude at 53°21′N, with the extremities of the coast bearing from me the same as in the morning. Nothing more new. Thanks be to God.

24th to Monday 25 July 1774 We proceeded on under full sail, turning to a course SSE, with light winds East, varying regularly to the NE. The weather overcast with clouds of varied hues; the sea rather quiet out of the South. At one the sky was shrouded in light fogs. At 4 it began to rain, and immediately we prepared to receive the buffeting with which the disagreeable weather in these latitudes of the Lord beset us. In the first place, the two topsails were secured with both reefings and we furled the lesser sails. At 6 in the afternoon an apprentice seaman died named Salvador Antonio, without a surname, a native of Guaynamota, married to María Juliana of the same town.[44] At 8 in the morning, on St. Ann's day, he was buried ✠.

At nightfall the horizons were very gloomy and continued squally all night and day. The weather was the same at dawn. At 4 the wind was diminishing, swinging around to the SE, for which reason at 6:30 we tacked to go in search of the coast, heading the bow NE1/4E. At 9 the wind was turning to SSE with heavy showers, but fresh. Considering myself 4 or 5 leagues from the coast, I gave orders to come about. While in the said maneuver there was a sudden shift in the wind to the SSW, very strong, which obliged me to furl the topsails, remaining with the two mainsails. Nothing more new. Thanks be to God.

25th to Tuesday 26 July 1774 We proceeded on with the two mainsails and foresails, turning to a course W; the wind out of the SSW, varying frequently to the South. The weather is extremely disagreeable; the sea turbulent on the said course. The storm continued with strong wind and showers. We worked the mainsail on the half-hour, and on occasions the leeward corner of the mainsail was hauled aloft. In this way, we passed this arduous night. At 10:45 the wind swung around to SW1/4S, at which we hauled the mainsail aloft, and we came about on a course SE1/4S. At 3 in the morning, seeing that the wind had calmed down somewhat and the sea was mostly from the S and SE, we loosened the topsails over two reefings, and they were left on the masthead caps. At 5 we experienced strong showers. At 7 the weather moderated, becoming drier, except for the sea which was very wild out of the S and SE. I ordered the topsails into use, and at 10 we loosened one reefing on both of them, and [loosened] the main topmast staysail. At midday I observed the latitude to be 52°59′N. According to the difference in latitude, distance, and course steered, I placed myself 8 leagues from the coast. Nothing more new. Thanks be to God.

26th to Wednesday 27 July [1774] We proceeded on with the four principal sails, the topsails on one reefing, and the main topmast staysail, turning to a course SSE. The wind SW, fair and variable; the weather fair, and the sea rough out of the South, SW and SE. At 8 I ordered the reefings taken in the topsails. At nightfall the horizons were foggy and the coast very overcast, so that it could not be seen. At dawn the horizons were squally in the 3rd [SW] and 4th [NW] quadrants, and as soon as the day cleared up we found ourselves near the coast.

At sunset the extremities observed from the S to the East were surveyed as being a distance of 18 leagues, and that of the NNW almost the same distance more or less, closer to the NE a distance of 5 leagues.

At 8 at night we were becalmed and remained so until 8 in the morning, at which hour we noticed a fair wind out of the S. I ordered the reefings and jibsails loosened. According to the survey today the coast was running SE–NW. At noon I observed the latitude at 52°41′N, in which latitude the extremities of the coast of *Los Cerros de San Cristóbal* were on the same bearing as when the sun set, because of [our] being becalmed by the slight wind. At 9 through to 12 it returned softly from the SSW. Nothing more new. Thanks be to God.

27th to Thursday 28 July 1774 We proceeded on under full sail, turning to a course SE. The wind, fair out of the SSW; the weather changeable, from clear to squally, and the sea rough out of the W and SW. At 7:30 we surveyed the most distant [point] at 18 leagues; that from S to E a distance of 7 leagues; and the nearest at 4 leagues. At the said hour the topsails were secured with both reefings because the horizons to the S, SW and W, were squally and overcast. At dawn it was the same. At one at night we furled the jibsail, not wanting to luff the ship. A reefing was loosened in the topsails, whereupon at 6 the most southerly part of the coast bore to the E a distance of 12 leagues, the most northerly NNW5°W a distance of 18 leagues, and the nearest 3 to 4 leagues. At 11 the wind swung around to the SE, for which reason we tacked to a course SSW.

At noon I observed the latitude at 52°20′N. Although it had not been to my satisfaction because of the overcast sky, it is not very far off its correct reading as the dead reckoning showed. Nothing more especially new. Thanks be to God.

28th to Friday 29 July 1774 We proceeded on with the 4 principal sails, the small sails, the topsails with one reefing, turning to a course SW. The wind SSE, variable; the weather overcast; the sea quiet out of the W and SW. At 7 it was determined that what was visible to the extreme N was NNW5°W a distance of 10 leagues, and that to the extreme South, E1/4SE the same distance.

At nightfall the horizons were covered with colorful clouds, and at dawn they were the same. From 8 at night to 12 we have experienced winds out of the NE, E and SE. At 6 in the morning the extremities of the coast visible to the S were determined to be E1/4NE a distance of 14 to 15 leagues. At the said hour we noticed a wind out of the SE, fair. At 8 we loosened the reefings in the topsails, jibsails, and the main staysails. At 11 we tacked, turning from the coast, the wind having veered to the SSE. Nothing more especially new. Thanks be to God.

29th to Saturday 30 July 1774 We proceeded on under full sail, turning from the coast, with the wind out of the SSE, fair and frequently varying to the SE. The weather was overcast, which prevented me from being able to observe [the latitude]. The sea was restless from the SW and W. At one the wind veered to the SE, and considering that this tacking back and forth was not advantageous, we put about in the said hour turning to a course SSW and S1/4SW. At 4 in the afternoon, seeing that the sky was becoming overcast with more gloominess than usual, its appearance anything but cheerful, and the wind increasing from the workings of the weather, I ordered the topsails secured with two reefings, and the jibsail and main topmast staysail furled. At nightfall the horizons were very dark and rainy. At 9 the sea was so excessively turbulent from the S and W that there was a danger that some of the spars might come down, and in order to avoid this danger I gave orders to furl the topsail.

Note: that at 6:30 I surveyed the remaining south [part] of the coast at ENE, a distance of 16 leagues. At 12 at night the wind and showers forced us to furl the main topsail, and in this fashion we greeted the dawn. At 8:30 the weather allowed for loosening the fore topsail and the main topsail. At noon I observed the latitude at 51°58′N, and having corrected today the last observation, which was the 27th of this month, the completed course sailed from my departure point, which was from 7 until noon today, was found to be to the SW and distant from the coast 87 miles or 29 leagues.[45] The difference in latitude: 60'S. Departure: 61'W. Distance: 197 miles. Latitude by dead reckoning: 51°58′N. Departure: 75'E. Observed latitude: 51°58′N. Departure: 14°E, and distance from the meridian, 1°41′. Nothing more especially new. Thanks be to God.

[*30th to Sunday 31 July 1774*] We continued on, turning to a course SW1/4W, the wind out of the S1/4SE, fresh and variable, with the four principal sails, the topsails secured with two reefings. The weather was extremely bad because of frequent wind squalls, quite strong and showery. At nightfall the horizons were in the said condition. At one the wind swung around to the SW, whereupon at one-thirty we came about, turning to a course SSE. At 4 the wind changed to the WSW, with the same force as before. At dawn the horizons were just as they were at nightfall. At 8 the sky was clear and beautiful, so that at 9 we loosened a reefing in the topsails and staysails. Nothing more new. Thanks be to God.

[*31st to Monday 1 August 1774*] We proceeded on our voyage with the 4 principal sails, the topsails with one reefing, turning to a course SSE; the wind WSW, fresh and regularly varying from the West and 4th [NW] quadrant. The weather was beautiful, although there was no lack of large clouds, and the sea was restless from the SW. The horizons were rather overcast at nightfall, and they were the same at dawn. At 4 I gave orders to steer SE, at which time we loosened the reefings in the topsails, spritsail and fore studding sail. At noon I observed the latitude at N50°20′, at which time I gave orders to steer E1/4SE in search of the coast. Nothing more new. Thanks be to God.

[*1st to Tuesday 2 August 1774*] We proceeded on under full sail turning to a course E1/4SE in search of the coast, with the wind out of the WNW, a constant fresh breeze. At 6:45 the small sails were furled. At 7 the sky was covered by very dense fog, which looked like rain, whereupon I gave orders to take in two reefings on the fore topsail and one on the main topsail, and the corner of the mainsail hauled aloft. The fore topsail remained lowered because it would not fill. I gave orders to steer ESE, and in said condition we sailed until midnight, when the course steered was SE1/4E. At 4 we steered to the ESE. At dawn we were in the same situation as at nightfall, enveloped in fog. At 8:30 we loosened the reefings in the fore and main topsails, and the starboard corner of the mainsail was hauled aft. At noon I observed the latitude at 49°24′N. According to the course sailed and the difference found in latitude from yesterday to today, a variation is shown of 22 1/2° from N to E, although the observation has not been satisfactory because of the dense fog. Thanks be to God.

[*2nd to Wednesday 3 August 1774*] We proceeded on with the 4 principal sails, turning to a course East in search of the coast, with the wind NNW, fresh. The weather was very gloomy because of the mist; the sea rather rough out of the said direction. At 2 in the afternoon, seeing that the weather was extremely gloomy, the wind gathering strength, and although we might have been in the vicinity of the coast, being unable to search for it, I determined to run before the wind to the SE. At 2:30 two reefings were taken in the topsails and we hauled the mainsail aloft. At 5 in the afternoon the sky cleared up, at which time I gave orders to steer to the E, and to loosen a reefing in the topsails and the minor sails, with the intention of sighting the coast if possible. At 8 the reefing was taken again in the topsails, and we furled the small sails and hauled the mainsail aloft. At 9 the wind obliged us to furl the topsails. At 12 the sky became overcast again with fog, accompanied by strong wind that obliged us to lay to with the mainsail, the bow headed WSW. At 4 in the morning we loosened the topsails and steered to the E. At 8 they were furled again, and with the foresail we fell off leeward to the ESE, because of the gloominess of the weather. Nothing more new. Thanks be to God.

[3rd to Thursday 4 August 1774] We proceeded on with the foresail, turning to a course ESE; the wind out of the NNE, varying regularly to the NE; the weather extremely overcast with fog; and the sea turbulent on the said course. At 1 in the afternoon the sky cleared, and the horizons became hazy. We immediately hauled the mainsail tack aboard, and we loosened the topsails, hauling all the wind possible with the intention of getting close to the coast. At sunset I took a bearing and found the western variation 20°34′ from West by North. The horizons at nightfall were clear and beautiful, and they were the same at dawn. The eastern bearing at sunrise was found to be 22°10′, and without doubt there are two quarters which are 22°30′ from N to E. At 7 we loosened a reefing in the topsails and lesser sails. At 10 the wind slackened, and at noon I observed the latitude at 48°34′N. Nothing more especially new. Thanks be to God.

[4th to Friday 5 August 1774] We proceeded on under full sail, except that a reefing was taken in the topsails. We continued in the said manner toward the coast, steering ENE and NE, hauling all the wind possible, with the intention of reaching the highest point, having not been able to do so. At nightfall the horizons were clear and beautiful, and they were the same at dawn. At 4 we loosened the reefings in the topsails. We have experienced in these 24 hours wind from the NE, fair and varying regularly in the 4th [NW] quadrant. At 11:30 we descried the coast with high and snowy peaks, the nearest part being to the NE a distance of 15 to 16 leagues.[46] Nothing more new. Thanks be to God.

5th to Saturday 6 August 1774 We proceeded on under full sail toward the coast, steering a course NE1/4N; and the wind out of the NW, fair; the sea quiet on the said course. At 7 I gave orders to take in both reefings on the topsail and to furl the minor sails, and to haul up the mainsail, with the intention of waiting for morning to be able to obtain a very careful close examination of the coast. At sunset I took a westerly bearing and found the variation of the compass to be 19°20′ from West by North.

The horizons were clear and beautiful at nightfall. At 11:30 at night the fog closed in. It looked exactly like a rain shower, so obscure that one could hardly see from stem to stern. With a dead calm and under these same conditions it dawned. I took a bearing on the coast by the same NE direction, because its extremities could not be descried due to its being very hazy; the distance is 8 leagues. Nothing more new. Thanks be to God.

6th to Sunday 7 August 1774 We continued becalmed; the weather overcast with fog; the sea quiet out of the E. This afternoon we have been engaged in mending our topsails and the mainsail. The horizons at nightfall were in the same condition as I described at dawn. At 4 we noticed a wind out of the ESE, fair, whereupon we hauled the tack aboard to starboard, and we loosened a reefing in the jibsail and in the main topmast staysail, steering to the NE in search of the coast. Nothing more new. Thanks be to God.

7th to Monday 8 August 1774 We continued sailing under full sail in search of the coast, steering to the N; the wind out of the SE, fresh; the sea smooth; the sky overcast. At 3 in the afternoon canoes began coming out from the land; three of them were nearby and up to five of them collected together, but without wanting to come near regardless of how much they were called. From the said hour we were sounding frequently, and the first depth was 25 *brazas*. From this depth we came to 15, 16 and 19 *brazas*, and from this to 25 *brazas*, very dark sand and green slime, where we anchored, giving it the name of *Surgidero de San Lorenzo* [St. Lawrence's Roadstead].[47] This maneuver was done at 7 in the evening, at which time a bearing was taken of *Punta de Santa Clara* [St. Clara's Point] to the NW,[48] a distance of 4 leagues, and that of *San Estevan* to the SE, a distance of 2 leagues, and the middle [point] or inside angle to the E a distance of one league.[49] This was all judged by the compass, the variation of which is 16° to the NE. The wind went calm. As darkness came on the sea was smooth, the sky and horizons overcast. Although it was night, the canoes did not cease to come, but without [the natives'] coming on board.

The night was calm. It dawned clear and beautiful, with a west wind trying to blow. A launch was immediately put in the water fitted out with sails and masts, with the purpose of locating a good anchorage, this one being unsheltered from the wind, and being anchored with a stream cable. At the time the launch was put in, a number of canoes were around, and immediately when they saw it they fled; but they returned giving us their advice. Seeing the appearance of the weather clear, we began weighing anchor confident of some shelter from *Punta de San Estevan.*

Note: The land sighted at noon a distance of 3 leagues, in latitude 49°30′N and longitude 20°11′W of San Blas, with the prow NE, is a hill similar to that of Puerto de San Diego. From the NW part of it a point of low land projects out about 3/4 of a league, entirely of rock, with the sea breaking in much surf.[50] From this point, referred to as *San Estevan*, the land continues to the NW, and a point was visible to the N which was called *Santa Clara* and runs with *San Estevan* NW–SE. All the land between these two points is moderate, but inland it is high, mountainous and covered with very luxuriant forests down to the water's edge. We anchored in the middle as I have said, and not trusting the place, we began weighing anchor. But it could not be finished because of the troublesomeness of the stream anchor. The wind freshened out of the W, and we were in danger of running aground on a foul coast, for which reason I ordered the stream anchor cut, and we sailed under full sail, leaving the launch tied with a stout rope and towed from our stern. This was done and happened between 5 and 7 in the morning. By this sailing we tried to get ourselves out by endeavoring to back off from the ledge of rocks that projected out, as I have said, over 3/4 of a league running South. It was frightening to see in so short a time the entire sea become angry, stirred up by the blowing wind.

The Indians then came within speaking distance,[51] and they started their trading by an exchange of furs for shells which our men brought from Monterey.[52] They [the sailors] got in return various sea otter skins and many sardines. The Indians differed in appearance from those at *Santa Margarita*, the pelts [they wore] not being placed against the body.

There is copper in their land, for various strings of beads were seen (similar to glass beads) that were made of animal teeth, and at their ends they had some eyeholes of beaten copper, which had certainly been grains extracted from the earth and later pounded, implying that they had some mines of this metal. These Indians are very docile, for they gave up their furs even before they were paid for them. They are very robust and white as the best Spaniard.[53] The two women whom I saw had the same appearance as the others. Some Indians wore rings made of bone in their ears. It did not appear that they had experienced or seen civilized people before. As many as 15 canoes collected around.

At 11 a survey was taken of *Loma de San Lorenzo* [St. Lawrence's Hill],[54] finding the said hill at latitude 49°30′N and at longitude 20°30′W of San Blas, bearing N a distance of 6 leagues. At noon I observed [the latitude] at 49°12′ North. Nothing more new. Thanks be to God.

8th to Tuesday 9 August 1774 We proceeded on with the foresail and the topsails made fast with both reefings until 12:30, at which time the force of the wind obliged us to furl them. We remained with the foresail steering a course SSE; the wind very strong out of the WNW; the sea turbulent on the said course; the weather clear. At 4:30 we hauled the mainsail aboard. The horizons were clear at nightfall, and at 11:30 they clouded over to the SW. At sunrise they were the same. At 4 in the morning we loosened the topsails under two reefings; at 6 we loosened one reefing. I gave orders to steer ENE, returning to the coast which I discovered bearing to the N 18 leagues at the greatest distance, and the rest S to East the same distance. We hauled the mainsail aloft. At 7:30 the 2nd reefing was loosened in the topsails, and at 8 the wind went calm. The latitude by dead reckoning was 48°17′N; west variation 18°14′; longitude made, 4°52′W; longitude from the meridian of San Blas 20°47′. Nothing more new. Thanks be to God.

9th to Wednesday 10 August 1774 We continued with the foresail and topsails, turning to a course NE; the wind out of the WSW, light; the weather overcast; the sea smooth. At one-thirty I gave orders to haul down the topsails with the purpose of mending them, and in place of them we hoisted, at a quarter to 4, new ones that had been fashioned. At sunset I took a bearing on the closest part of the coast to the NNE, a distance of 14 leagues. The horizons at nightfall were threatening and dark, although it came to nothing, everything dissolving into a calm. We took two reefings in the topsails.

It was calm the greater part of the night, with some light variable winds out of the W. At dawn the horizons were clear from the NE to the South, and dark in the 3rd [SW] and 4th [NW] quadrants. I took a bearing on the [land] that was sighted to the extreme E to E1/4SE a distance of 18 leagues and the opposite to the N a distance of 14 leagues. The reefings were loosened in the topsails, said work being done at sunrise. At noon I observed the latitude at 48°09′N, in which parallel bore a very high peak all covered with snow,[55] and from afar there appeared to be an island to the E1/4NE a distance of 12 leagues from the said peak.[56] The coast runs NW–SE, a moderately low land, densely forested. It [the peak] is in latitude 48°05′N and longitude 24°20′W of San Blas, and it is named *Santa Rosalía*.[57] Nothing more new. Thanks be to God.

10th to Thursday 11 August 1774 We proceeded on with the foresail, the main topsail and fore topsail, turning to a course ENE in search of the coast; the weather clear and beautiful; the wind out of the WNW, fair; and the sea quiet out of the W. At 3 in the afternoon I gave orders to steer East. At 6 I took a bearing on the most southerly part of the coast at E5°SE, a distance of 8 leagues. At 7:15 a reefing was taken in the topsails, and at the said time I gave orders to steer SE. At nightfall the horizons were beautiful and clear. At one the sky clouded over and became dark toward the South. At the said hour we noticed a wind out of the said direction, rather fresh. At the same time it began to rain, and it has continued [to do] so most of the night and until noon. At 4 in the morning we were tacking ahead. At 11 we came about, tacking off and on, because I did not want to tack ahead, the wind having swung around to the SW. Although by noon it stopped raining, an observation has not been obtained. Nothing more new. Thanks be to God.

11th to Friday 12 August 1774 We proceeded on, turning to a course SE, with the four principal sails, the two topsails with one reefing. The wind was out of the SW, fair; the sea choppy out of the W and SW; the weather overcast. At 5 in the afternoon we were tacking ahead, turning to a course WSW, the wind out of the South. At 8 the 2nd reefing was taken in the topsails because of the threatening and dark appearance noticed on the horizons. At 11 at night we came about, tacking off and on, turning to a course SE; the wind out of the SSW. We have operated in this fashion for 24 hours. Rain squalls continue, and the winds are varying frequently from the SE to the South and SW.

At dawn the horizons were the same as they were at nightfall, with rain squalls. At 5 in the morning the weather settled down somewhat, whereupon I gave orders to loosen the reefs in the topsails and minor sails, considering that the wind shifted to the W. At 8 it returned to the S, with rain squalls. I took a sighting on the extreme S part of the coast to the E a distance of 8 leagues, and the *Cerro de Santa Rosalía* to the N a distance of 10 leagues. At 11 we noticed a fresh wind and rain squall out of the SW, which made us take in the two reefings on the topsails. At 12 one of them was let out because we found ourselves being drawn onto the coast. Nothing more especially new. Thanks be to God.

12th to Saturday 13 August 1774 We proceeded on along the coast with the 4 principal sails and the topsails with a reefing, turning to a course SSE. The wind was SW, fresh; the sea turbulent on the said course; the weather squally; distance from the coast 6 to 7 leagues. At 7 in the evening, seeing that the sea swell was increasing and the wind abating, I gave orders to steer S1/4SE. At nightfall the horizons were squally, of which we have noticed frequent rain showers and moderate winds. At the hour of 7 we furled the main topmast staysail, and hauled up the mainsail because of a squall, which came close on the windward side. Nothing happened except for some drops of rain that fell. Afterward, sailing was resumed.

At 11 the same maneuver was accomplished with respect to another squall that burst with strong winds and some heavy showers. After it was over, the sails were hauled aft again.

At dawn the horizons were in the same condition as at nightfall. At 5:30 the mainsail was hauled up, the wind having swung abaft, and the 2nd reefing was loosened in the topsails. At 7 we discovered on the coast a hill that looked like that at Puerto de San Diego,[58] bearing ENE a distance of 10 leagues.

At 11 the wind changed to NE, fair. At noon I observed the latitude at 46°8′N.[59] Nothing more especially new. Thanks be to God.

13th to Sunday 14 August 1774 We proceeded on along the coast with the foresail, and the main and fore topsails under one reefing, turning to a course SSE. The wind was N, fresh; heavy swell out of the W; the weather clear. At sunset, the coast was found to be so hazy that we were able to see only that part directly in front of the ship, which bore ENE a distance of 7 to 8 leagues. At nightfall the horizons were clear and beautiful; they were the same at dawn. As daylight came on, the south extreme of the coast was perceived to bear SE a distance of 18 leagues; the N extreme bore N the same distance, a little more or less. The said coast runs NNW–SSE; nearest to the coast 4 leagues, ENE. At 7:30 we loosened the spritsail. At 9:30 the starboard corner of the mainsail was hauled aft. The reefings in the fore topsail and minor sails were loosened. At 11 they were furled again. At 12 I observed the latitude at 44°35′N.[60] The S extreme of the coast bore SE1/4S, and that on the NW [bore] NW1/4N; nearest distance 5 to 6 leagues, ENE. From the aforesaid latitude the coast runs NNW-SSE. The land is high and mountainous for a distance of about 12 leagues and very heavily forested up to the mountain summits. It then runs in the same direction at a more moderate height, beginning with a point that slopes steeply into the sea. It is massive and has a very prominent cliff that is between white and yellow in color.[61] Nothing more new. Thanks be to God.

14th to Monday 15 August 174 We proceeded on along the coast with the foresail, main and fore topsails, and the starboard corner of the mainsail, turning to a course S1/4SE. The wind N, fresh; the weather clear; and the sea choppy out of the N and W. At 4 in the afternoon I gave orders to haul up the corner of the mainsail and to steer South. At 7 land was sighted in the same direction as the bow,[62] whereupon I gave orders to steer SSW. At sunset the west bearing was 8°53'W by N. At 8 I gave orders to steer South. The horizons at nightfall were hazy in the 4 quarters, an indication of wind in these parts; and in fact we experienced such most of the night. At 9 we hauled up the mainsail, since we were unable to steer the ship. Dawn came on in the same condition, except that the wind was more moderate. At 5 we steered SE1/4S; at 6, SSE, and at the said hour we loosened the reefing in the topsails and those taken in the fore topsail at 5 in the afternoon, and those in the main topsail at 6 in the same evening. The mainsail was hauled aft to starboard. The coast was not visible this morning because it was very hazy. At 11 the wind went calm, and at 12 I observed the latitude at 42°38'N.[63] By correction I find myself a distance of 172 leagues from Puerto de Monterey, bearing SSE, and the longitude from the said port 3°18'W. The nearest coast is 12 leagues to the ENE, although I have been unable to see this said [coast] today because of the fog. Nothing more new. Thanks be to God.

15th to Tuesday 16 August 1774 From noon we continued becalmed, as already said, and it stayed that way until 11:30 at night, at which time we noticed a wind out of the NNW, fair. I gave orders to steer South, and it began to freshen so much that at 3:30 the main topsail tore, obliging us to furl both [topsails]. At 4 in the morning, concluding the said procedure, we continued on with only the foresail, and judging from the force of the wind it should be sufficient. At dawn the horizons were foggy, and they were the same at nightfall. At 8 the sky began to clear. At 6 we hauled aft the port corner of the mainsail, which was hauled aloft at 8:30 because of the poor steering the ship was experiencing.

Note: At sunset we took a west bearing, and the variation was found to be 5°31′W from the N, the same as the Chinese have found in the parallel of Cabo Mendocino.[64] At noon I observed the latitude at 41°27′N,[65] whereupon I gave orders to steer SSE. Nothing more especially new. Thanks be to God.

16th to Wednesday 17 August 1774 We proceeded on with the foresail, turning to a course SSE, with the wind out of the NNW, fresh, although not with the force it blew in the morning. When the sun was at its noon zenith, we observed that the wind was blowing a little, whereupon at 1 the fore topsail was loosened with its two reefings, and we hauled the corner of the mainsail aft. At the same time, the main topsail yardarm was hauled down to repair it. The weather remained clear, but a substantial sea continued from the N. At nightfall the horizons were clear. At 8 in the evening I gave orders to steer SE1/4S, and at 12, SE. It dawned with very thick fog that stayed on until one, at which time it cleared up. At 4 in the morning we loosened a reefing in the main topsail, as well as the main topmast staysail. At 10 we were almost becalmed. At noon we had no opportunity to observe because of the aforesaid fog; nor was it possible to see the land because of the fog. Nothing more new. Thanks be to God.

17th to Thursday 18 August 1774 After noontime we continued with the four principal sails, the topsails with a reefing, and the main topmast staysails, turning to a course SE, with light winds out of the NNW, fair. The weather was clear at one, except that the strong wind yesterday has left a heavy sea out of the N and NW. At sunset it seemed that there was some indication of a fresh wind, whereupon I gave orders to secure the topsails with the 2nd reefing, and at the same time the main topmast staysails were furled. The weather has been the opposite of what was expected, resulting in calm and a light fog. The horizons were hazy at nightfall, although it was clear overhead. At 11 the mainsail was hauled aloft, because of the wind's having abated completely; later it clouded over. At 10 a wind was noticed out of the SE, very light, at which the port rigging was hauled aboard, and we steered SSW. At noon we hauled up the mainsail because of having become becalmed at the said time. Finding the weather heavily fogged in, an observation could not be made, Nothing more new. Thanks be to God.

18th to Friday 19 August 1774 After noontime the calm and darkness continued, with a very quiet sea out of the N and NW. We have remained in the said condition for these 24 hours, with continual very humid fog that looks like rain with snow, and so cold that it has made nearly all of us sick. Counting today, it has been 3 days since we have been in this gloomy calm, the cold of which we have felt more in 40° than in 55°.

The entire crew is disheartened. Some 14 to 16 are much afflicted by scurvy and in very serious condition.

It has not been possible to make observations during these 3 days. At noon today I caught a glimpse of the sun and made out 39°48′[N],[66] which has not been to my satisfaction, [although] it is not very far off its [true] position. Nothing more especially new. Thanks be to God.

19th to Saturday 20 August 1774 We continued in the same condition as Friday, with the foresail, main topsail, and fore topsail double-reefed, in a dead calm and shrouded in fog. At 6 I gave orders to haul up the foresail, and the topsails were lowered over the masthead caps. We braced the opposite yardarms on the bow to port, and those on the stern to starboard. We continued in the said condition until twelve-thirty, at which time we noticed the wind out of the SE, whereupon the topsails were set, and we hauled the main tacks on board to port. At 5 it went calm again, and the mainsail was hauled up. At 10 we came about to a course ENE, and we hauled the main tack on board.

At 12 I took a partial observation that was found to be 39°30′N. I was unable to be sure whether it was exact or not, because that marvelous instrument failed me at the critical moment.[67] But considering how the sea has drifted us from N to S, and having sailed to the SSW since 12:30, I am not very far from the [correct] position. Nothing more especially new. Thanks be to God.

20th to Sunday 21 August 1774 We proceeded on with the 4 principal sails, the topsails double-reefed, turning to a course ENE. The wind SE, fair; the weather heavy with fog; the sea quiet out of the N and NW. It was extremely cold, so much so that the cold and damp of the fog made nearly all of us sick. There was not a man who did not have his complaint, some with aching bones, others with headaches, others taken with colds, and still others who have inflammations in their mouth and throat, none of which happened in 55 degrees.

We sailed this night in search of the coast on the said course of ENE, the wind light out of the SE. At 2 the sky cleared, and at 4 it clouded over again from the SW. Toward the beginning of the day, we sighted Cabo Mendocino bearing NNW5°W, a distance of 8 leagues, and other [land] was sighted to the SE toward San Francisco, SE 1/4E, a distance of 12 to 14 leagues, the nearest part of which was 3 leagues to the NE.

At sunrise we came about to a course SSW, at which time I ordered the reefings loosened and the minor sails set. At noon I observed the latitude at 39°46′N, and according to the bearing I took of Cabo Mendocino it bore NW5°N, corrected for a variation of 11°15′N by NE. I find the cape situated in 40 09'N, according to its distance of 12 leagues. That [land] which could be sighted far off in the distance to the SE, [I] thus [take] for San Francisco, bearing to the ESE5°S the same distance, a little more or less.[68] Nothing else new. Thanks be to God.

21st to Monday 22 August 1774 We continued on under full sail, turning to a course SW1/4S. The weather beautiful; the wind out of the SE1/4S, very fair; the sea smooth. At 3:30 in the afternoon we came about to a course ENE, and at 5 we put about again tacking on a course SW1/4S, with the wind out of the SE1/4S, very weak. At 6 the topsails were double reefed, and the small sails were furled. At 6:30 the slight wind went calm and the mainsail was hauled up.

The horizons were overcast at nightfall, and they were in the same condition at dawn. At 10 the SE [wind] began to freshen. At 8 in the evening a quiet sea came upon us out of the W.

It was not possible to make an observation at noon because of the weather's being overcast. Nothing else especially new. Thanks be to God.

22nd to Tuesday 23 August 1774 We proceeded on with the foresail, main topsail, and fore topsail, all double-reefed, turning to a course SW1/4S. The wind was cool and fresh out of the SE1/4S; the weather cloudy and changeable. We have experienced some sprinkles, although nothing significant. The horizons were overcast and gloomy at nightfall. At 9 we hauled the main tack on board, and at 10 the course was SE1/4S, the wind out of the E1/4NE, fair and regularly varying out of the NE. At 11 the course was SE1/4E. At one the wind swung around to the N, and one reefing was loosened in the topsails, which was taken in again at 4, because of the wind's having freshened. At dawn the horizons were overcast, although the sky was clear overhead.

At 5 one reefing was loosened in the topsails and spritsail. At 7 the sky was overcast and threatening in the 3rd [SW] quadrant. Some heavy showers appeared to be falling. At 8 the stay sail was furled, and the wind was dying down. At 10 it freshened again moderately. At noon there was no opportunity to make an observation because of the overcast sky. Nothing more new. Thanks be to God.

23rd to Wednesday 24 August 1774 We proceeded on with the four principal sails, the topsails with a reefing in both, heading on a course SSE. The wind was out of the NNW, fair; the weather overcast, and a rather quiet swell out of the N and NW. At 6 in the evening we furled the spritsail, and the topsails were secured with the second reefing. We hauled up the mainsail and swung the rigging around, the light wind having veered to the NW.

At nightfall the horizons appeared threatening, very dark and squally, with some raindrops falling. The same conditions prevailed at dawn. *Note:* in the first part of the evening, around 9 or 10 we experienced frequent lightning flashes in the direction of the E; the same thing was observed early this morning in the said direction. At 7 we noticed the wind from the SE, fair. At 10 it was out of the ESE, fresh, whereupon we hauled the starboard tack on board, heading on a course NE in search of the coast. At noon, I observed the latitude at 38°32′N, being a distance of 15 leagues from the coast, which was not seen because of the sky and horizons' being dark and overcast. Nothing more new. Thanks be to God.

24th to Thursday 25 August 1774 We proceeded on with the foresail, the main topsail, and the fore topsail, heading on a course ESE. The wind was out of the N, which had just begun to blow very lightly at 12:15. At 3 it swung around again to the ESE, fair, whereupon we hauled the port tack on board, heading South. We were in this condition, struggling between two winds, with the weather gloomy, and a heavy swell from the N and NW. At 6 the wind changed to the NNW, fair, whereupon I gave orders to steer ESE, and at 8, to the SE1/4E, because of finding the weather very overcast with fog. At dawn the horizons were in the same condition. At 3:30 a reefing was loosened in the topsails and spritsail. At 4 I gave orders to steer ESE, with the wind fair out of the NW, variable within the 4th [NE] quadrant. At 10 we sighted the Farallones over to the W of Puerto de San Francisco,[69] lying to the SE a distance of 2½ leagues, whereupon we steered SSW, and loosened the 2nd reefing until rounding them—which was at 12. At that time we steered SE, and the Farallones were seen nearer the Puerto [de San Francisco],[70] lying to the SE1/4E a distance of 2 leagues. At one I gave orders to steer SE1/4E in search of the coast. With the weather so overcast, no observation could be made. Nothing more new. Thanks be to God.

25th to Friday 26 August 1774 We proceeded on with the foresail, the main and fore topsails, heading for the coast steering to SE1/4E. The wind was NW, fresh; the sea swell heavy on the said course; the weather so gloomy that the coast could not be seen at two leagues. At sunset I gave orders to steer SE1/4E in search of Punta de Año Nuevo, which we reached at two in the morning, at a distance of two leagues. The course was changed to SSE, and at sunrise it was observed on a bearing of NE5°N, a distance of two short leagues. At 7 we loosened the reefing in the main and fore topsails, remaining with one reefing, at which time I gave orders to steer SE1/4E in search of the hill that marks Puerto de Monterey. At 10:30 we sighted said hill bearing ESE5°S, a distance of 6 leagues. At noon I observed the latitude at 36°55′N, and according to the said latitude Punta de Pinos bore in the same direction. At 2 the wind changed to S, which made it necessary to brace and secure the lines with all our strength. At 4 in the afternoon the wind obliged us to anchor in 9 *brazas* of water with all sails hauled up, rather far from the regular anchorage, which caused us to resort to warping, with the launch conveying the anchor for said warping. And so we remained until Sunday, 28 August, when after mass we finished securing the ship. Nothing else especially new. Thanks be to God.

Having arrived at the Puerto de San Carlos de Monterey, may it be to the greater honor and glory of God and of the Most Holy Mary of Bethlehem.

By calculations I made, the direction from *Santa Margarita* to Puerto de Monterey is South 29° East, and a distance of 423 leagues, longitude 16°20′ from the meridian of San Blas. I signed it on 28 August 1774. It is a copy of the original that I am forwarding.

Juan Pérez

I certify that this diary is a literal copy of the original kept and written by the hand of ensign, frigate grade, said Juan Pérez who has daily shown me his work. Everything expressed in it is certain and true, and therefore as it happened. So that this is clear, I signed it in the capacity of second captain and pilot, and as an eyewitness, in Monterey, 29 August 1774.

Estevan Josef Martínez

The officers of the frigate *Santiago*, also called the *Nueva Galicia*, which sailed from Puerto de San Blas on 24 January for Puerto de Monterey and other places, swear to what is expressed in this diary.

We certify that ensign, frigate grade, Don Juan Pérez, captain and first pilot of the aforesaid frigate, read to us daily the events of this voyage, telling us the main happenings of each day; and that the aforesaid diary is a literal copy of the original. We are sure that whatever is in it is true. We sign it at the request of the said captain and in order to record it; done in Monterey, 30 August 1774.

As boatswain, Juan Pérez
As second [boatswain] Carlos Ortega
As first boatswain's mate, Francisco Fernández
As first carpenter, Manuel de Rojas
As first caulker, Francisco Alvarez y Rua.

As surgeon of the aforesaid frigate of his Majesty, named *Santiago*, and also called *Nueva Galicia*, I certify that ensign, frigate grade, Don Juan Pérez, captain and first pilot of the aforesaid frigate, has daily communicated to me the events of this voyage, showing me the main happenings of each day; and that the aforesaid diary is a literal copy of the original. Being sure of what is expressed in it, I signed it at the request of the said captain in Monterey, on 30 August 1774.

Pedro Castán y Hoyos

I certify that this is a copy of the original that remains in the secretary's office of the viceregency, which is under my supervision. [City of] Mexico, twenty-sixth of November, seventeen hundred and seventy four.

Melchor de Peramas

Extract from Esteban José Martínez's "Diario" for 20–21 July 1774

A copy of what pilot first class of the Department of San Blas, Don Estevan José Martínez, states in his diary of the voyage of discovery from Monterey concerning events of the twentieth and twenty-first of July of this year [1774].

20th to 21 July 1774 We continued on as I have related, endeavoring to approach the previously mentioned island (which it was not),[1] so that at one we were very close, but having sounded we found no bottom. Since 9 in the morning we had fresh weather, so that at noon it looked as though we might find a place where we could anchor, which was behind three off-shore rocks. But seeing that each time the land extended farther inside, we continued along the coast, and we observed that the land that receded inward formed a kind of inlet which we were unable to examine, for the wind failed us and went calm.[2] Having not found bottom at 65 *brazas*, I do not believe we would have found it at 100 [*brazas*]. As for the situation of this coast, it looks like a cliff consisting of sheer rocks, and above them various species of trees grow, such as pine, many beech trees, large white poplars, and other species that I did not see. I say this because I saw it [the wood] in various implements used by these Indians, such as arrows, a paddle that I handled and that was seen very plainly. As I said, we remained becalmed. We experienced a furious current on this coast which for a while flowed athwart the ship, proving as the experience shows that the currents in this inlet are very great, and that perhaps they arise from some rivers that empty into it. As we remained becalmed, the Indians took the opportunity to satisfy their desire to trade with us, and we with them. For the rest of the afternoon they gathered about us in 21 canoes, which according to my count had in total some 150 Indians, all stocky, robust, and past the age of majority. Two canoes arrived full of women and some babies that were nursing at the breast, and some that were older. The women are good looking; they wore a tablet in the mouth that looked like the lip of a painted shell.[3] They had the lower lip pierced where they attached the tablet, a very ugly thing. They wore bracelets of iron or lead, and also of copper, and many small rings. In one large canoe there came someone representing [himself] to be the king or captain,[4] with 22 Indians, accompanied by the jingling of tambourines, all dancing and shouting. This king, or whatever he was, took a fancy to my red cap. I gave it to him and he presented me with the cloak that he was wearing, which is a blanket that I will forward to Your Excellency on my arrival. It is beautiful for being handmade by people without culture. Various other things were obtained by my companions. I also noticed in their canoes some small plates of iron and some other stone implements. But what surprised me was to see among them half of a bayonet and another [Indian] with a piece of a sword made into a knife. They were not much inclined to this [last mentioned] instrument, and indeed they asked by signs for swords and large knives. All trade was reduced to the sailors' giving them some old clothes for blankets of coarsely woven wool and pelts of wolf as well as otter, which is the clothing they wear wrapped about the body. The women were dressed the same way, and they wore their hair like the Spaniards. As for the men, they wear their's in a shoulder knot like the soldiers, tied with wool strips and very thin rawhide.

I asked them a thousand questions, all having to do with whether we could cast anchor, but they did not understand me, and their replies were to say that they had plenty to eat and drink if we would come ashore. Some of our men got into their canoes; they gave them presents and two of them came on board, to whom were given presents of bread and cheese. It was a very pleasant afternoon, but we had wanted to cast anchor. However, there was nowhere in this place it could be done because of the heavy breakers along the coastline. The Indians also use hats, but they are of straw like [those of] the workmen at the Santa Barbara Channel. I also saw a wooden spoon, and I picked up two first-rate arrows, unlike those used by other Indians in New Spain. We always hoped to plant the cross of Christ in this place, but the weather deprived us of this wish, as was said before.

The afternoon ended with the canoes withdrawing, and us becalmed, with only a little wind. We parted, and as night came on the sky was covered with fog so that the land was not visible. The current carried us along toward some land that bears NW1/4N. The land was not visible at nightfall. This land is very high, and it forms the inlet with *Punta de Santa Margarita*. It was named *Santa María Magdalena*. From the inner corner of this inlet, the land runs to the E and ENE farther down, and it was joined to *Magdalena*. This land is at about 55 degrees and 30 minutes, and it is the same place where the lieutenant of captain Bering, *Monsr.** Chirikov, lost his launch and crewmen in the same month of July in the year 1741.[5] I believe that the iron possessed by these Indians may be relics from the unfortunate men who embarked in said launch. The Indians told us not to go to that land, for they [the natives there] shot arrows and killed [people]. In their actions and appearance they [the natives here] were very compliant and good-natured, for they embraced those [Spaniards] who went in their canoes and invited them to eat and sleep ashore.

As mentioned before, finding ourselves caught in the inlet at *Magdalena*, the weather threatening, and the current very strong, now from the SE, now from the NW, the wind to the SE, we determined to get out. The topsails were reefed, and thus was concluded the day's run. With nothing more new. Thanks be to God.

This is a verbatim copy of what second pilot Don Estevan Josef Martínez expressed in his diary which remains in the secretary's office of the vice-regency, which is in my charge, and which I certify. [City of] Mexico, twenty-sixth of November, one thousand seven hundred and seventy-four.

Melchor de Peramas

* Apparently an abbreviation of the Spanish word *monseñor*, which means monseigneur, an ecclesiastical title—one that Chirikov is highly unlikely ever to have held.

Francisco Mourelle's Narrative of Pérez's Voyage in 1774

Voyage from Puerto de S. Blas to Monterey and the Northern Coast of California
*by Ensign, Frigate Grade, D. Juan Pérez**

Departure from Puerto de San Blas, situated in 21°21′ latitude North, and West of Tenerife 88 degrees and 6 minutes, toward [Puerto] de Monterey which is found in latitude 36°40′ and West of San Blas 17°00′.

The 25th of January, 1774, at midnight, the *Santiago* set sail from Puerto de San Blas under the command of ensign of the Royal Navy Don Juan Pérez, for discoveries on the northern coast of California, with the usual winds that blow from the N West in those vicinities, varying only at night to the Northeast, which are land breezes. It continued its course in order to pass north of the Islas Marías,[1] the northern point of which is in 21°46′ latitude, 29 leagues from said harbor. Later it anchored several times, in order not to lose [due to currents] during the calms the distance gained on its voyage. It was obliged on the 31st at midnight to separate itself from them [las Islas Marías] for the vicinity of the Southeast point which is found below latitude 21°18′ North, and 22 leagues from San Blas.

From then on, it continued hauling the wind as much as possible on courses spread between West and Northwest, because in its passage away

* This title appears in the index of Mourelle's collection of documents concerning Pérez's voyage in 1774.

from the coast those [winds] from the Northwest veered to the North Northeast, with seas that were continually choppy in that part until the 20th. At 26 degrees of latitude and West of San Blas 20 degrees 51 minutes, it began to experience calms and variable weather that blew undependably in the 3rd [SW] and 4th [NW] quadrants, in which case it managed to gain latitude North and stay on a course in the 1st [NE quadrant] that diminished [the ship's] longitude very little. But as the seas were often severe and the winds so fluctuating that the ship could not be properly steered, the cross-beams of both masts were sprung. For this reason, on the 28th of February, being at 33°18′ latitude and West of San Blas 17°41′, forty-five leagues from land, it was resolved to enter Puerto de San Diego, which is found at 66 minutes south of [the ship's] parallel, in order to attend to repairing said damage.

From that place, the winds were veering from Northeast to North Northeast more or less, depending on the distance from land, along which they usually blow following its direction to the Southeast.

On 6 March, the sunrise was visible across the land northeast of the Santa Barbara Channel a distance of eight leagues. [The ship] entered between the Farallón de Lobos and Isla Santa Rosa, which is the most westerly of them [the Channel Islands];[2] and in which place it is always advisable to draw away from the said farallón, because in its vicinity there are many rocks, hidden as well as exposed to view.

This islet is situated almost in the middle of the mouth formed by the referred-to Isla Santa Rosa with the mainland, which is considered an opening of eight leagues. Each ship that runs through that channel should draw near the coast, considering that in its vicinity there are anchorages sheltered from the northwesters, and one can easily seek water and firewood, and remedy whatever mishap that might have happened.

The islands that form the Santa Barbara Channel are: Santa Rosa, the most westerly; Santa Margarita, the middle one;[3] and Santa Cruz, the easterly one, which is high and large in relation to the others. At [the Channel's] easterly head there is an islet called Santo Tomás which is distant five leagues from the coast.[4] All four run East and West with little deviation.

On the 7th, three canoes from Isla Santa Cruz came alongside with fish that they sold to the crew; and pleased with the sale they had made, they returned to the island.

In this place, the islet of Santo Tomás and Isla Santa Cruz run through 84 degrees of the 2nd [SE] and 4th [NW] quadrants a distance of 9 leagues.

no. 5 159.

Dias del Mes

Salida del Puerto de Sn. Blas situado en 21º.. 21 de latd. Nte. y al Oeste de Tenerife 88 gs. o 6 ms. para el de Monte Rey que se halla en la latitud de 36º.. 40' y al Oeste de San Blas 17º.. 0á

Henero de 1774. 25.

El 25 de Henero de 1774 á las 12 dela noche se puso á la vela del Puerto de San Blas, la Fragata Santiago al mando del Alferez dela Rl. Armada Dn. Juan Perez, para los descubrimientos dela Costa septentrional de Californias, y con los vientos generales, que corren del Noruese en aquellas inmediaciones, variando unicamente por la noche á los Nordestes, que son los terrales, Continuó su derrota para rebazar al Norte delas Islas Marias, cuya punta septentrional está en 21º. 46' de latd. á 29 leguas del Dho Puerto, y despues de dar fondo varias veces para no perder durante las calmas, las distancias ganadas en su navegacion, se vió precisado el 31, á las doce dela noche á separarse de ellas por la immediacion á la punta del Sueste que se halla bajo la latd. de 21º. 18' nte. y 22 Leguas de San Blas.

31.

Desde entonces continuó ciñendo los vientos qto. le fue posible, por los rumbos comprendidos entre el Oeste, y el Noruese, pues al paso que se alexaba delas Costas se llama=

6 Febrero de 1774.

145

INITIAL PAGE of Mourelle's Narrative of the Pérez voyage in 1774. (*Colección de diarios, noticias y papeles varios* [MM 401], The Bancroft Library, University of California, Berkeley)

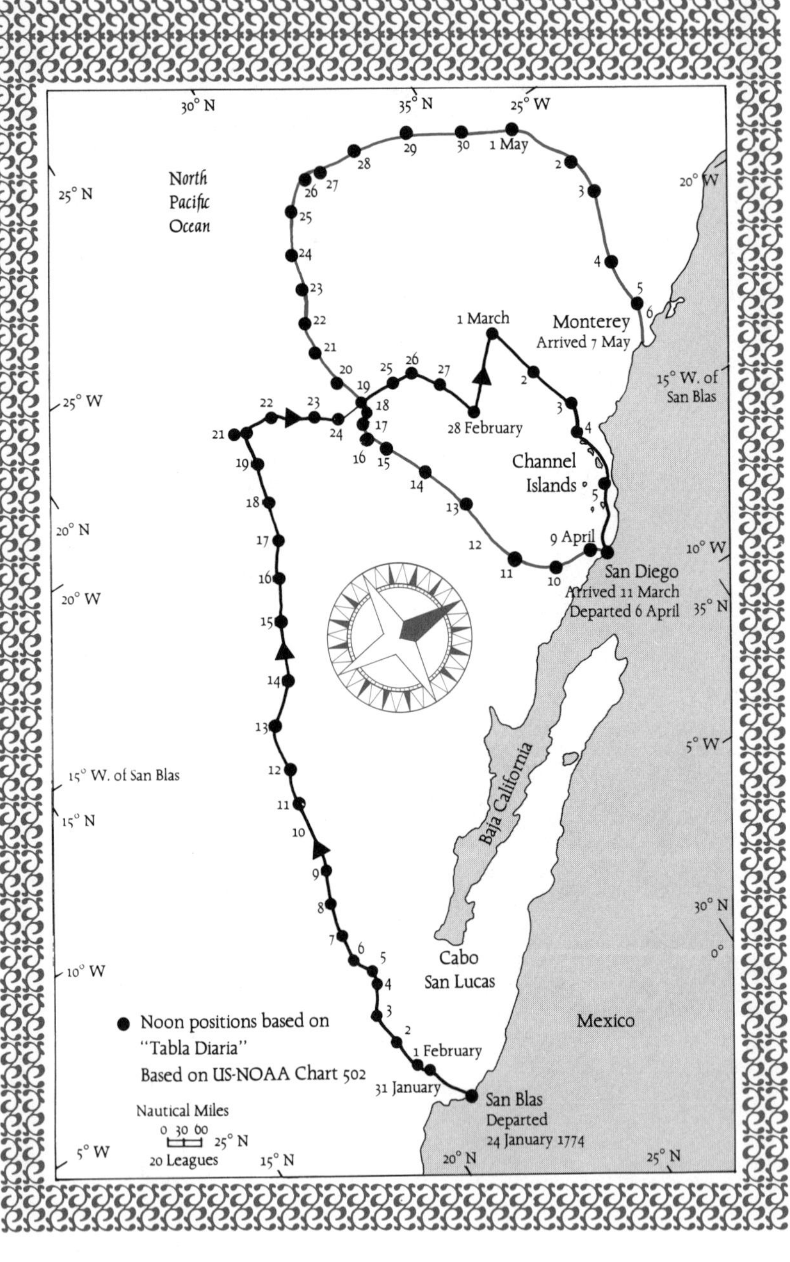
THE COURSE OF THE SANTIAGO
24 January to 7 May 1774
North
Pacific
Ocean
Monterey
Arrived 7 May
1 March
28 February
1 May
Channel
Islands
9 April
San Diego
Arrived 11 March
Departed 6 April
Baja California
Cabo
San Lucas
Mexico
1 February
31 January
San Blas
Departed
24 January 1774
Noon positions based on
"Tabla Diaria"
Based on US-NOAA Chart 502
Nautical Miles
20 Leagues

The hill of Bahía de San Pedro [runs] with the aforesaid Santa Cruz through 66 degrees 30 minutes of the 2nd [SE] and 4th [NW] quadrants the same distance,[5] having observed the latitude at 33 degrees 56 minutes.

The winds in these locations were nearly slack in the West, and often calm, for which reason [the ship] set various courses in the 2nd [SE] quadrant, passing between the [main] land and Isla Santa Catalina, where four canoes of Indians arrived alongside full of curiosity. It anchored on the 10th in the mouth of the Puerto de San Diego, securing itself on the 11th in the inner anchorage that is found at 32°44′ of latitude N, and West of San Blas 31 degrees 10 minutes.

This harbor has its mouth directly to the South, which opening is about a mile and one-half. The channel runs to the North Northeast for the space of a league inclining to the East, at which place it takes its direction to the Southeast in such a form that finding one offering more shelter or a better anchorage is impossible.

Departure from the Establishment and Puerto de San Diego toward [Puerto] de Monterey.

After 25 days of delay in Puerto de San Diego, employed in the necessary work to which they* devoted themselves there, sail was set 5 April 1774. Being ready for sailing from the coast, [the ship] experienced calms, squalls and very slack, variable winds with ominous aspects that took them between the islands of San Clemente and Santa Catalina until the 9th; and which thereafter began West to Northwest. It followed courses in the 3rd [SW] as those [winds] permitted, suffering henceforth very choppy seas of the 4th [NW] quadrant which obliged them to shorten sail out of regard for working the ship.

The winds were increasing toward the North, and to the Northeast, so that [the ship] was separated from the land. When it found itself on the 27th at about 31°49′ of latitude, and 26 degrees 17 minutes East of San Blas, 180 leagues from the nearest coast, [the winds] wheeled around to the 2nd [SE] quadrant almost to the South, with which it steered North Northeast heading in this manner to Puerto de Monterey. But having gone up to 37 degrees, the winds changed to the 3rd [SW] quadrant up

* Throughout Mourelle's narrative, "they," "them" and "their," when lacking antecedents, should be taken as referring to the ship's company.

to the North, and at times they blew with such strength that it required sailing with limited sail.

At sunrise on the 7th of May the coast of Monterey was sighted, and Punta Año Nuevo was noted to the Northeast a distance of 7 leagues.

From there, slack winds blew from the West Northwest, and marshaling all the force possible to gain the anchorage, it anchored on the 8th at 3 in the afternoon in six *brazas* of water in good anchoring ground.

This harbor, which is found in 36°40′ latitude, and East of San Blas by dead reckoning 16°21′, does not have such handsome qualities as that of San Diego. But nevertheless, with some precaution taken with the moorings, it has sufficient sheltered security from the winds that are capable of damaging ships.

Departure from Puerto de Monterey for Discoveries on the Northern Coast of California.

After 26 days of unloading and stowing the ship for the voyage that would be undertaken, sail was set on 6 June with light winds that were now from the 4th [NW quadrant], now sometimes from the 3rd [SW] quadrant. They were prevented from departing the bay at Monterey until the 16th, at which [time] they found themselves free of its points [Punta de Pinos and Punta de Año Nuevo]. With winds out of the Northwest to West, it followed courses in the 3rd [SW] quadrant, separating itself from the coast as much as it was able, so as to seek out favorable weather that blows out beyond it.

The 24th of said month it found itself at about 33 degrees 44 minutes of latitude, and West of Monterey 7 degrees 29 minutes, 127 leagues from the nearest land. The winds veered from the North to the Northeast, and then wheeled around to the 2nd [SE] quadrant, when [the ship] was in 37 degrees 30' of latitude, considered then 170 leagues from the coast.

The said winds stayed constant from South to East, with some interruption of calms and perpetual fogs so dense that they looked like small rain showers. They were prevented almost entirely from seeing the horizons until they went up to 47°32' of latitude. Finding themselves 162 leagues from the land, [the winds] blew from the South and West, and [the ship] endeavored henceforth to steer in the 1st [NE] quadrant in order to lessen that large distance.

The 15th at about 51 degrees, 42 minutes of latitude, and West of Monterey 18°17′, a meeting of the pilot [Martínez] and the ship's officers was held, in which the need to find the coast was explained, because it was necessary to seek in timely fashion a secure harbor in order to renew the water supply and [refresh] the ship's crew, which suffered from the bad weather. There apparently was general approval of this, and as a consequence it was ordered that their courses be set toward it [the coast], with the indicated winds, very fair, [the sea] calm, and [the horizons] less gloomy than those of the 2nd [SE] quadrant.

The 18th at eleven in the morning,[6] land was discovered when [the ship] was at about 53°53′ of latitude, and considered 14°40′ to the West of Monterey, from which point it endeavored to coast northward with the purpose of finding an anchorage where, with the ship secured, it would be easy to attend not only to the necessities of navigation, but also their instructions. The gloominess of the foggy and rainy weather, together with the Southeast winds, prevented attaining this objective. Although [the ship] ran along the coast a distance of three to four leagues, it was lost to view many times because of the thick fog and continual bad weather, which always required taking precautions necessary in unknown localities, [namely] laying to and furling their sails, depending on the clearness or gloominess of the horizons.

At noon on the 19th, orders were given to turn to a course East Northeast toward a point jutting seaward where the land ended, to which was given the name *Santa Margarita*. Having not taken an observation, it was considered to be at about 55° of latitude, and 14 degrees 8 minutes West of Monterey. The land, from the point at which it was discovered, runs half to the North Northwest and the other half to the North up to *Santa Margarita*.

From *Punta de Santa Margarita* a hill runs southward extending for the space of three leagues, which appears divided from the mainland, but which nevertheless is not an island. At its southerly end, a distance of half-a-league to sea, there is an island a league in circumference. Outside it an equal distance is a rock six or eight *varas* high, a musket shot from where are seen four or five small rocks on which waves are seen breaking at a great distance.[7]

There are also three small islets a musket shot from the aforesaid *Punta de Santa Margarita*, near which vicinity [the ship] passed without discovering anything dangerous.[8]

It remains now to be said that the coast runs to the South from the *Cabo de Santa Margarita* to a high, snowy mountain, and from there the land goes down to a point resembling a tongue;[9] from where it goes to the South Southeast.

From the *Punta de Santa Margarita*, along its north side, the land runs to the East a distance of 10 leagues, low and heavily forested.

Besides that, they might have discovered beaches along its shores, on which there is interposed a low point forming a small hill where two rocks are out of the water.[10] Between this point and the [main] land, it appeared to them that there was an inlet sheltered from all weather. The strength of the currents prevented them from reconnoitering it, because they had four hours of calm in their vicinity. [The ship] found itself six or seven leagues at sea, where it remained four days, having struggled notably in order to carry out its reconnaissance. But it was useless against the constancy of the winds out of the 2nd [SE] quadrant and the terrible thrust of the waters.

Eight leagues to the North of the *Punta de Santa Margarita*, a cape of land, large and plunging steeply into the sea, was seen, which was named *Santa Magdalena*.[11] Between these points without a doubt there is a large gulf, because the enormous volume of its waters are unable to flow out of so wide a mouth without producing those violent currents, which with a wind of six to seven miles [an hour] impeded entry.[12]

It was also seen that six leagues West of *Santa Magdalena* there is an island five or six [leagues] in circumference, which was named *Santa Christina*,[13] and which runs Northwest-Southeast with *Santa Margarita* the exact distance of seven leagues.

On the 21st the latitude was observed at 55 degrees North, and seeing that the winds and weather were not improving, and in order to seek an anchorage with the purpose of taking on water, for the ration had been cut, and not having a crust of bread for pressing farther North, it was determined to return, coasting along the land in order to reconnoiter it, and to find a place suitable for getting the ship into better trim.

Trade with the Natives of that Coast during the Stopover in Sight of *Punta Santa Margarita*.

On the 19th, being near *Punta de Santa Margarita*, much smoke was seen in the hills, and three canoes approached [the ship]. Repeating the visit on the following day, twenty-one [canoes came] of different sizes, amongst which there was one 25 or 30 *codos* long, with many more persons inside. But in the rest there were only 7 to 15 [persons], and two of them had only women and children aboard.[14]

It was then observed that they were of robust stature, cheerful in appearance, with beautiful eyes and handsome faces. The hair consisted of a queue, although some simply had it tied up. They have beards in the manner of the Chinese; they are white in color, and many of them have blue eyes. The women are good looking; they have the lower lip perforated, in which incision is inserted an object that is a different size depending on whether [the wearer] is young or old; it appeared that only the married ones had them.[15] Both sexes exhibited docility and agreeableness; the women were dressed in pelt tunics fitted to the body, with bracelets of copper or iron, and rings of the same metals.

After finding themselves in the frigate's vicinity, they sang their songs in unison; they danced to the accompaniment of a jingling tambourine brought by one of them, apparently the principal chief on board the largest canoe.[16] They cast feathers on the water, and standing up, they extended their arms, and then crossed them on their chest in demonstration of friendship.

These actions concluded, they came close to begin their trading. They showed remarkable perspicacity at it, for it was necessary to give them agreed-upon trifles in advance, and in the event they liked them, they were in the habit of requesting more, threatening not to deliver up the pledge agreed upon.

Trade was reduced to pelts of seals, sea otters and bears. They also have white wool of an unknown kind, from which are woven beautiful, though small, blankets. The commander bought four as specimens. The sailors obtained in all a remarkable quantity by [trading] mother-of-pearl shells that they had brought from Monterey, old pieces of cloth, and some knives. Although at first this seemed to them little, wanting [instead] large pieces of iron, they [the Indians] nevertheless finally received what the crew offered.

Half a bayonet and a fragment of a sword were seen in their hands, which the pilot [Martínez] conceived were from the men whom captain Chirikov had sent [ashore] in a launch in this same place, and who never returned.[17] They carried in their canoes boxes in order to divide up the goods according to their custom.

In these meetings, [the Indians] were asked many questions, of necessity by signs, in order to investigate everything for which the Instructions had prepared them; but they were never understood. And then, the sailors went down into their boats, increasing the bonds of friendship, and two [Indians] also came aboard the frigate, where they were well entertained in order to gain their goodwill.

The canoes appeared to be well made from a single piece [of wood], with a washboard over the gunwales. They were very swift, rowed with bladed-paddles a *vara*-and-one-half long, well made and lustrous.

Continuation of the Voyage Made to the South Reconnoitering that Coast.

After reflecting well on the reasons that obliged them to return to Puerto de Monterey, their courses were set in the 2nd [SE] and 3rd [SW] quadrants, depending on what the winds blowing from the South permitted, with the same fogs, rain, threatening appearances, and choppy seas that follow from the Southwest.

On the 23rd, at 6 in the evening, a snow-capped mountain range, which was seen earlier and named *San Cristóbal* for its great elevation, was newly discovered.[18] It is said that the north head is in 54°40′ latitude, from where it takes its direction to the South Southeast for a distance of 33 leagues in such a manner that its southern end stops at 53°08′.

On the 25th, [the latitude] was observed at 53°21′ in sight of the *Sierra de San Cristóbal*, in the absence of which the winds might have had more variation than from the Southeast to Southwest. They sailed along tacking, and on the 28th they observed [the latitude] at 52°41′, five leagues from the land they descried 16 [leagues] to the North Northwest and 14 [leagues] to the East Northeast.

From the 29th to 30th, they were becalmed in sight of the coast; although the wind then returned, it was always out of the 2nd [SE] and 3rd [SW] quadrants. This obliged them to continue tacking along the land from 51°30′ until the 2nd of August, when [the winds] were blowing Southwest, East, Northwest and North Northwest. But with threatening appearances, rain and fog, they were prevented from getting close until the east winds cleared the horizon, and they saw the land 15 leagues to the North, finding themselves in 48°50′ of latitude. Although the winds varied in the 2nd [SE] and 3rd [SW] quadrants, they tried very hard to get in close with the purpose of anchoring, which they effectively succeeded in doing on the 7th at 3:00 in the afternoon. Sounding first in 25 *brazas* of water, which lessened to 15 [*brazas*], then increased to the same 25 [*brazas*], in black sand and mud, a league from the closest land, they stopped with a stream anchor, hoping to look for a better shelter with [the ship's] launch.

That point of its anchorage, which they named *San Lorenzo*, was found to be in 49°30′ of latitude North, and they considered it West of Monterey 3 degrees 51 minutes.[19]

Six leagues to the Northwest of there was a point that was called *Santa Clara*.[20] There was another, two leagues to the Southeast, which they named *San Esteban*,[21] from where a point of rocks extended three-quarters of a league seaward, which took its direction to the Northwest and caused large breakers.

In that place, they were approached by fifteen canoes of Indians who began trading with the ship's crew, from whom they received mother-of-pearl shells for pelts and sardines, which they handed over before receiving the agreed-upon price with neither suspicion nor deceit.

Once again they saw small items of copper, which was an indication to them of mines of that metal. The natives asked for cutting intruments.

The people are said to be very robust and as white as the whitest Spaniard.[22] It was the same with the only two women they saw, the dress of both sexes being pelts that without other arrangement cover their backs. [The sailors'] having requested to know of them [the Indians] if they had knowledge of other civilized people, they apparently had never seen any.

The lands on those shores were moderately elevated, but in the interior they were high and covered with forests.

The commander resolved to seek suitable shelter for their tasks. The launch was put in, and when it was ready the wind blew from the West exactly abeam, for which reason he sought to weigh anchor and set sail with the aim of avoiding the danger that threatened. But the wind freshened quickly, obliging him to cut the stream cable and make ready to sail immediately, in which case he followed a course South Southeast while the winds wheeled around to the 4th [NW] quadrant.

A remark is found in the pilot's diary that says that a distance of five leagues from the anchorage of *San Lorenzo* there is a stepped sandbank where the least depth is 25 *brazas*, and which is five or six leagues from North Northwest to South Southeast, beyond which the sounding continues with much unevenness and a bad anchoring ground.

Afterward they continued sailing in sight of the coast, hoping for improvement in the weather, searching for shelter in which to enter. The 11th, being in 47°47′ of latitude, they saw a high mountain covered with snow, very perceptible, standing out alone, because the lowland stretching on all sides was heavily forested and populated with people as indicated by the multitude of smokes they saw. They named this mountain *Santa Rosalía*, considering it to be in 48°07′ of latitude.[23]

From that place, they continued on with winds of the fourth [NW] quadrant on a course Southeast and South Southeast, following the direction of the coast, and in sight of which they sailed until the 16th, when they measured the sun in 44°00′ of latitude. As the storm clouds and seas abeam increased incessantly, they lost sight of it until 40°08′ [latitude] in which they found a cape [on the] 22nd. By its configuration and the [identifying] signs that Cabrera Bueno gives, they believed it might be the one called Mendocino, the first discoverers of which placed it one degree 37 minutes farther North.[24]

In this parallel they were at pains to explain the progress that scurvy had made, the bad weather, and the continuous cold they suffered since 30 June, in going up to that same place, ensuring that they now had only six or seven sailors for watch, because the scarcity of water and salted foods hastened the unavoidable symptoms of that illness [scurvy].

Although the winds were quite variable, they were always steadier from the Southwest to Northwest, and with them they continued on. Without the fogs and haziness of the horizons, they might have been permitted to see the land until the 26th, when they found themselves in the vicinity of the Farallones de San Francisco. Continuing on courses in the 2nd [SE] quadrant, they saw on the 27th Punta de Año Nuevo, which is the most northerly [point] of Monterey [Bay], in which anchorage they cast anchor at 4:00 in the afternoon.

They were in that harbor until the 29th of October,[25] which was agreed to at a meeting of its harbor pilot and the ship's officers, with the purpose of passing the effects of the equinox in safety. In the interim, the commander communicated to His Excellency, the Viceroy, his arrival from the voyage that His Excellency had entrusted to his service, offering to remit the diaries later when he anchored in San Blas.

Departure from Puerto de Monterey toward Puerto de San Blas.

On the 9th of October, sail was set with the wind out of the 2nd [SE] and 3rd [SW] quadrants, nearest the South, from which part they blew until the 13th, when [the ship] found itself in 36°16′. Continuing variable until the 18th, when they observed the latitude at 34°57′, [the winds] were now from the 4th [NW] quadrant; and with them, on the 24th, they

THE COURSE OF THE SANTIAGO

9 October to 5 November 1774

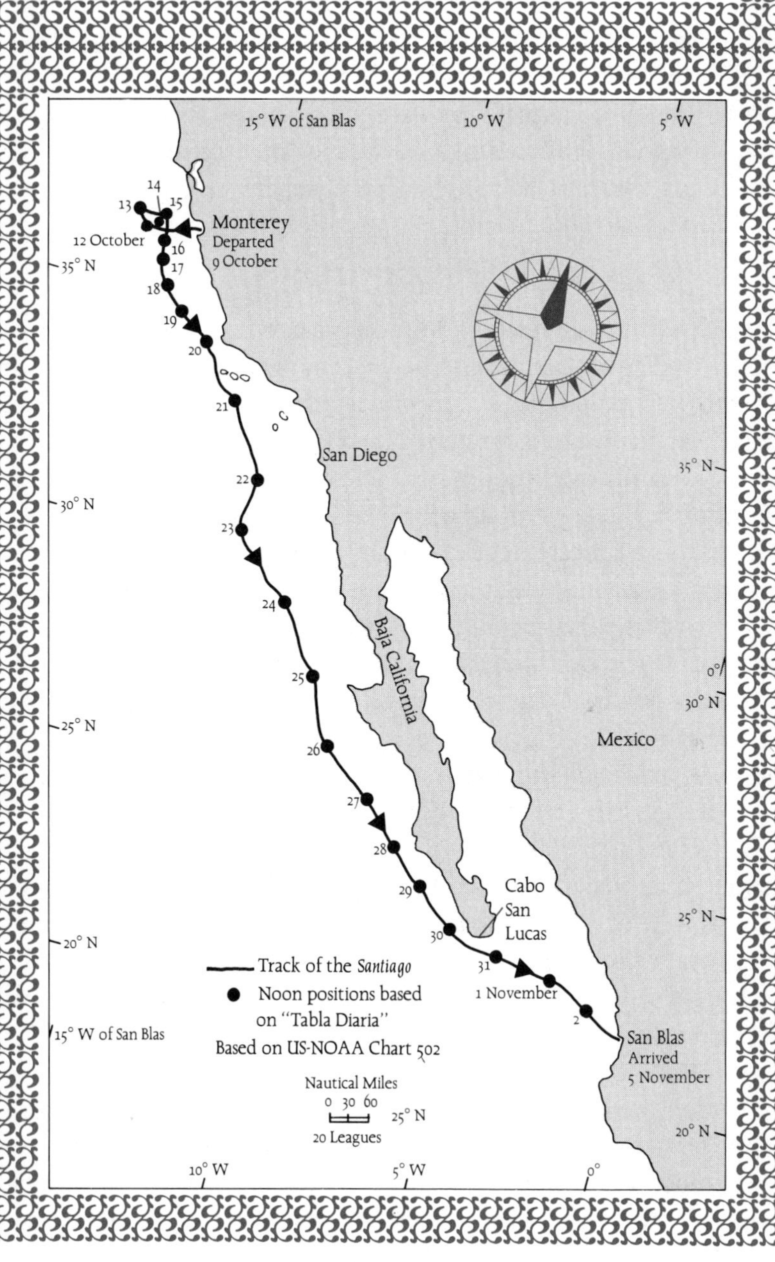

passed between Islas Navidad and Cerros [Cedros?], which are at the north head of Old California.[26]

On the 27th, [the ship] passed within six leagues of Cabo San Lázaro, which is found in 25 degrees of latitude. Coasting along the west side of [Baja] California, it arrived in the vicinity of Cabo San Lucas, which is in 22 degrees 52 minutes of North latitude, and West of Tenerife 93 degrees 14 minutes.

After doubling the said cape, and crossing the mouth of the Sea of Cortés [Gulf of California], land was sighted on 2 November north of the Islas Marías, close to Isla Isabela, between which [the ship] went, casting anchor in the harbor of San Blas on 3 November 1774.

Editor's Notes[27]

The little fruit that resulted from this voyage is immediately apparent from a reading of their diary accounts. They departed from Monterey on the 6th of June, and they returned there on the 27th of August, resulting in little more than two and one-half months at sea. Despite [the fact that it was] so short a time, they did not hesitate to call attention to the water shortage they suffered, making it almost the principal cause of their turning back. It is scarcely credible that in leaving Monterey they would fail to bring six months of water, which is the same as was carried on subsequent voyages. Likewise, they were persuaded by the advance of scurvy, and one or two deaths on the voyage, of having to leave Monterey for San Blas 15 days from [the ship's] arrival, without anyone sick's opposing it.

The earnest desire they had, according to what they say, to seek out an anchorage on all the coast, had been [pressed] with very little resolution, because there are on it havens, inlets, rivers and harbors that would have fulfilled all the purposes of the Instructions. [This is] in addition to having made landfall right at the mouth of sheltered bays and harbors, such as were at 55°00′, which promised them the best anchorages, and from where the Entrada de Bucareli is seen, which is only a distance of eight or nine leagues.[28] [There is] also the anchorage of *San Lorenzo*, which is found right at the mouth of Nootka [Sound], where five years afterward captain Cook careened [his ships].

In the days right after they discovered the coast, they were doing no work [concerning] its point [*Santa Margarita*],[29] and the entire description they made of it is in approximate terms, which characterize the insufficiency of the commander and pilot, in whose diaries these results are found.

So says Martínez:

"According to the latitudes and longitudes of the places we have reached, I state that one will be able to sail the coast without major error in the following manner.

"From Cabo San Lucas to Cabo Mendocino: to the Northwest, corrected, one will find very little difference in longitude.

"From said cape [Mendocino] to *Punta de Santa Margarita*, one will be able to sail Northwest ¼ North, 2°30′ farther West, assured that the difference will be very slight."

Their letters and knowledge are reduced to these two annotations, leaving us no other documents of so extensive a coast, after a voyage that cost the Royal Treasury plenty. And so, up to Cabo Mendocino we already had very particular information given by the best pilots; but except for finding out that the coast continues to the northwest, we remained almost in the same ignorance after the voyage.

One ought to note that there are hardly any observed [compass] variations during the course of the voyage, and they never did any work [concerning] its point [*Santa Margarita*] after they sighted land. Earlier, there are notes in the diary of the pilot [Martínez] in which are seen orders of the commander not to enter in the log those observations found most clearly inscribed in the "Tabla Diaria."[30]

Francisco Mourelle's "Tabla Diaria" of Pérez's Voyage in 1774

Tables of the Latitudes, Longitudes, Variations and Winds Observed on Said Voyage*

Tabla Diaria, which contains the latitudes and longitudes, [compass] variations and winds for each twenty-four hours on the voyage of discovery in 1774.

Month	*Day*	*Latitude North*	*Longitude West of San Blas*	*Observed Variation North East*	*Winds that blew during the 24 hours*
Jan.	24	[21°24′]	[0°]	[–]	[–]

On the 24th of January, they** made sail at 12 midnight from Puerto de San Blas, situated in 21°24′ latitude N, and West of Tenerife 88°14′. Afterward, they endeavored to gain all possible [distance] westward with the Northwesters blowing during the day, and the Northeasters, which are the land breezes that blow at night. Anchor was cast during the hours of calm in order not to lose to the current what [the ship] had advanced. Although it endeavored to pass north of the Islas Marías, that was not possible to attain, for which reason it departed from the southeasternmost of them on the 31st, at 12 midnight.

Jan.	31	20°45′	01°6′	5°00′	The winds were from North to Northwest

*This title appears in the index of Mourelle's collection of documents concerning Pérez's voyage in 1774.

**Throughout the "Tabla Diaria," "they," when lacking an antecedent, should be taken as referring to the ship's company.

Month	Day	Latitude North	Longitude West of San Blas	Observed Variation North East	Winds that blew during the 24 hours
Feb.	1	20°29′	1°28′	ditto	From North to NNW
	2	20°18′	2°38′	"	From NW to NNW
	3	20°12′	3°35′	"	From NW to NNE
	4	20°38′	4°28′	"	From NE to NW1/4N
	5	20°40′	4°39′	"	Calm and breezes from N to East
	6	20°25′	5°10′	"	Calm and breezes from NE to NW.
	7	20°25′	6°11′	5°00′	From NW to N1/4NE
	8	20°37′	7°18′	"	From North to NNE
	9	21°02′	8°19′	"	From North to NNE
	10	21°07′	9°28′	"	North and N1/4NE
	11	21°18′	10°25′	"	North and N1/4NE
	12	21°38′	11°20′	"	North and NNE
	13	22°04′	12°41′	"	NE
	14	23°12′	13°48′	"	NE and NNE
	15	23°55′	15°09′	"	NE and N1/4NE
	16	24°28′	16°23′	"	NE and NNE
	17	25°03′	17°38′	"	NE

Tabla diaria que contiene las latit. longit. variaciones, y vientos de cada veinte y quatro horas en el viage de 1774 a los descubrimientos.

179

	Dias.	Latitudes N.	Longit. al O. de S.n Blas.	Variacion NE.	Vientos que corrieron en las 24 horas.
Enero.	24.	El 24 de Enero de 1774 a las 12 de la noche se hicieron a la vela del Puerto de S.n Blas situado en 21°. 21' de lat. N. y al Occid.te de tenerife 88°. 14' desde entonces procuraron ganar acia el Oeste todo lo posible con los noruestes que corrian por el dia, y los nordestes q.e son los terrales y soplaban p.r la noche Dando fondo en las horas de calmas p.a no perder con la corr.te lo q.e tenia adelantado; y aunq.e procuró pasar al Norte de las Islas Marias no le fue dable conseguirlo, p.r cuya razn. dejó la punta del Sueste de ellas el 31 a las 12 de la noche.			
	31.	20° 45'	01° 06'	5° 06	Los vientos fueron del norte al nor noruoeste.
Febrero.	1.	20 29	1 28.	5o.	Del N.te al nno.
	2.	20 18	2 36.	"	Del no al nno.
	3.	20 12	3 35.	"	Del no al nne.
	4.	20 32	4 28.	"	Del ne al no ¼ n.
	5.	20 40	4 37.	"	Calmas y ventolinas del n.te al Oeste.
	6.	20 25	5 10.	"	Calmas y ventolin.s del ne al no.
	7.	20 25	6 11.	"	Del no al n ¼ ne.
	8.	20 37.	7 18.	"	Del N.te al nne.
	9.	21 02.	8 19.	"	Del n.te al nne.
	10.	21 07.	9 28.	"	N.te y N. ¼ ne.
	11.	21 18.	10 25.	"	N.te y N. ¼ ne.
	12.	21 38.	11 20.	"	N.te y nne.
	13.	22 04.	12 41.	"	NE.
	14.	23 12.	13 48.	"	NE y nne
	15.	23 55.	15 09.	"	NE y n ¼ ne.
	16.	24 28.	16 29.	"	NE y nne
	17.	25 03.	17 38.	"	NE
	18.	25 29.	18 35.	"	N ¼ ne y nne
	19.	25 53.	19 49.	"	N y N ¼ ne
	20.	26 04.	20 51.	"	Del no al n ¼ ne
	21.	25 40.	20 51.	"	Calmas y vientos al N.te
	22.	26 49.	20 51.	"	Sur y sso.
	23.	27 45.	20 03.	"	Del oso al n ¼ no
	24.	28 32.	19 38.	"	Del Sur al Oeste.
	25.	30 13.	19 38.	"	SSE
	26.	30 56.	19 39.	"	Sur, Oeste, no. y ne.
	27.	31 21.	18 57.	"	NO. y nno.
	28.	31 49.	18 33.	"	N.te N ¼ no - O ¼ no y sso
Marzo.	1.	33 14.	19 29.	"	Sur = sso = so = y no
	2.	33 48.	17 41.	"	Ono - no = y nnb.
	3.	34 07.	16 21.	"	nno, nne, y so.

165

INITIAL PAGE of Mourelle's "Tabla Diaria" of the Pérez voyage in 1774. (*Colección de diarios, noticias y papeles varios* [MM 401], The Bancroft Library, University of California, Berkeley)

Month	*Day*	*Latitude North*	*Longitude West of San Blas*	*Observed Variation North East*	*Winds that blew during the 24 hours*
Feb.	18	25°29′	18°35′	″	N1/4NE and NNE
	19	25°53′	19°49′	″	N and N1/4NE
	20	26°04′	20°51′	″	From NW to N1/4NE
	21	25°40′	20°51′	″	Calms and winds to the North
	22	26°49′	20°51′	″	South and SSW
	23	27°49′	20°03′	″	From WSW to N1/4NW
	24	28°32′	19°38′	″	From South to West
	25	30°13′	19°38′	″	SSE
	26	30°56′	19°38′	″	South, West. NW and NE
	27	31°21′	18°57′	″	NW and NNW
	28	31°43′	18°33′	″	North, N1/4NW–W1/4NW and SSW
March	1	33°14′	19°23′	″	South–SSW–SW–and NW
	2	33°48′	17°41′	″	WNW–NW–and NNW
	3	34°07′	16°21′	″	NNW, NNE and SW
	4	33°56′	15°29′	5°00′	From North to NNE
	5	33°54′	13°45′	″	From NNW and NW

Month	*Day*	*Latitude North*	*Longitude West of San Blas*	*Observed Variation North East*	*Winds that blew during the 24 hours*
March	6	34°10′	11°57′	″	North
	7	33°46′	15°47′	″	NNW and NW

On the 7th, at 6 in the morning, the coast of the Santa Barbara Channel was sighted to the Northeast, 8 leagues distant. Steering between the Farallón de Lobos and the islands extending along the Channel, and steering between the [main]land and the Isla de Santa Catalina, [they reached] Puerto de San Diego, where anchor was cast on the 11th, and the ship secured on the 12th of March inside the harbor.

April 6

On the sixth of April, 1774, [the ship] departed from San Diego for Monterey, and in those vicinities the winds became variable and slack, and [the sky] appeared threatening, which obliged it to remain between those [Channel] islands until the 9th, when having made the last sighting of the hill of San Diego, their courses were pursued in the 3rd [SW] quadrant.

April	9	32°32′	12°25′	″	
	10	31°20′	12°25′	″	Had calms and winds from the WNW
	11	30°33′	13°04′	8°30′	NW slack
	12	30°23′	14°20′	8°30′	North
	13	30°20′	15°36′	″	From the NW to 1/4NE
	14	29°47′	17°02′	″	From the NW
	15	29°14′	18°03′	″	From the NNW to NW
	16	29°01′	18°55′	″	From NW to North

Month	Day	Latitude North	Longitude West of San Blas	Observed Variation North East	Winds that blew during the 24 hours
April	17	29°05′	19°21′	″	Calms and slack winds from the North
	18	29°24′	19°28′	″	From NW to NE with calms
	19	29°30′	19°49′	″	From the WNW to NW1/4N; laid to
	20	29°05′	20°36′	″	From the NNW, slack
	21	29°03′	21°38′	8°30′	From the North
	22	29°09′	22°27′	″	From the North to NNE
	23	29°36′	23°26′	″	NNE
	24	29°56′	24°33′	″	NE1/4N and NNE
	25	30°33′	25°47′	″	From the NE
	26	31°16′	26°10′	″	NE and NE1/4E
	27	31°49′	26°17′	″	NE–SE–South, with calms
	28	32°48′	26°17′	8°00′	South and SE
	29	34°14′	25°55′	″	South and SE
	30	35°34′	24°59′	″	South and SSW
May	1	36°42′	24°10′	″	South and SSW
	2	37°34′	22°35′	″	SSW–SW–W–WNW and NNW

Month	*Day*	*Latitude North*	*Longitude West of San Blas*	*Observed Variation North East*	*Winds that blew during the 24 hours*
May	3	37°37′	21°19′	″	N1/4NW–North
	4	37°06′	19°11′	″	North
	5	37°11′	17°55′	″	North
	6	36°55′	16°50′	″	North
	7	37°06′	16°35′	″	From WNW to N1/4NW

On the seventh at sunrise, they saw the land a distance of 7 leagues. They anchored and secured the ship in the anchorage of Monterey, which they consider 16°21′ West of San Blas, and about 36°30′ latitude North.

June 7

On the 7th of June they set sail from Puerto de Monterey. As the winds were always slack from WNW to SSW, it was impossible for them to depart that bay until the 15th. On the 17th, they made the last sighting of the land that they consider [to be] in 36°09′ of latitude, and 16°56′ West of San Blas.

June	18	35°45′	16°51′		From WNW to NW
	19	34°57′	18°11′		NW
	20	34°22′	18°45′		From NW to NNW
	21	34°08′	20°25′		From NW to N1/4NW
	22	34°07′	21°41′		From North to NW
	23	33°46′	22°33′		NW and NNW
	24	33°44′	23°49′		From NW to NNE
	25	34°26′	25°15′		From NNE to ENE

Month	*Day*	*Latitude North*	*Longitude West of San Blas*	*Observed Variation North East*	*Winds that blew during the 24 hours*
June	26	35°37′	26°45′	5°00′	From NE1/4N to ESE
	27	35°59′	27°12′		SE–North–and calms
	28	36°26′	28°17′		From North to NE1/4N
	29	37°20′	29°35′	10°19′	From NNE to ENE
	30	38°35′	30°19′		From ENE to ESE
July	1	39°43′	31°08′	7°42′	ESE–SE and calms
	2	39°54′	31°15′		SW–W1/4NW–and calm
	3	40°34′	31°54′		N–NE–ENE–ESE–SE–E
	4	41°41′	32°48′		ESE–SE
	5	42°48′	33°36′		SE
	6	43°46′	34°18′		SE and SSW
	7	44°14′	34°27′		W1/4SW and North
	8	44°25′	34°47′		N1/4NE–NE1/4N–NE
	9	45°00′	34°59′		SE and calm
	10	45°35′	35°20′		SE and SSE, slack
	11	46°23′	35°58′		SSE
	12	47°32′	36°52′		South and West
	13	48°55′	36°09′		From West to NW

Month	Day	Latitude North	Longitude West of San Blas	Observed Variation North East	Winds that blew during the 24 hours
July	14	50°21′	36°09′		WNW–SW1/4W–SSE and SW
	15	51°42′	34°37′		From the South to W1/4SW
	16	52°41′	33°22′		SW and SSW
	17	53°13′	32°21′		SSW
	18	53°53′	31°00′		SSW, SE and West

On the 18th, at 11:30 [A.M.], they sighted the coast to the NE a distance of 16 leagues. They then endeavored to sail North along the coast seeking a harbor for their operations. But the bad weather and the Southeast winds did not permit it, despite running [along the coast] at a distance of 3 or 4 leagues, having to lay to frequently as a necessary precaution.

July 19

On the 19th, a point of land was neared that was named *Santa Margarita,*[1] and which is said to be found in 55° of latitude, and West of San Blas 14°8′. To the North of this point a cape was seen that was named *Santa Magdalena*[2] from where the coast went to the North 16 leagues. To the West of this cape there is an island that was named *Santa Cristina,*[3] which was distant from *Santa Margarita* seven or eight leagues. Between *Santa Margarita* and *Santa Magdalena* there is a large gulf from where issue currents so strong that with a wind six or 7 miles [per hour] they cannot be breached.[4]

July 22 — The winds were from the South to E

Seeing the difficulties they were having in order to find an anchorage, it was determined on the 22nd to return to the South from 54°23′ of latitude and 32°26′ of longitude in which they found themselves that day.

July 23 — 53°48′ — 31°17′ — East–SSW and West

The land was seen in the afternoon, and there were some high, snow-covered mountains that were named *San Cristóbal,*[5] the north head of

Month	*Day*	*Latitude North*	*Longitude West of San Blas*	*Observed Variation North East*	*Winds that blew during the 24 hours*

which they considered to be in 54°41′ of latitude, and the south one in 53°8′.

July	24	51°21′			They saw the coast, and the winds were from E1/4SE and calms

25
They did no work,[6] and with the fogs, they did not see the land. Slack winds E, NE, SSE and SSW.

July 26 52°59′
They did not see the coast; and the winds were variable from the 3rd [SW] quadrant.

July 27 52°41′
On rounding the *San Cristóbal* mountains, 5 leagues distant, the slack winds were from the 3rd [SW] quadrant.

July 28 52°20′
At 4 leagues from the coast the winds were from the South to West.

July 29
They did no work, and did not see the land; the breezes were from the SE to NE.

July 30 51°58′
They saw the coast a long way off; the winds were from the ESE to SSE.

July 31 51°35′ 28°50′
They did not see land; the winds were from the South to WSW.

August 1 50°29′ 27°41′
They did not see land; winds from WSW to WNW.

August	2	49°24′	26°11′	221/2°	Land was not seen; winds from WNW to NNW

Month	*Day*	*Latitude North*	*Longitude West of San Blas*	*Observed Variation North East*	*Winds that blew during the 24 hours*
August	3	48°52′	25°30′	20°34′	Land was not seen; winds from NW1/4N to N
	4	48°34′	22°23′	20°10′	Land was not seen; winds from NNE.
	5	48°50′	21°05′	19°37′	Land seen at 16 leagues, with high snow-covered mountains; winds from NW1/4N to NNE.
	6	They did no work	19°21′		Land seen at 8 leagues to NE; winds NW, NE, and calms.

7

No work done; course to NE with calms and breezes from the East; continued to the vicinity of the coast, sounding 25 to 15 *varas* [*sic*], but later they went down to 25 [*varas*?] in black sand, 1 league from land, where anchor was cast at 7 in the evening.[7] Called *San Lorenzo*, it is found in 49°30′. Here [Pérez] wanted to send the launch out to search for a harbor, but the wind from the West obliged him to order the stream anchor cable cut. Canoes of the Indians came alongside. This place is exactly at the mouth of Nootka [Sound].

August	8	49°12′			They saw the coast to the North, 6 leagues distant; wind from the West.
	9	48°17′	20°17′	18°18′	Land seen a long way off; winds from WNW.
	10	48°09′	19°45′		They saw the coast a long way off; winds West and WSW

Month	*Day*	*Latitude North*	*Longitude West of San Blas*	*Observed Variation North East*	*Winds that blew during the 24 hours*
August	11	47°47′	19°35′		They saw land 7 or 8 leagues to the E; winds from the West to SSE.
	12	47°26′	19°32′		The coast, 6 leagues distant; winds from the South to WSW.
	13	46°06′	19°32′		Land 6 leagues distant; winds from WSW to North.
	14	44°33′	18°35′		Land sighted is all little elevated; winds from the North.
	15	42°37′	16°46′		They no longer saw land; observed 9°30′ deviation; wind, North.
	16	41°23′	19°26′	5°30′	They did not see the coast; winds from the North.
	17				They did no work, and did not see the coast; winds from the North.
	18				They did no work, and did not see the coast; had continual calms.
	19	39°48′			They did not see the coast; had calms.
	20	39°30′			Land was not seen; had calms and breezes from the SE.

Month	*Day*	*Latitude North*	*Longitude West of San Blas*	*Observed Variation North East*	*Winds that blew during the 24 hours*
August	21	39°46′	no longitude	11°15′	They saw a cape, which they considered to be Mendocino, and which they located at about 40°09′ latitude; winds from the SE; land, 3 leagues distant.
	22				No observation; they did no work, and did not see land; winds from the SE, slack.
	23				They neither exerted themselves nor made observations due to the cloudy weather; winds from the SE, cool.
	24	38°32′			The coast was considered 15 leagues away; the winds, WNW.
	25				They neither made observations nor did work; they saw the Farallones de San Francisco, 1 league distant.
	26	36°55′	no longitude		They found themselves on a course for the bay within Puerto de Monterey. The winds those days were from the NW. At 4 in the afternoon, they anchored in 9 *brazas* of water within the anchorage into which they warped, resting secure on the 28th of August. It concluded a voyage of discovery

Month	*Day*	*Latitude North*	*Longitude West of San Blas*	*Observed Variation North East*	*Winds that blew during the 24 hours*
					from which little information could be extracted.

August [28]

The commander [Pérez] says in conclusion that *Punta de Santa Margarita* is on a bearing of 29° in the 2nd [SE] and 4th [NW] quadrants, a distance of 423 leagues [from Monterey]. The pilot [Martínez] gives the following directions as result of the voyage: From Monterey to *Punta de Santa Margarita* the coast runs through 36° of the 2nd [SE] and 4th [NW] quadrants, a distance of 457⅔ leagues. According to their operations, one can sail the coast without much error as follows: From Cabo San Lucas to Cabo Mendocino: to the NW, corrected. From Cabo Mendocino to *Punta de Santa Margarita*: to the NW1/4N, 2 degrees farther to the West, which ensures there will be plenty of sailing room.

For the most part, it appears to the editor that [the voyage] was of little usefulness, and that it characterizes the inefficacy of one voyage in such matters.

Sept.
After having stopped over at Monterey sixteen days in order to rest the crew, [Pérez] endeavored to leave on the 12th of September. But as the appearance [of the sky] and the variable breezes foretold stormy weather, a council was convened, and in it they resolved to stay put until the [. . .]

Oct. 9
[. . .] 9th of October, when sail was set on a course West, with the wind to the SSW.

	10	36°48′			No work. Had variable winds from the 2nd [SE] and 3rd [SW] quadrants, with calms.

Month	*Day*	*Latitude North*	*Longitude West of San Blas*	*Observed Variation North East*	*Winds that blew during the 24 hours*
Oct.	11	36°33′			They did not work; within view of land—calms and breezes from the 2nd [SE] quadrant.
	12	36°14′	18°03′	11°00′	Winds slack from SE1/4S
	13	36°27′	18°14′		Winds from SSW to SE, slack
	14	36°16′	17°42′		Wind SW1/4S and South
	15	36°19′	17°42′		Calms
	16	35°59′	17°23′		Breezes to the 4th [NW] quadrant & calm
	17	35°45′	17°23′		Breezes from the 2nd [SE] and 4th [NW] quadrants
	18	35°11′	17°08′		Breezes from the 2nd [SE] and 3rd [SW] quadrants, and winds from the West to NW
	19	34°57′	16°41′		Calms and breezes from WNW to S1/4SW
	20	34°17′	15°38′		Breezes from the SW and winds from the NW to the North
	21	33°13′	14°42′		Wind NW
	22	31°48′	13°26′		Wind WNW and NW
	23	30°21′	13°37′		Wind NW and NNW
	24	29°07′	11°51′		NW and NNW

Month	*Day*	*Latitude North*	*Longitude West of San Blas*	*Observed Variation North East*	*Winds that blew during the 24 hours*
Oct.	25	27°49′	10°39′		NW, NNW and North

This night they passed between the Isla[s] de Cerros [Cedros] and Navidad, which channel is 3 to 4 leagues wide.

Month	*Day*	*Latitude North*	*Longitude West of San Blas*	*Observed Variation North East*	*Winds that blew during the 24 hours*
	26	26°10′	9°54′		NNW, NW and NW1/4N
	27	25°09′	8°18′		NW and NNW
	28	24°16′	7°13′		From North to NW1/4W; they sighted the coast
	29	23°35′	6°13′		From North to NW1/4W
	30	22°55′	5°07′		From West to North; near Cabo San Lucas
	31	22°37′	3°56′		From West to NNE
Nov.	1	22°28′	2°21		NE1/4N –North
	2	21°57′	1°14′		From North to NNW; 4 leagues to NW of [Isla] Isabela.
	3				

SE of [Isla] Isabela a distance of 3 leagues.

	4				

In the vicinity of Piedra Blanca.

	5				

At sunset, they anchored at San Blas, and they remitted the diaries to his Excellency, the Viceroy.

APPENDICES

APPENDIX 1

Where Pérez Sailed

Long after the *Santiago* had returned from its northern voyage in 1774, a variety of controversies and misunderstandings arose as to where (and even when) it had sailed. The ship's track in general has never been in much dispute, but discrepancies and ambiguities in the several accounts of the expedition have left some details in doubt. Although seemingly minor, they are of considerable importance because the value of the expedition's ethnographic observations depends substantially on an accurate understanding of where they were made. The following discussion examines these issues, to establish as precisely as possible the localities Pérez visited, and when he visited them, on his voyage in 1774.

DISCREPANCIES IN DATES

Writing in 1937, Henry R. Wagner noted that the accounts of Pérez and Martínez "were a day early in their dates" compared with those of the chaplains; for reasons unexplained, he decided to use Crespi's dates "as being most probably the correct ones."[1] The assertion that the ship's commander and its principal navigational officer had the dates of the voyage wrong is, if true, more than a little surprising. Wagner may have reached this conclusion by overlooking the fact that Pérez and Martínez, as naval officers, made entries in their diaries according to nautical or ship's time (noon to noon) instead of civil time (midnight to midnight). Thus their diary entries are dated by notations reading, for example, "17th to Saturday 18 June 1774" (*Día 17 al Sábado 18 de Junio de 1774*). Observations of the sun were made each midday, weather permitting, concluding a twenty-four-hour period that had begun at noon the previous day. Consequently, the latitudes they recorded refer to the second date (in this example, 18 June). Both Crespi and Peña, however, made entries in their diaries on the basis of the midnight-to-midnight day to which, as landsmen, they were accustomed. Under these circumstances, the possibility of confusion over dates is easy to appreciate.

However, a careful comparison of the Pérez, Peña and Crespi accounts reveals that differences between them as to dates (and the corresponding observations of latitude) are not quite what Wagner thought. For the period between noon, 11 June (when the *Santiago* got underway at Monterey), and noon, 17 June, dates in all three diaries agree—a period during which no observations of latitude had been possible because of overcast skies. At last, on Saturday, 18 June, the sun was visible at noon, and Pérez observed the latitude as 35°44′N—information that apparently was not shared with the chaplains, for their accounts make no mention of this.[2] They recorded the latitude for that day as 34°57′N, the observation the ship's officers recorded for the following day (19 June). Evidently, Crespi and Peña, being unsure of how seamen kept time, made an error that briefly made their accounts appear one day behind Pérez's. Two days later, they seem to have realized their mistake, and from noon, 21 June, to noon, 18 July, the diaries are once more in essential agreement on dates and their corresponding observations of latitude.

The late morning of 18 July was no ordinary occasion, for it was then that the expedition made its first landfall on an unexplored coast. Pérez's navigation table for 17–18 July places this event at 11:30, while his accompanying description of events (*acaecimientos*) states that it was at 11:00 o'clock.[3] Peña gives the time as 11:00 o'clock, while Crespi places it at 11:30.[4] All three accounts agree that the sighting of land occurred some time in the hour before noon on 18 July.

The next day, a somewhat mystifying discrepancy arises between Pérez's *Diario* and those of the chaplains. The expedition's first encounter with natives is recorded by the captain at 4:30 P.M. of 19 July, while the Peña and Crespi diaries say this happened a day later, in the afternoon of 20 July.[5] All the accounts of the episode differ in some detail, but they almost certainly describe the same event. Who, then, had gone astray in reckoning dates, the captain or the chaplains? That may never be known conclusively; yet it seems most likely that the latter, being less experienced in nautical timekeeping, and excited over the expedition's first landfall and contact with natives, may have inadvertently entered the events of 19 July in their diaries under the following day. Whatever the case, entries in the chaplains' diaries are henceforth one day ahead of both Pérez's and Martínez's.

The situation seems to have prevailed until the end of the voyage. Peña and Crespi both record sighting the Farallon Islands (off the Golden Gate) at 10:00 A.M. on Friday, 26 August, while Pérez says it was 10:00 A.M. on the previous day. The chaplains have the *Santiago* anchoring off Monterey on Saturday, 27 August, while the captain's diary says it was on Friday, 26 August—although, adding to the confusion, elsewhere in a letter to Viceroy Bucareli (*see* p. 55), he says it was at 4:00 P.M. on 27 August. Pérez adds that the wind forced him to anchor "rather far from the regular anchorage,"[6] necessitating use of the launch to warp the ship into Monterey harbor—an operation that evidently took all of Saturday to accomplish. Whatever their reasons, the chaplains say nothing about this. Surprisingly enough, all three accounts conclude and were signed on the same day, Sunday, 28 August 1775.

None of the diarists mentions or acknowledges discrepancies in dates between their respective accounts, probably because the naval officers' diaries were not compared with those of the chaplains either during, or soon after, the voyage. The consequences of the mix-up have not been serious, but Wagner's contention that all the chaplains' dates are one day ahead of the naval officers' is only partially true, and there is little reason to suppose that Crespí's dates (or Peña's) should be regarded as more authoritative than those logged by the ship's naval officers.

TRACK OF THE VOYAGE NORTH

On leaving Monterey (noon, 11 June 1774), Pérez planned to head westward, putting as many miles as possible between himself and the coast in the hope of leaving behind the incessant summer northwesters to gain a northing. Instead, he had considerable difficulty with variable, uncooperative winds, punctuated by fog and calms, all of which put the *Santiago* on a none-too-favorable southward track for the first nine days of the voyage. But his luck changed on 20 June, and for the next forty-eight hours (until noon, 22 June) the *Santiago* sailed almost due west nearly one hundred and fifty nautical miles, averaging a little over three knots. In the next forty-eight hours, it continued more or less westward (bending only a few degrees to the southwest) at an average two and three-tenths knots. This was enough to allow Pérez to begin turning northwesterly in a broad arc, which by 3 July put the ship on a northward track.

The daily noon positions Pérez logged between 17 June and 3 July (expressed in latitude and longitude) are probably a reasonably accurate indication of the ship's track. However, there is reason to believe that some time around 4 July his dead-reckoning estimates of longitude began to overstate the ship's position westward of the coast.[7] This error seems gradually to have increased until the *Santiago* first made landfall off the Queen Charlotte Islands on 18 July, when his recorded longitude is clearly some 2°32′ too far west.

If Pérez's northward track is plotted on a modern chart, making allowances for his excessive longitude west, it is evident that from 3 July to the morning of 15 July the *Santiago* sailed more or less due north. Had it continued on this course it would have made landfall on the Alaskan coast somewhere slightly eastward of Yakutat Bay. Instead, at 8:00 A.M. on 15 July, Pérez, concerned (among other things) over the ship's low water supply, gave orders to sail northeast in the hope of encountering the coast. When he did glimpse land during the hour before noon on 18 July, he was off the northwestern part of Graham Island, the largest of the Queen Charlotte archipelago.

Until then, there is little doubt as to where the *Santiago* had sailed. It next coasted briefly northward along Graham Island, "heading for a point surrounded

THE COURSE OF THE SANTIAGO
11 June to 28 August 1774

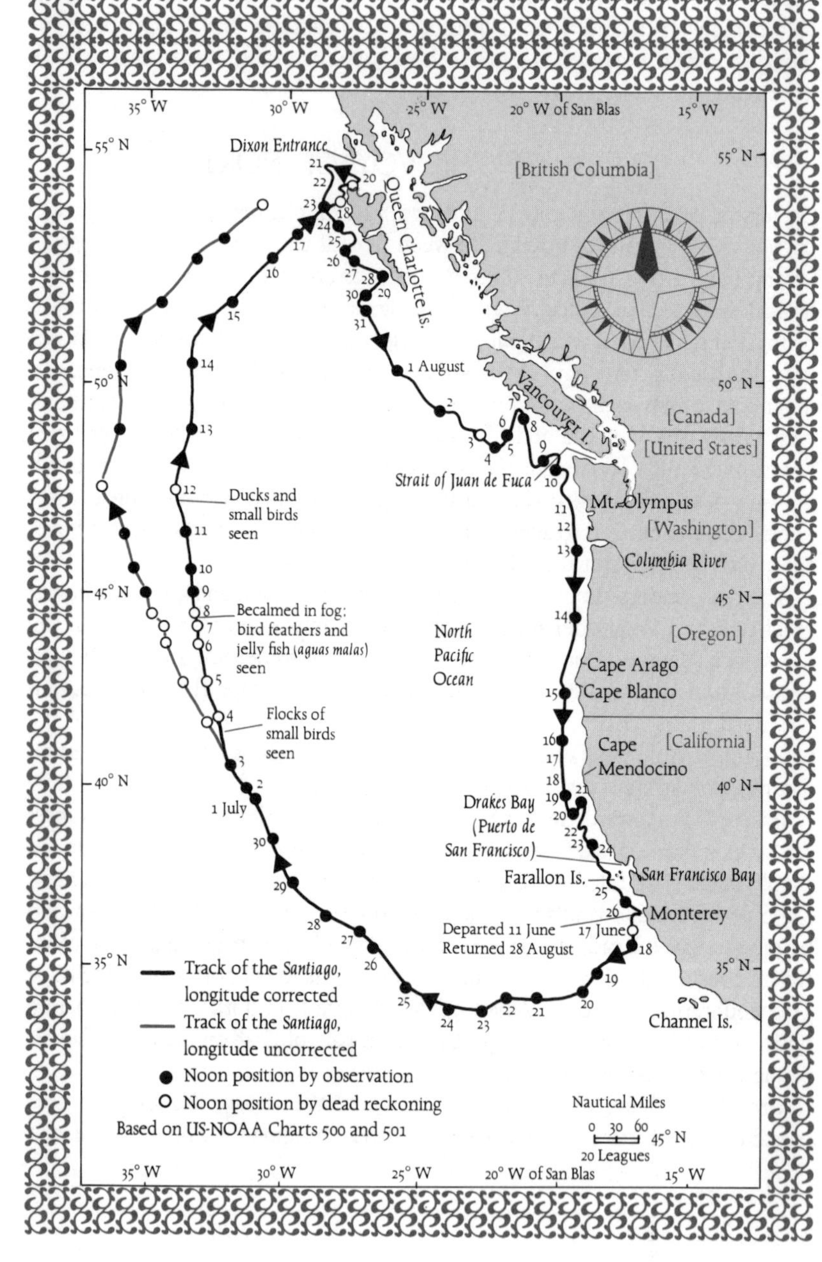

by the sea,"[8] to which Pérez gave the name *Santa Margarita*. There the problems began that have given rise to certain misconceptions about the voyage.

PÉREZ AT SANTA MARGARITA

Most probably, Pérez's *Punta de Santa Margarita* refers to a point on an island, today called Langara, that lies just off the northwest tip of Graham Island. These two islands, separated by a narrow channel named Parry Passage, are so situated that their division is not easily discerned. Overcast and rainy weather, such as that experienced there by the *Santiago* in 1774, would have increased the illusion that the islands were connected.

From a distance, Pérez at first seems to have believed that *Punta de Santa Margarita* was on an island, for he wrote (19–20 July entry) that "it jutted out from an extended hill and was about 3 leagues long, appearing separated from the coast and looking like an island from a distance."[9] Writing a more complete description of this point later in his diary, he revises his first impression, remarking that it "looks from a distance of four to five leagues like an island (although it is not)."[10] Martínez (judging by remarks in his *Diario* for 20–21 July) at first also thought *Santa Margarita* was on an island, only to conclude later that it was not.[11] Peña, on the other hand, refers to this landmark as consisting of three islands, which, he contends, Pérez named the *Islas de Santa Margarita* (although the captain's *Diario* refers only to *Punta de Santa Margarita*). Crespi also speaks of three islands.[12] All four diarists thus had some difficulty deciding the nature of the place Pérez had named *Santa Margarita*.

Most confusing of all are the captain's assertions about the latitude and longitude of *Santa Margarita*. Twice he expressly states its latitude as 55°N, claiming to have made an observation at that parallel at noon on 21 July.[13] As for the longitude, Pérez says it is "14°08′ West of Monterey"[14]—departing from his usual practice of stating longitude in reference to San Blas. Plotted on a modern chart, however, this position lies in mid-ocean, no closer than about eighty nautical miles west of the nearest land (Cape Bartolome, on Baker Island in the Alaskan Panhandle). It can hardly be the location of *Santa Margarita*.

Pérez's tendency to overstate longitude west has already been described, and thus his mislocating *Santa Margarita* substantially too far west is not surprising. There is less reason for his latitudinal reckoning's being drastically off the mark, since on other occasions he had demonstrated his ability to establish latitude within a margin of error usually no greater than ten minutes (or ten nautical miles). But the fact remains that his description of *Santa Margarita* is impossible to reconcile with any islands or land features in the vicinity of 55°N. Clearly, he was describing Langara Island and the adjacent terrain on the northwest corner of Graham Island, all of which lie between 54°10′ and 54°16′N.[15]

Why had Pérez so misjudged the latitude of *Santa Margarita*? No conclusive answer to this question may be forthcoming, and we can only speculate. Considering the poor weather reported by all the diarists at *Santa Margarita*, one may

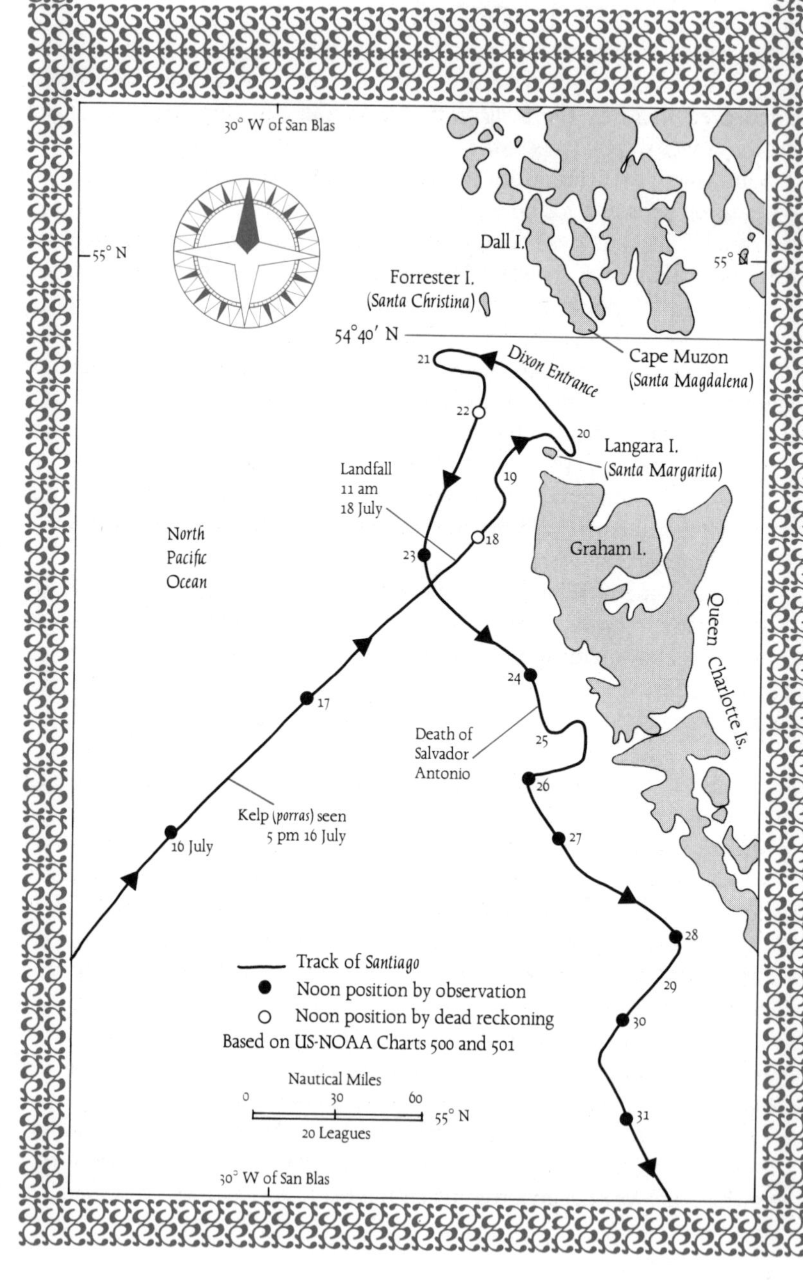
THE COURSE OF THE SANTIAGO
16 July to 31 July 1774
30° W of San Blas
55° N
Dall I.
55° N
Forrester I.
(Santa Christina)
54°40′ N
Dixon Entrance
Cape Muzon
(Santa Magdalena)
21
22
20
Langara I.
(Santa Margarita)
Landfall
11 am
18 July
19
18
23
North
Pacific
Ocean
Graham I.
Queen Charlotte Is.
24
17
Death of
Salvador
Antonio
25
26
Kelp (porras) seen
5 pm 16 July
16 July
27
28
Track of Santiago
Noon position by observation
Noon position by dead reckoning
Based on US-NOAA Charts 500 and 501
29
30
Nautical Miles
0
30
60
55° N
20 Leagues
31
30° W of San Blas

THE COURSE OF THE SANTIAGO
20 July 1774

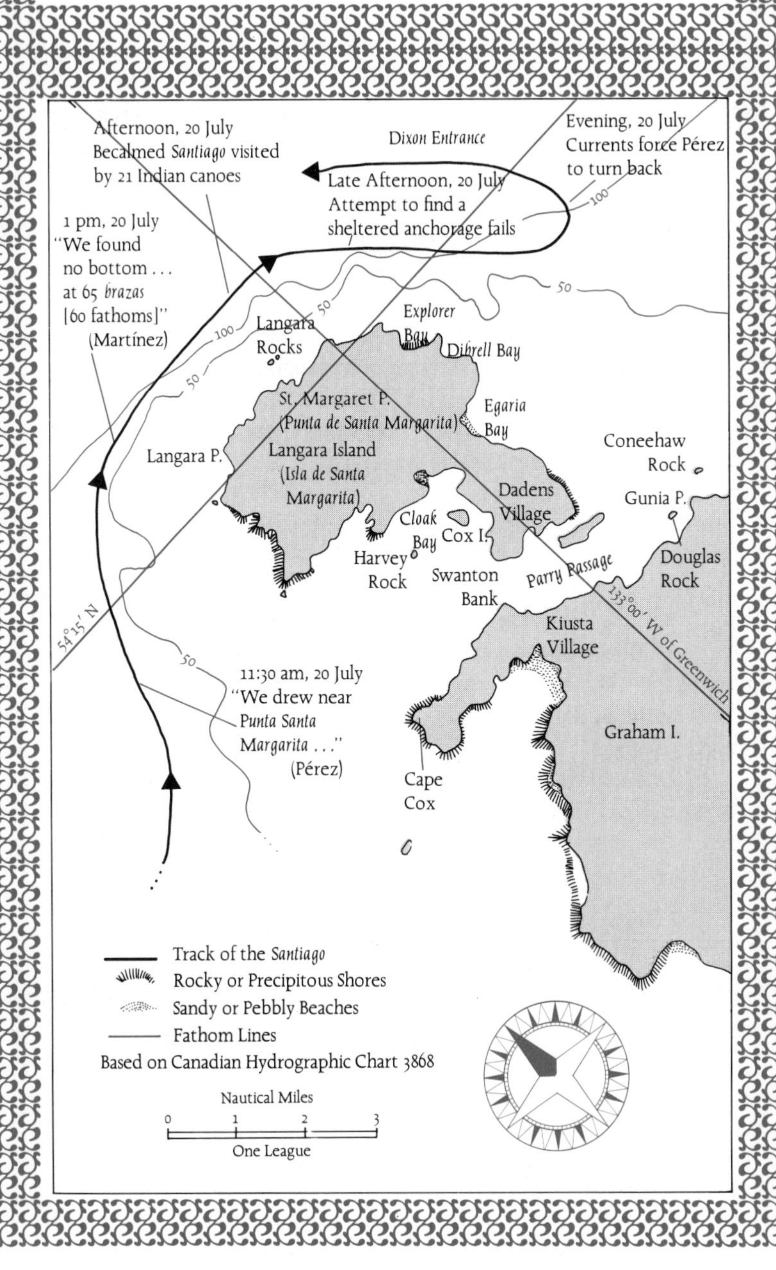

reasonably wonder whether Pérez observed the sun as he says—and, if so, whether he saw it well enough for an accurate determination of latitude. Having plainly failed to reach 60°N, as ordered, he was under some compulsion to minimize the disparity between Viceroy Bucareli's goal and the actual latitude the *Santiago* had reached—even if it meant stretching the truth a little.

All this would have been of minor importance had not Pérez's claim of reaching latitude 55°N been taken literally by some later interpreters of the voyage, and had not the expedition's highly significant first encounters with natives occurred at *Santa Margarita*. This combination of circumstances has led at least two students of the ethnographic aspects of the voyage to suggest—mistakenly, in this writer's view—that Pérez made contact with Haida Indians considerably north of Dixon Entrance.[16] Nothing in the four eyewitness accounts supports contentions that the Haidas occupied islands north of the Queen Charlottes in 1774 except the captain's questionable assertion that *Santa Margarita* was at latitude 55°N. In most other respects, the evidence points unmistakably to Langara Island as the scene of the *Santiago*'s historic first contacts with Northwest Coast Indians. And it is to that locality that the ethnographic data recorded by the expedition between 19 and 21 July is properly assigned.

When the *Santiago* rounded the north side of Langara Island, Pérez was looking for a secure anchorage on its eastern (inward) shore. Instead, he encountered a "current that gripped me and set me westward with so much velocity that it drifted me away from the coast some 6 or 7 leagues."[17] This current, which must have been the powerful ebb tide flowing out of what is today called Dixon Entrance, eventually seems to have propelled the *Santiago* in a northwesterly direction, allowing the Spaniards to glimpse at least two landmarks on the entrance's north side. First, they sighted a rugged, precipitous cape, six to eight leagues north of *Santa Margarita*. They named it *Santa María Magdalena*. This was unquestionably the southernmost tip of Dall Island, known today as Cape Muzon. Then, some six leagues west of this landmark, they caught sight of an island which they named *Isla de Santa Christina*. This was almost certainly what is now Forrester Island. However, any suggestion that the *Santiago* may have visited the localities north of Dixon Entrance and there made direct contact with natives is nowhere borne out in Pérez's diary.[18]

PÉREZ AT SAN LORENZO

Turning south from Dixon Entrance on 22 July, the *Santiago* began its return voyage of some twelve hundred nautical miles to Monterey. Pérez made an effort to reconnoiter the western coasts of the Queen Charlotte Islands, but succeeded only in gaining a few glimpses of their mountainous spines from some distance at sea. He called them collectively *Los Cerros de San Cristóbal*; today they are known as the Queen Charlotte Ranges.

After following a generally southeasterly course paralleling the Queen Charlottes for five days (23–28 July), Pérez gave orders to turn southwesterly, away from the scenic and mountainous lands they had been coasting. Two days later, the *Santiago* resumed a southeasterly heading, which by 3 August brought it to a point some seventy nautical miles off the central west coast of Vancouver Island. There the captain decided to seek the coast again by first heading due east, then northeasterly. According to his account, on 5 August, at 11:30 A.M., they first sighted "high and snowy peaks, the nearest part bearing to the NE a distance of 15 to 16 leagues."[19] These were peaks of what today are called the Vancouver Island Mountains; the ship was headed for the vicinity of what we know as Nootka Sound.

The *Santiago* approached the coast under full sail on a course NE 1/4N. But on 5 August, at 11:30 P.M., a dense fog enveloped it, so that, as Pérez phrased it, "one could hardly see from stem to stern."[20] The ship remained becalmed and fog-bound until the early morning of 7 August, when a wind sprang up from the east-southeast, enabling the *Santiago* to resume its northeasterly course. Later, in the early afternoon of 7 August, Pérez put the ship on a course due north, whereupon, at 3 o'clock "canoes began coming out from the land."[21]

Frequent soundings were made as the ship edged north toward what appeared a possible anchorage. At first their sounding lead indicated a depth of 25 *brazas* (23 fathoms). Then, as Pérez describes: "From this depth we came to 15, 16 and 19 *brazas* [13.8, 14.7 and 17.5 fathoms, respectively], and from this to 25 *brazas*, very dark sand and green slime, where we anchored, giving it the name *Surgidero de San Lorenzo*."[22] In only one place in the vicinity of Nootka Sound could a ship approaching from the south (as the *Santiago* was) have attained this particular series of soundings. That place (lat. 49°26′N, long. 126°371/2'W) is near the southern extremity of Nootka Sound's outer harbor, some two nautical miles west of the Hesquiat Peninsula's southwesterly shore, more or less midway along a submerged rocky ledge extending seaward west-northwesterly, some five nautical miles. Closer to shore, the rocks of this ledge become progressively exposed and washed by breakers. Aptly enough, today they are called Perez Rocks, honoring their European discoverer.[23]

From where the *Santiago* anchored, Pérez describes distances and directions to two points of land. One, he says, bore "to the NW, a distance of 4 leagues,"[24] while the other was two leagues away in the opposite (southeasterly) direction. He named these points *Santa Clara* and *San Estevan* respectively, and there is little doubt that the former is today's Bajo Point (lat. 49°37′N, long. 126°491/2W). As for the latter, it is most likely a point bearing on modern charts the name of Estevan Point (lat. 49°23′N, long. 126°321/2'W). Pérez's distances and directions from the ship's position to these two points suggest convincingly that the *Santiago* anchored at or near a location (lat. 49°27′N, long. 126°371/2'W) some three nautical miles west of the interior corner of a cove called Barcaster Bay, on the Hesquiat Peninsula's west coast, and about one nautical mile north of the submerged rock ledge his soundings had found.

Evidence that Pérez and the *Santiago* were at Nootka Sound in 1774 has also been noted in oral accounts attributed to the area's indigenous inhabitants. Pos-

THE COURSE OF THE SANTIAGO

7–8 August 1774

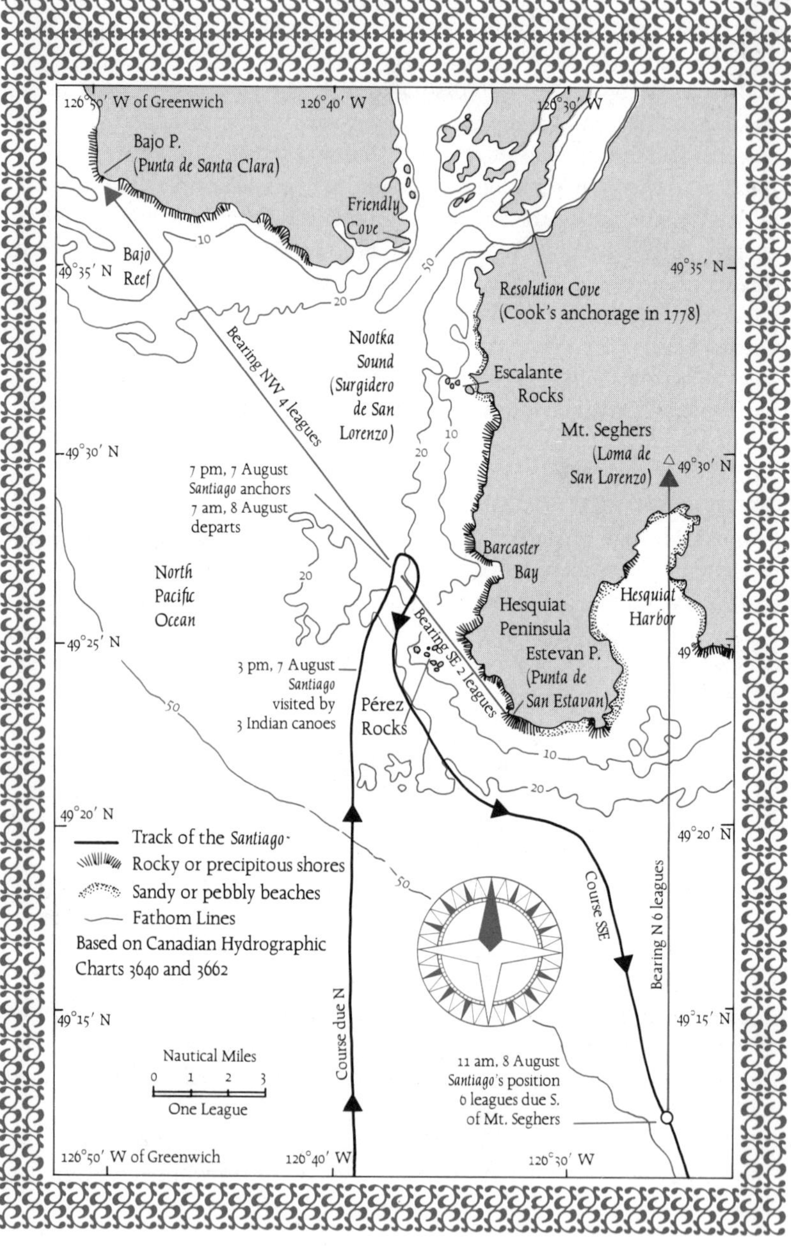

sibly the most interesting such case is found in a document written some time in the spring of 1789 by Joseph Ingraham, first mate of the Boston ship *Columbia Rediviva* (then captained by John Kendrick), which had spent the winter of 1788–89 at Nootka. Ingraham seems to have made it his purpose to learn as much as possible about the sound's climate, geography, flora, and fauna, as well as the culture and language of its native human population. When the Spanish vessel *Princesa* entered Nootka Sound in May 1789, its commander, Esteban José Martínez, evidently struck up a friendship with Ingraham and convinced him to set down his observations in writing. Essentially an undated letter addressed to Martínez, the document was originally written in English and later translated into Spanish. It concludes with a description by Ingraham of what the Nootka natives had told him about the first European ship to visit them.[25]

According to their account, this had occurred approximately forty months before James Cook's visit in March and April, 1778. They went on to specify that the ship had anchored near some rocks on the east side of the sound's entrance, remaining there four days. This jibes closely with what is known from other sources about the *Santiago*'s anchorage, though differing slightly as to date (closer to forty-four months before Cook's visit) and duration of the visit (no more than two days). On balance, these discrepancies are minor—certainly what one might expect in an oral transmission of the story over some fifteen years. It seems likely that Ingraham was told an authentic—if not quite accurate—recollection of the first contacts the natives of Vancouver Island had with Europeans.

In 1792, a botanist and naturalist named José Mariano Moziño, who visited Nootka Sound as a member of Bodega y Quadra's so-called Boundary Expedition (*expedición de los límites*), also attested to a tradition among the Nootka natives of the *Santiago*'s presence there eighteen years earlier.[26] And should any uncertainty remain as to the whereabouts of *Surgidero de San Lorenzo*, Pérez logged its latitude at 49°30′N,[27] within 2½ minutes of the ship's anchorage as indicated by the independent evidence of soundings, bearings and distances to landmarks. Although doubts have been raised by various interpreters of the voyage, especially Henry Wagner and, to a lesser extent, Henry Oak,[28] as to whether the *Santiago*'s anchorage was really at Nootka Sound, these now appear largely if not entirely groundless.

When Pérez cast anchor off the Hesquiat Peninsula, he was not long in realizing that he needed a safer, less exposed place. Promptly at dawn on 8 August, the ship's launch, equipped with masts and sails, was lowered into the water to search for a more secure anchorage. Pérez, in remarking that he was "confident of some shelter from *Punta de San Estevan*," may have intended to seek a haven in what is today called Hesquiat Harbor.[29] If the launch's crewmen had been able to go northward two or three leagues, they would no doubt have discovered the entrance to Nootka's inner harbor, as well as one of the several well-protected coves (such as the one in which Cook's ships anchored in 1778). But luck was against them, and before they could get under way, whatever direction they had

THE COURSE OF THE SANTIAGO
2–14 August 1774

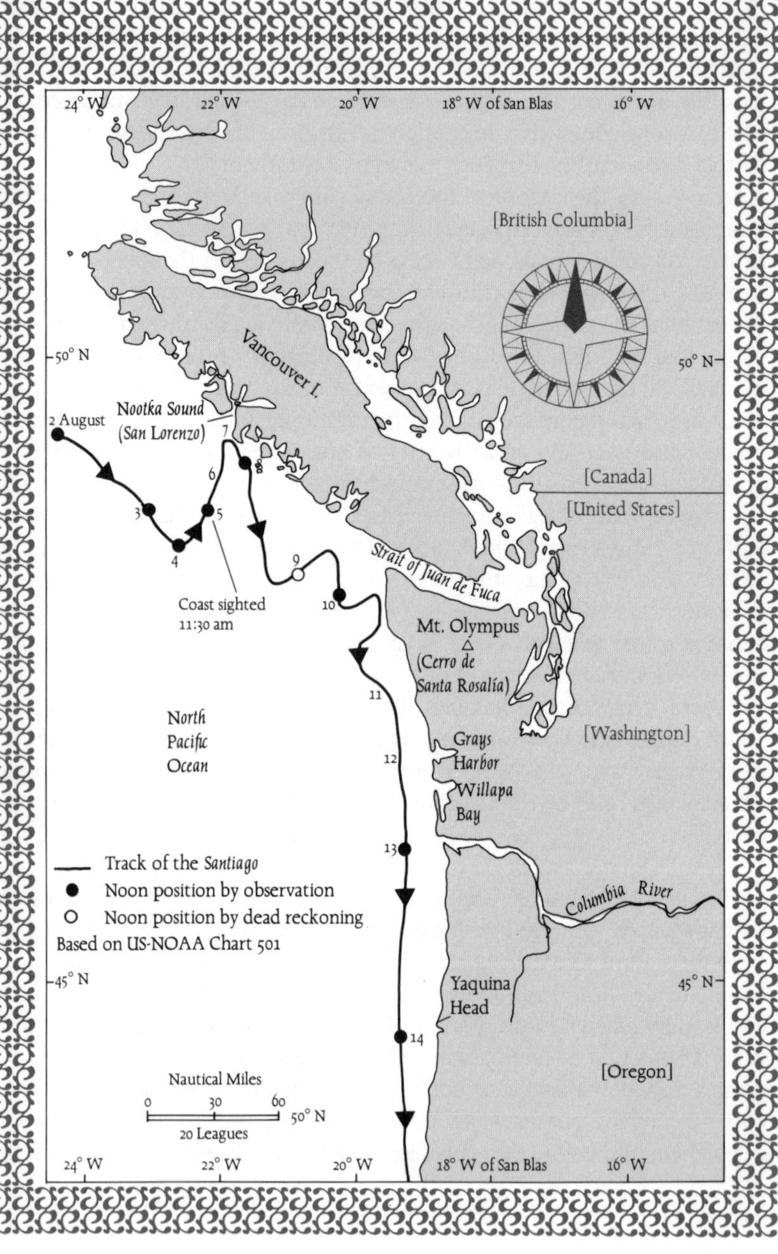

been ordered to go, a brisk west wind came up, threatening to drive the *Santiago* on to the rocky, wave-dashed shore of the Hesquiat Peninsula. Difficulties in retrieving the stream anchor further complicated their precarious situation, forcing Pérez to order the anchor cable cut so that the ship could, as sailors say, claw off this dangerous lee shore and avoid being cast ashore. Thus the expedition left Nootka under hurried and harried conditions that deprived Pérez of any further opportunity to explore or take formal possession of it in the name of Carlos III—although the anchor they left may still be there today.

PÉREZ ON THE WASHINGTON–OREGON COAST

The *Santiago*'s track during the four days after its departure from Nootka Sound (8–11 August) is among the more controversial parts of the voyage. In 1789, Pilot Martínez made claims about "an entrance which I had seen in the distance in 1774 on my return to the department [of San Blas]."[30] If he did glimpse such an "entrance," it must have been during the four days immediately after leaving the precarious anchorage off the Hesquiat Peninsula. That was the only time the *Santiago* was within sight of the coast near latitude 48°20′N, with which his statement associated the sighting.

Nothing in Pérez's account explicitly corroborates Martínez's claim, but the commander's entry for 9–10 August does contain remarks suggesting, however tenuously, that some such sighting may well have occurred. At noon on 9 August, Pérez logged the latitude by dead reckoning at 48°17′N, and ordered the ship to turn from a south-southeasterly course to one northeast. If his dead-reckoning latitude was even approximately correct, the *Santiago* was sailing more or less directly toward the seaward opening of what is today the Strait of Juan de Fuca (latitude 48°30′N). The weather, he says, was overcast; at 1:30 P.M., he ordered the topsails hauled down for repair and replacement. At sundown, the coast could be seen bearing north-northeast, fourteen leagues distant, whereupon the ship settled down for a nearly calm night with only light, variable winds out of the west. When dawn broke on 10 August, the horizons were "clear from the NE to the South,"[31] permitting Pérez to take bearings on land "sighted to the extreme E to E1/4SE a distance of 18 leagues and the opposite to a distance of 14 leagues."[32] The land he saw to the east could only have been near Cape Flattery and the northernmost coast of what is now Washington State; to the north, Vancouver Island's coast, somewhat east of Barkley Sound. One is almost forced to conclude that he was looking directly into the twelve-mile-wide seaward opening of the Strait of Juan de Fuca, even if, despite having clear horizons, he unaccountably failed to recognize it for what it was.

The remainder of the *Santiago*'s voyage southward along the coast to Monterey is neither mysterious nor especially eventful. Uncooperative weather and an understandable reluctance to test his luck further in coastal fog banks prevented Pérez from recording more than a few glimpses of coastal topography south of the Strait of Juan de Fuca. Nevertheless, off the coast on 14 August, he sighted and described a "massive and . . . very prominent cliff that is between white and yellow in color."[33] The observed latitude for that day was 44°35'N, only six minutes south of Yaquina Head; without question that was the landmark Pérez saw. It was to be the first European description of any feature on the coast of what we know as Oregon that can be identified with certainty.

APPENDIX 2

Rosters of the Santiago's Officers, Crew and Passengers January 1774

The following two rosters were prepared by The Department of San Blas' commissary officer, Francisco Hijosa, and his assistant, Joseph Faustino Ruíz. The first, dated 22 January 1774, lists the names of the ship's officers and crew, together with their respective ranks and salaries. The second, dated 23 January 1774, lists the families and unmarried persons who had booked passage to Monterey, where they intended to settle as colonists. Originals of the documents are in Mexico City's Archivo General de la Nación, Ramo (Division): Historia, 61: fojas (folios) 225–28. Microfilm copies in the Oregon Historical Society's manuscript collection have been used in making the translations that follow.

List of the officers, gunners, seamen, apprentice seamen, cooks and cabin boys who are manning Your Majesty's frigate named *Santiago*, alias *Nueva Galicia*, on the present voyage which is going to be made to Puerto Monterey.

Rank	*Personnel*	*Salary*
Captain	Don Juan Pérez, in conformance to the new regulations promulgated by Your Excellency, to enjoy each month	70 p[esos]
Second in Command	Don Estevan Martínez, to enjoy a salary of	50 "
Chaplain	The Reverend Fray Pablo de Mugártegui	———
Surgeon	Don Pedro Castán, to enjoy a monthly salary of	30 [pesos]
Boatswain	Manuel López, to enjoy a monthly salary of	24 "

Rank	*Personnel*	*Salary*
Boatswain's Mate	Pasqual de Esa, to enjoy a monthly salary of	20 [pesos]
Mate	Juan Hernández, to enjoy a monthly salary of	16 "
Carpenter	Manuel de Rojas, to enjoy a monthly salary of	19 "
Mate	Diego Nicolás, to enjoy a monthly salary of	15 "
Caulker	Francisco Rua, to enjoy a monthly salary of	19 "
Mate	Joseph Matthes, to enjoy a monthly salary of	15 "
Steward	Joseph Anglada, to enjoy a monthly salary of	19 "
Mate	Christóbal Rodríguez, to enjoy a monthly salary of	12 "
Master Gunner	Ramón Padilla, to enjoy a monthly salary of	10 "
Coxswain	Carlos Ortega, to enjoy a monthly salary of	14 "
Gunners	Juan Melión Pérez, to enjoy a monthly salary of	12 "
"	Bacilio Silva, same	12 "
"	Geronimo Ruéz, same	12 "
"	Joseph Casimiro, same	12 "
"	Ignacio Marques	12 "
"	Joseph Figueroa	12 "
"	Francisco Santa María, same	12 "
"	Santiago Agudo, same in total	12 "
"	Joseph Miguel, same in total	12 "
"	Antonio Marmolejo, same	12 "
"	Joseph Antonio Rodríguez	12 "

Rank	*Personnel*	*Salary*
″	Jusito Guardado	12 [pesos]
″	Mattheo de la Cruz	12 ″
″	Ignacio Díaz, same in total	12 ″
Seamen	Juan Sevastián Robledo	10 ″
″	Juan Reyes, same in total	10 ″
″	Juan Joseph Ervaes, same	10 ″
″	Domenico de los Santos, same	10 ″
″	Ignacio Cortés, same	10 ″
″	Bonefacio Ocampo, same	10 ″
″	Miguel Hidalgo, same	10 ″
″	Antonio María Beas, same	10 ″
″	Patoriano Torres, same	10 ″
″	Joseph Britio, same	10 ″
″	Antonio Prive, same	10 ″
″	Salvador Angel, same	10 ″
″	Leandro Estanislas, same	10 ″
″	Manual Martínez, same	10 ″
″	Antonio Mendisaval, same	10 ″
″	Diego Melchor, same	10 ″
″	Lorenzo Resa, same	10 ″
″	Pasqual de la Cruz, same	10 ″
″	Nicolás Tolerano, same	10 ″

Rank	*Personnel*	*Salary*
Apprentice Seamen	Antonio Sabalso, eight pesos	8 [pesos]
"	Joseph Manuel Silva	8 "
"	Joseph Taburio, same	8 "
"	Juan Secundino, same	8 "
"	Indian Joseph, same	8 "
"	Joseph Antonio Dávila, same	8 "
"	Augustín Sovarano, same	8 "
"	Joseph Manuel, same	8 "
"	Raymundo Aparicio, same	8 "
"	Alejo Feliciano, same	8 "
"	Luis María, same	8 "
"	Joseph Romero, same	8 "
"	Joseph María Martínez, same	8 "
"	Miguel Gutierrez, same	8 "
"	Manuel Antonio, same	8 "
"	Joseph Miguel Phelipe, same	8 "
"	Juan Joseph Carpio, same	8 "
"	Joseph Pinuelas, same	8 "
"	Juan Engenio Rosalío, same	8 "
"	Joseph Rodrigo, same	8 "
"	Francisco Blas, same	8 "

Rank	*Personnel*	*Salary*
Apprentice Seamen	Miguel Nicacío, same	8 [pesos]
"	Pablo Marques, same	8 "
"	Joseph Bonifacio Salasar	8 "
"	Joseph Miguel Velez, same	8 "
"	Juan Atencio Martínez, same	8 "
"	Feliciano Santiago, same	8 "
"	Lorenzo Antonio, same	8 "
"	Salvador Antonio, same	8 "
"	Francisco Hernández, same	8 "
Cooks	Francisco Ponce de León, same	10 "
"	Ignacio Gonsales, same	10 "
"	Marcos Saravía, eight pesos	8 "
"	Domingo Gallo, same in total	8 "
Cabin Boys	Tomás de la Cruz, six pesos	6 "
"	Antonio Marcolino, same	6 "
"	Juan Acencio Pérez, same	6 "
"	Pablo Sambrano, same	6 "
"	Pedro Joseph Romero, same	6 "
"	Pedro Díaz, same	6 "

San Blas, 22 January 1774, Francisco Hijosa, Joseph Faustino Ruíz.

List of the families who booked passage to Monterey in the frigate named *Santiago*, alias *Nueva Galicia*, under the command of Juan Pérez, frigate-grade ensign of the Royal Navy.

Loans		*Persons*
	Don José Joachin Dávila, with his wife, Doña María Josefa Caravajal, and his son, José Favian Sebastián	3
	Fernando Antonio Chamorro, blacksmith, married to Ana María Hurtado de Mendoza; and two daughters, maidens 18 to 20 years old, one named Cipriana and the other María del Carmen	4
	Phelipe Romero, blacksmith, from Guadalajara, unmarried; and his mother, María Petrona Garcia Yuida	2
Received 24 p[eso]s	Veino, from Tepic	1
	Manuel Dávila, from Guadalajara, married to Geronima Montaña, with four children: one José Antonio; another José Estamilos; another María Josefa; another José Mariano; all from 6 to 12 years old	6
	Josefa, sister of Manuel Dávila, a maiden lady	1
	José Lorenzo, a Spaniard from the town of Aguas Calientes, carpenter, unmarried	1
	José Manuel Rodrigues, from Guadalajara, carpenter, unmarried	1
	José Francisco Ramírez, from Aguacatlan	1
Received 24 p[eso]s	An unmarried farmer	1
	Juan Conrrado, Indian servant of *padre presidente* Fray Junípero Serra	1
	Juan Ebangelista, the same	1

Loans		*Persons*
	Juan María Trinidad, a boy from the village of Guaynamota	1

It conforms to the review that I, Don Francisco Hijosa, made of the aforesaid persons in Puerto de San Blas on 23 January 1774. Francisco Hijosa, [and] with my supervision, José Faustino Ruíz.

APPENDIX 3
Pérez's Navigation Tables

During three distinct periods of Pérez's 1774 voyage, the entries in his *Diario* include tabular summaries of the navigation data for each day's run (noon to noon), in addition to his narrative of events. The initial such period began at noon on 17 June, about the time clearing skies first permitted solar observations of their latitude, and extended until noon on 18 July, shortly after land was sighted off the Queen Charlotte coastline. Pérez did not keep such tables during the succeeding four days (18–22 July, noon to noon), but at noon on 22 July he resumed them for the next forty-eight hours, or until noon on 23 July. Then, for unexplained reasons, he failed to keep daily tables for the next seven days, as he tried somewhat unsuccessfully to regain his navigational bearings and reconnoiter the Queen Charlotte coast on his way south. On 31 July he resumed his tabular summaries, only to suspend them for the third and final time on 5 August, before reaching Nootka Sound. There would be no further tables between then and the *Santiago*'s return to Monterey at the end of August.

To avoid disrupting the diary's narrative flow, the tables have been moved from their original context and grouped together in this Appendix. For the reader interested in the data they contain, a few words of explanation may be helpful.

Each table is divided into left- and right-hand components. On the left are seven headings under which data are entered:

"Hr," or *horas* (hours);

"Mi," or *millas* (miles, probably nautical);

"½ Mi," or *medias* (half miles);

"Br," or *brazas* (.92 fathoms of length);

"*rumbos*" (courses);

"*vientos*" (winds); and

"*abatim[ien]to*" (drift or leeway).

The tables thus provide, for each twenty-four-hour period, an hourly record of the ship's estimated distances sailed in *millas*, half-*millas* and *brazas*, and of its compass bearings, together with wind direction and an estimate of the effects of drift or leeway.

The right-hand component bears a heading that gives the two dates on which each twenty-four-hour run falls (noon to noon). Indicated are the date the run commenced (at noon), and the name and date of the following day when the run was completed (at noon). Below these dates, a brief sentence usually introduces the following information:

1. *Distance*: The distance in *millas* traversed by the ship in a given twenty-four-hour period (noon to noon).

2. *Difference in Latitude*: The degrees and minutes of latitude gained (north) or lost (south) in a given twenty-four-hour period (noon to noon).

3. *Departure*: The degrees and minutes of longitude gained (west) or lost (east) in a given twenty-four-hour period (noon to noon), relative to a meridian Pérez established for the departure point he used to plot the voyage north. This reference point was at longitude 16°51'W of San Blas and latitude 35°44'N, or about thirty-five nautical miles off the Big Sur coast, some sixty nautical miles SSW of Monterey. Later in the voyage, he sought to establish another such departure point off the Queen Charlotte Islands by which to plot his return voyage. Entries in this category after 22 July seem to refer to that point's meridian. However, his inability to fix its longitude with any accuracy may have been chiefly responsible for his abandoning efforts to keep detailed navigation tables on the return voyage south.

4. *Latitude by Dead Reckoning*: The degrees and minutes of latitude for the ship's position, as determined by a plot of the ship's position based on direction and distance sailed, unaided by a noon sighting of the sun.

5. *Observed Latitude*: The degrees and minutes of latitude for the ship's position, as determined by a noon sighting of the sun, in addition to a plot of the ship's direction and distance sailed.

6. *Distance from the Meridian*: The degrees and minutes of longitude for the ship's position west of the first departure point's longitude (or meridian) at

16°51′W of San Blas. This seems the case for both the outbound and return segments of the voyage.

7. *Longitude Made*: The degrees and minutes of longitude for the ship's position west of the meridian of Point Pinos at Monterey, which Pérez believed was at longitude 15°55′W of San Blas.

8. *Longitude from San Blas*: The degrees and minutes of longitude for the ship's position west of San Blas, at Pérez's prime (or zero) meridian.

In some instances, other data are included, namely: magnetic compass variations; east longitude from the city of Cádiz (Spain); and bearing, distance and time of the expedition's first landfall in the Queen Charlotte Islands. The various data coincide with the end of each run, or noon of the second date given in the tables.

Hr	Mi	½Mi	Br	Courses	Winds	Drift
1						
2						
3						
4						
5						
6	We got under way at this time					
7	2	0	1-1/2	North	W1/4NW	
8	2	1/2	0			
9	2	0	0			
10	1	1/2	2	N1/4NE	NW1/4W	
11	1	0	0		NW	
12	1	0	0	SW1/4W		
1	1	0	2			
2	1	1/2	0			
3	1	1/2	2			
4	2	0	0			
5	1	1/2	1	SW	WNW	
6	3	0	0			
7	3	0	0			
8	3	0	1			
9	3	0	1			
10	3	1/2	2			
11	3	1/2	2			
12	3	1/2	2			

Hr	Mi	½ Mi	Br	Courses	Winds	Drift
1	3	1/2	2	WSW9°S	NW	1/4
2	3	1/2 2				
3	4	1/2	0			
4	3	1/2	1			
5	3	1/2	2	WSW 1/4	NW1/4W	
6	4	0	2			
7	4	0	2			
8	4	0	0			
9	4	0	0			
10	4	0	0			
11	4	0	0			
12	4	0	0			
1	4	0	0			

17th to Saturday 18 June 1774

Latitude observed 35°44′ N

Longitude of the meridian 16°51′ West

18th to Sunday 19 June 1774

Course to the South	50°West
Total distance	48 leagues

Hr	Mi	½Mi	Br	Courses	Winds	Drift
2	4	0	0			
3	4	0	0			
4	4	0	0			
5	4	0	0	WSW6°	W	
6	3	1/2	1			
7	3	0	0			
8	3	1/2	0			
9	3	1/2	0			
10	3	1/2	0			
11	3	1/2	0			
12	3	1/2	0			

Hr	Mi	½Mi	Br	Courses	Winds	Drift
1	Steering			WSW	NW	6/4
2						
3						
4	2	1/2	2	W1/4SW	NW1/4N	
5	2	1/2				
6	2	1/2				
7	3	0				
8	Steering			WSW	NW1/4N	5/4
9						
10						
11						
12						
1						
2						
3						
4						
5	2	1/2	0	West	NNW	
6	3	0				
7	3	0	3	W1/4SW	NW1/4N	
8	3	1/2	2		NW	
9	3	1/2	2			
10	4	0	0			
11	3	0	0			
12	3	0	0			

Difference in latitude	1°33′S
Departure	1°57′
Observed latitude	34°57′N
Latitude by Dead Reckoning	34°57′N
Distance from the Meridian	1°51′
Longitude made	2°16′W
Longitude from San Blas	18°11′W

19th to Monday 20 June 1774

Course South angle of	38°W
Distance	45 miles
Difference in Latitude	35′S
Departure	28′W
Latitude by Dead Reckoning	N34°23′
Observed Latitude	N34°22′
Distance from the Meridian	2°19′W
Longitude made	2°50′W
Longitude from San Blas	18°45′W

Hr	Mi	½Mi	Br	Courses	Winds	Drift
1	3	1/2	0	W	NNW	1/4
2	4	0	0			
3	3	1/2	0	W1/4SW	NW1/4N	
4	3	1/2	1			
5	5	1/2	0	WSW5°W	NW	
6	5	1/2	0			
7	5	1/2	0	W1/4SW	NW1/4N	
8	4	1/2	0			
9	4	0	2	W5°S		
10	3	0	2			
11	3	0	3	West	NNW	
12	3	0	3			
1	3	0	2	W1/4NW	N1/4NW	
2	3	0	2			
3	3	0	0			
4	2	1/2	2			
5	3	0	1			
6	3	0	2			
7	3	0	0			
8	3	0	0			
9	3	0	1			
10	3	0	0			
11	3	0	0			
12	3	0	1			

Hr	Mi	½M	Br	Courses	Winds	Drift
1	3	1/2	2	W1/4NW	N1/4NW	1/4
2	3	1/2	2			
3	3	1/2	1			
4	3	0	2			
5	3	1/2	0	WNW5°	W	
6	3	1/2	0			
7	3	0	1	WNW	North	
8	2	1/2	1			
9	2	1/2	2			
10	2	1/2	0			
11	2	1/2	0			
12	1	1/2	2	West	NNW	
1	1	1/2	0			
2	1	1/2	0			
3	1	1/2	0			

20th to Tuesday 21 June 1774

According to the observed latitude I found the direction sailed these 24 hours to be South 81°West.

Distance	86 miles
Difference in Latitude	14′S
Departure	85′W
Latitude by Dead Reckoning	34°9′North
Observed Latitude	34°8′North
Distance from the Meridian	3°44′W
Longitude made	4°30′W
Longitude from San Blas	20°25′W

21st to Wednesday 22 June 1774

According to the observed latitude the direction sailed for these 24 hours was found to be West.

Distance	63 miles
Difference in Latitude	00

Hr	Mi	½Mi	Br	Courses	Winds	Drift
4	1	1/2	0			
5	1	1	0			
6	2	2	0			
7	2	2	0			
8	2	2	0			
9	2	2	0	WSW	NW	
10	2	2	1			
11	2	2	2			
12	2	2	0			

Hr	Mi	½Mi	Br	Courses	Winds	Drift
1	2	1/2	3	WSW	NW	15°
2	2	1/2	2			
3	3	0	0			
4	3	1/2	0			
5	3	0	0			
6	3	0	1	W1/4NW	NW1/4N	
7	2	1/2	1			
8	2	1/2	0			
9	2	0	0	W5°SW	NNW	
10	1	0	2			
11	1	0	0			
12	1	0	2			
1	1	1/2	0			
2	1	1/2	0			
3	1	1/2	0			
4	1	0	0			
5	2	0	0	W5°NW		
6	1	1/2	0			
7	1	1/2	0			
8	3	0	0	West		
9	2	0	0			
10	1	1/2	2			
11	1	1/2	2			
12	1	1/2	0			

Hr	Mi	½Mi	Br	Courses	Winds	Drift
1	2	1/2	2	WSW	NW	1/4
2	2	1/2	1			
3	2	1/2	2			

Departure	63′West
Latitude by Dead Reckoning	34°7′North
Observed Latitude	34°7′North
Distance from the Meridian	4°47′West
Longitude made	5°46′West
Longitude from San Blas	21°41′West

22nd to Thursday 23 June 1774

According to the observed latitude the direction steered was found to be South an angle of 65°West.

Distance	49 miles
Difference in Latitude	21′South
Departure	44′West
Latitude by Dead Reckoning	33°45′N
Observed Latitude	33°46′N
Distance from the Meridian	5°31′W
Longitude made	6°38′W
Longitude from San Blas	22°33′West

23rd to Friday 24 June 1774

Hr	Mi	½Mi	Br	Courses	Winds	Drift
4	3	0	0			
5	2	1/2	2	W5°S	NW1/4N	
6	2	1/2	0			
7	1	1/2	0			
8	1	1/2	0			
9	2	0	0	W1/4SW		
10	2	0	0			
11	1	1/2	0			
12	1	1/2	3			
1	2	1/2	0	W1/4NW	N1/4NW	
2	2	1/2	1			
3	2	1/2	0			
4	2	1/2	0			
5	3	1/2	0	WNW	North	
6	2	1/2	0			
7	3	0	2			
8	2	1/2	2			
9	3	0	0	NW	NNE	
10	3	0	0			
11	3	1/2	0			
12	3	1/2	0			

Hr	Mi	½Mi	Br	Courses	Winds	Drift
1	3	1/2	0	NW	NNE	1/4
2	3	0	0			
3	3	1/2	0			
4	3	1/2	0	NW1/4W	N1/4NE	
5	4	0	0			
6	4	0	0			
7	3	1/2	1	NW	NNE	
8	3	0	0			
9	3	0	1		NE	
10	3	0	2			
11	3	1/2	0			
12	3	1/2	2			
1	3	0	2			
2	3	0	0			
3	3	0	0			
4	3	0	0		NE	
5	3	1/2	0			
6	3	0	0			

According to the observed latitude the direction sailed was found to be S an angle of 87°West.

Distance	62 miles
Latitude	S 03′
Departure	62′W
Latitude by Dead Reckoning	33°44′N
Observed Latitude	33°44′N
Distance from the Meridian	6°33′W
Longitude made	7°54′W
Longitude from the Meridian of San Blas	23°49′

24th to Saturday 25 June 1774

According to the observed latitude the completed course sailed was found to be North an angle of 59° West.

For a distance of	84 miles
Difference in Latitude	43′N
Departure	71′West
Latitude by Dead Reckoning	34°28′N

Hr	Mi	½Mi	Br	Courses	Winds	Drift
7	3	0	0			
8	4	0	0			
9	4	0	0			
10	4	0	0			
11	4	0	0			
12	4	1/2	0			

Hr	Mi	½Mi	Br	Courses	Winds	Drift
1	4	1/2	0	NW	NE1/4N	12°
2	4	1/2	2			
3	4	1/2	3			
4	4	0	1/2			
5	5	0	0			
6	4	0	2			
7	4	1/2	1	NW1/4	NE	
8	4	1/2	1		East	
9	4	1/2	2			
10	4	1/2	2		ESE	
11	5	0	0			
12	4	0	0			
1	4	0	1			
2	4	0	0			
3	3	1/2	0			
4	3	0	0			
5	3	1/2	0			
6	3	1/2	2			
7	4	1/2	0			
8	4	1/2	0			
9	4	1/2	0			
10	4	0	1			
11	3	1/2	0			
12	3	0	1			

Hr	Mi	½Mi	Br	Courses	Winds	Drift
1	3	1/2		NW1/4N	SE	
2	2					
3	1	1/2	2			
4	2	0	0			
5	2		1			
6	1					

Observed Latitude	34°26′N
Distance from the Meridien	7°44′W
Longitude made	9°20′W
Longitude from the Meridian of San Blas	25°15′W

25th to Sunday 26 June 1774

According to the observed latitude the completed course sailed was found to be N an angle of 46°West

Distance	102 miles
Difference in Latitude	71′North
Departure	73′West
Latitude by Dead Reckoning	35°40′N
Observed Latitude	35°37′N
Distance from the Meridian	8°57′W
Longitude made	10°5′W
Longitude from San Blas	36°45′W
Variation to the East	05° from North

26th to Monday 27 June 1774

Hr	Mi	½Mi	Br	Courses	Winds	Drift
7			Calm			
8						
9						
10						
11						
12						
1						
2						
3						
4						
5	1			WNW	North	
6	1	1/2				
7	1	1/2				
8	1	1/2	1			
9	1	1/2	2			
10	1	1/2	0			
11	1	1/2	0			
12	1	1/2	0			

Hr	Mi	½Mi	Br	Courses	Winds	Drift
1	1	1/2	0	WNW	North	14°
2	1	1/2	2			
3	1	1/2	1			
4	1	1/2	0			
5	1	1/2	1			
6	1	1/2	1			
7	1	1/2	1	NW6°	NNE	
8	2	1/2	2			
9	2	1/2	3			
10	2	1/2	2			
11	2	1/2	3	WNW	N	
12	3	0	0	NW1/4W	N1/4NE	
1	3	0	0			
2	3	0	0	NW	NNE	
3	2	1/2	0			
4	3					
5	3					
6	2					
7	2					
8	2	1/2	2	NW1/4N	NE1/4N	
9	3	1/2	1			

According to the observed latitude the completed course sailed was found to be North an angle of 45°West

and a Distance of	31 miles
Difference in Latitude	22′N
Departure	22′W
Latitude by Dead Reckoning	36°1′N
Observed Latitude	35°59′N
Distance from the Meridian	9°19′W
Longitude made	11°17′W
Longitude from San Blas	27°12′

27th Tuesday 28 June 1774

According to the observed latitude I found the completed course sailed to be N an angle of 63° West and a distance of 58 miles

Difference in Latitude	27′N
Departure	52′W
Latitude by Dead Reckoning	36°27′N
Observed Latitude	26°26′N

Hr	Mi	½Mi	Br	Courses	Winds	Drift
10	2	1/2	2			
11	3					
12	3	1/2				

Hr	Mi	½Mi	Br	Courses	Winds	Drift
1	3	1/2		NW	NNE	1/4
2	3		1			
3	3					
4	3	1/2		NW1/4N	NE1/4N	
5	3	1/2				
6	3		1			
7	2	1/2	3			
8	3	2				
9	3	0				
10	2	1/2	2			
11	3					
12	3					
1	3					
2	3		1			
3	3		2			
4	3					
5	3	1/2				
6	3	1/2	2			
7	3	1/2	2			
8	3	1/2	2			
9	3	1/2			NE	
10	4	1/2	2		ENE	
11	4	1/2	0			
12	4	1/2	0			

Hr	Mi	½Mi	Br	Courses	Winds	Drift
1	3	1/2	1	NW1/4N	ENE	
2	3	1/2				
3	3	1/2				
4	4		2			
5	4		1			
6	3		2		East	
7	3					
8	3					

Distance from the Meridian	10°11′W
Longitude made	12°22′W
Longitude from the Meridian of San Blas	28°17′W

28th to Wednesday 29 June 1774

According to the distance sailed and the difference in latitude, which I have found by observation, the course sailed was found to be N an angle of 49°W, and for a distance of 82 miles.

Difference in Latitude	54′N
Departure	62′W
Latitude by Dead Reckoning	37°20′N
Observed Latitude	37°20′N
Distance from the Meridian	10°21′W
Longitude made	13°40′W
Longitude from the Meridian of San Blas	29°35′W
Eastern variation from North to East	10°19′

29th to Thursday 30 June 1774

Hr	Mi	½Mi	Br	Courses	Winds	Drift
9	3	1/2			ESE	
10	4		2			
11	4	1/2	2			
12	4	1/2	2			
1	4		3			
2	3	1/2				
3	3	1/2				
4	3	1/2				
5	3	1/2	2			
6	4				ESE	
7	3	1/2	3			
8	2	1/2	0			
9	2	1/2				
10	2		2			
11	1	1/2	2			
12	2					

Hr	Mi	½Mi	Br	Courses	Winds	Drift
1	3			NW1/4N	ESE	
2	3	1/2				
3	3	1/2				
4	3		2			
5	3		2			
6	3	1/2				
7	4		1			
8	3	1/2	1			
9	3	1/2	2			
10	3	1/2				
11	3				SE	
12	2	1/2	1			
1	3					
2	3		1			
3	2	1/2				
4	2		2			
5				Calm		
6						
7	2		2			
8	2					
9	3					
10	2	1/2	2			
11	2	1/2	2			
12	2	1/2	2			

According to the distance and the difference in latitude sailed, the course sailed was found to be N an angle of 25° to the W and a distance of 83 miles

Difference in Latitude	71′N
Departure	35′West
Latitude by Dead Reckoning	38°34′N
Observed Latitude	38°35′N
Distance from the Meridian	10°56′W
Longitude made	14°24′W
Longitude from the Meridian of San Blas	30°19′W

30th to Friday 1 July 1774

According to the distance sailed and the difference in latitude found by dead reckoning, the completed course sailed was found to be N an angle of 28° to the E, and the distance 77 miles.

Difference in Latitude	59′
Departure	31′W
Latitude by Dead Reckoning	39°34′N
Observed Latitude	39°43′N
Distance from the Meridian	11°32′W
Longitude made	15°11′W
Variation of the Compass from the North to the NE	7°42′

Hr	Mi	½Mi	Br	*Courses*	*Winds*	*Drift*
1	3			NW1/4N	SW	
2	2	1/2	3			
3	2					
4	2					
5	Calm					
6						
7						
8						
9						
10						
11						
12						
1						
2						
3						
4						
5				N1/4NW	W1/4NW	
6	1	1/2				
7						
8						
9						
10						
11						
12						

Hr	Mi	½Mi	Br	*Courses*	*Winds*	*Drift*
1						
2						
3				NW1/4W	N1/4NE	
4	1					
5	1					
6	1			NW1/4N	NE	
7	1					
8	1					
9	1	1/2				
10	1	1/2			ENE	
11	1	1/2	2			
12	2	1/2	1			
1	3		1			
2	3		3			
3	3		4			
4	4				East	

1st to Saturday 2 July 1774

According to the distance sailed and the difference in latitude, the completed course sailed was found to be North an angle of 32° W, corrected, a distance of 13 miles

Difference in Latitude	11′N
Departure	7′W
Latitude by Dead Reckoning	39°54′N
Observed Latitude	39°54′N
Distance from the Meridian	11°39′W
Longitude made	15°20′W
Longitude from the Meridian of San Blas	31°15′

2nd to Sunday 3 July 1774

According to the distance sailed and the difference in latitude by observation, the completed course sailed in these 24 hours was found to be N an angle of 37° W,

for a Distance of	50 miles
Difference in Latitude	40′N
Departure	30′E
Latitude by Dead Reckoning	40°33′N

Hr	Mi	½Mi	Br	Courses	Winds	Drift
5	3	1/2	2			
6	3	1/2	2		ESE	
7	3	1/2				
8	3	1/2			SE	
9	2					
10	1	1/2	2		ESE	
11	2	1/2				
12	3					

Hr	Mi	½Mi	Br	Courses	Winds	Drift
1	3	1/2	0	NW1/4N	ESE	
2	3		2			
3	3					
4	3					
5	3					
6	3		1		SE	
7	3		2			
8	3		1			
9	3		2			
10	3		1			
11	3		2			
12	3		1			
1	3		2			
2	3		1			
3	3					
4	3					
5	3					
6	3					
7	3		1			
8	3		1			
9	3					
10	3					
11	3		1			
12	3					

Hr	Mi	½Mi	Br	Courses	Winds	Drift
1	3			NW1/4N	SE	
2	3					
3	3					
4	2	1/2	2			

Observed Latitude	40°34′N
Distance from the Meridian	12°9′W
Longitude made	15°59′
Longitude from San Blas	31°54′W
Longitude East, from the city of Cádiz	134°23′

3rd to Monday 4 July 1774

According to the distance of 77 miles and the course sailed to the North an angle of 31° West, the difference in latitude was found to be 66′N

Departure	40′W
Latitude by Dead Reckoning	41°41′N
Observed Latitude	00 00
Distance from the Meridian	12°49′W
Longitude made	16°53′W
Longitude from the Meridian of San Blas	32°48′W

4th to Tuesday 5 July 1774

Hr	Mi	½Mi	Br	Courses	Winds	Drift
5	2	1/2	2			
6	2	1/2	3			
7	3					
8	3		2			
9	3	1/2	2			
10	3	1/2				
11	3	1/2	1			
12	3	1/2	1			
1	3	1/2				
2	3	1/2	2			
3	4					
4	3	1/2	2			
5	3	1/2	2			
6	3	1/2				
7	3		3			
8	2	1/2				
9	2	1/2	2			
10	2	1/2	1			
11	2		2			
12	2		3			

Hr	Mi	½Mi	Br	Courses	Winds	Drift
1	2	1/2		NW1/4N	SE	
2	2	1/2	2			
3						
4	2	1/2				
5	2	1/2	2			
6	2	1/2				
7	2	1/2				
8	2					
9	2		1			
10	2	1/2				
11	3					
12	3		2			
1	3		3			
2	3		1			
3	3		2			
4	3					
5	3		2			
6	3					
7	3		3			

According to dead reckoning, a distance of 76 miles was sailed on a course N at an angle of 28° west; the difference in latitude was found to be 67′. The other things are as follows:

Departure	36′West
Latitude by Dead Reckoning	42°48′N
Observed Latitude	00 00
Distance from the Meridian	13°25′W
Longitude made	17°41′
Longitude from the Meridian of San Blas	33°36′N

5th to Wednesday 6 July 1774

According to the distance traveled of 67 miles and the course sailed N an angle of 28° W, the completion of the other things by dead reckoning was found to be as follows:

Difference in Latitude	59′N
Departure	31′W
Latitude by Dead Reckoning	43°46′N

Hr	Mi	½Mi	Br	Courses	Winds	Drift
8	3					
9	2	1/2	2			
10	2	1/2				
11	3				SSW	
12	2	1/2				

Hr	Mi	½Mi	Br	Courses	Winds	Drift
1	3			NW1/4N	W1/4SW	1/4
2	2	1/2	1			
3	2	1/2	2			
4	3					
5	2					
6	1					
7	1					
8	1					
9	1					
10	1					
11	1					
12	1					
1	1					
2	1					
3	1					
4	1					
5	1					
6	1					
7	1			ENE	North	
8						
9						
10						
11						
12						

Hr	Mi	½Mi	Br	Courses	Winds	Drift
1						
2						
3						
4				W1/4NW	NE1/4N	
5	1					
6	1					

Observed Latitude	00 00
Distance from the Meridian	13°56′W
Longitude made	18°23′W
Longitude from the Meridian of San Blas	34°18′W

6th to 7 July 1774

According to the distance traveled of 29 miles and the course sailed north N an angle of 13° West, completion of the following things was found to be:

Difference in Latitude	28′N
Departure	6′W
Latitude by Dead Reckoning	44°14′
Observed Latitude	00 00
Distance from the Meridian	14°02′[W]
Longitude made	18°32′W
Longitude from the Meridian of San Blas	34°27′W

7th to Friday 8 July 1774

Hr	Mi	½Mi	Br	Courses	Winds	Drift
7	1					
8	1		2	NW1/4W	N1/4NE	
9	1					
10	1					
11	1		1			
12	1					
1	1					
2	1					
3	1					
4	1					
5	1			NW1/4N	NE	
6	1					
7	1					
8	1					
9	1					
10	1					
11	1					
12	1					

Hr	Mi	½Mi	Br	Courses	Winds	Drift
1	1			NW1/4N	SE	
2	1					
3	1					
4	1					
5	1					
6	1					
7	1					
8	1					
9						
10						
11						
12						
1	1					
2	1					
3	1					
4	1					
5	1					
6	1					
7	1					
8	1					

According to the distance of 19 miles and the course of N an angle of 52° W, the completion of the other things was found to be as follows, according to dead reckoning:

Difference in Latitude	11′N
Departure	15′W
Latitude by Dead Reckoning	44°25′N
Observed Latitude	00 00
Distance from the Meridian	14°17′W
Longitude made	18°52′W
Longitude from the Meridian of San Blas	34°47′W

8th to Saturday 9 July 1774

By having obtained today a good observation I have corrected since Sunday 3 July, which makes 6 days. Each thing was found to be as follows:

Course, angle from N	27°W
Distance	298 miles
Difference in Latitude	264′N
Departure	135′W
Latitude by Dead Reckoning	45°00′N
Observed Latitude	45°00′N

Hr	Mi	½Mi	Br	Courses	Winds	Drift
9	1					
10	1					
11	1					
12	1					

Hr	Mi	½Mi	Br	Courses	Winds	Drift
1	1	1/2		NW1/4N	SE	
2	1	1/2				
3	1	1/2				
4	1	1/2				
5	1	1/2				
6	1	1/2				
7	1	1/2				
8	1	1/2				
9	1	1/2				
10	1	1/2			SSE	
11	1	1/2				
12	1	1/2				
1	2					
2	2					
3	1	1/2	2			
4	1	1/2				
5	1		2	NW		
6	1	1/2	1			
7	1	1/2				
8	1	1/2				
9	1	1/2				
10	1	1/2				
11	2					
12	2					

Hr	Mi	½Mi	Br	Courses	Winds	Drift
1	2			NW	SSE	16°
2	2					
3	1	1/2	2			
4	1	1/2				
5	1		2			
6	1					
7	1					

Distance from the Meridian	14°24′W
Longitude made	19°04′W
Longitude from the Meridian of San Blas	34°59′W

9th to Sunday 10 July 1774

According to the observed latitude the completed course sailed was found to be N an angle of 23° W, corrected, and for a distance of 38 miles

Difference in Latitude	35′N
Departure	15′W
Latitude by Dead Reckoning	45°36′N
Observed Latitude	45°35′N
Distance from the Meridian	14°39′W
Longitude made	19°25′W
Longitude from the Meridian of San Blas	35°20′W

10th to Monday 11 July 1774

Hr	Mi	½Mi	Br	Courses	Winds	Drift
8	1					
9	1	1/2				
10	1	1/2				
11	2					
12	2					
1	3					
2	2	1/2				
3	1	1/2	1			
4	1					
5	1	1/2				
6	2		2			
7	2	1/2				
8	2	1/2	1			
9	3					
10	3					
11	2	1/2				
12	2	1/2				

Hr	Mi	½Mi	Br	Courses	Winds	Drift
1	3	1/2		NW	South	With the variation
2	3	1/2				
3	3	1/2				
4	3	1/2				
5	3	2				
6	3					
7	3		2			
8	3					
9	3		2			
10	3		2			
11	3		2			
12	3		2			
1	3	1/2	2			
2	3	1/2	1			
3	3	1/2				
4	3	1/2				
5	3	1/2		WSW		
6	2	1/2	1			
7	2	1/2	2			
8	2	1/2	2			

According to the observed latitude the completed course sailed was found to be N an angle of 29°W, and a

Distance of	55 miles
Difference in Latitude	8′N
Departure	27′W
Latitude by Dead Reckoning	46°24′N
Observed Latitude	46°23′N
Distance from the Meridian	15°06′W
Longitude made	20°03′W
Longitude from the Meridian of San Blas	35°58′W

11th to Tuesday 12 July 1774

According to what has been determined by dead reckoning, the completed course steered was found to be N an angle of 28°W.

Distance	78 miles
Difference in Latitude	69′N
Departure	37′W
Latitude by Dead Reckoning	47°32′N
Observed Latitude	00 00

Hr	Mi	½Mi	Br	Courses	Winds	Drift
9	3			NW1/4N	N1/4SW	
10	2	1/2				
11	3		3	NNW	West	
12	3					

Hr	Mi	½Mi	Br	Courses	Winds	Drift
1	4	1/2		NNW	West	
2	4	1/2				
3	4	1/2	2			
4	5			North	WNW	
5	5					
6	4	1/2				
7	4	1/2	1			
8	4					
9	3	1/2	2	N1/4NW	W1/4NW	
10	3		2			
11	3		2			
12	3	1/2	1			
1	3		2			
2	3		2			
3	3					
4	3		1	North	WNW	
5	3	1/2	2	N1/4NE	NW1/4W	
6	3			NNE	NW	
7	3					
8	3	1/2	2			
9	3	1/2	2			
10	3	1/2				
11	3		3			
12	3	1/2				

Hr	Mi	½Mi	Br	Courses	Winds	Drift
1	3			North	W1/4NW	2/4
2	3					
3	2	1/2	2			
4	2	1/2				
5	3	1/2				
6	3	1/2				
7	2		2	NW1/4W	SW1/4W	

Distance from the Meridian	15°43′W
Longitude made	20°57′W
Longitude from the Meridian of San Blas	36°52′W

12th to Wednesday 13 July 1774

According to the difference that has resulted from yesterday to today, by the good observation we obtained, the completed course steered was found to be N an angle of 19° East.

Difference in Latitude	80′N
Distance	88 miles
Departure	29′W
Latitude by Dead Reckoning	48°55′[N]
Observed Latitude	48°55′N
Distance from the Meridian	15°14′W
Longitude made	20°44′W
Longitude from the Meridian of San Blas	36°09′[W]

13th to Thurs. 14 July [17]74

Hr	Mi	½Mi	Br	Courses	Winds	Drift
8	1	1/2				
9	2	1/2	1	WNW	SSE	
10	3			NW1/4N		
11	3		2			
12	3		2			
1	3	1/2	2			
2	3	1/2	1			
3	3	1/2	2			
4	3	1/2	3		SW	
5	4		3			
6	4				W1/4SW	
7	3		3			
8	4					
9	3	1/2	2	NW1/4N		
10	4	1/2				
11	4		2	North		
12	3	1/2	2			

Hr	Mi	½Mi	Br	Courses	Winds	Drift
1	4		2	North	W1/4SW	
2	3	1/2	3			
3	3	1/2				
4	4	1/2			SW1/4W	
5	4	1/2				
6	4	1/2				
7	3	1/2	1			
8	3	1/2			SW	
9	3	1/2	2			
10	3	1/2	3		SSW	
11	3	1/2	2		South	
12	3		3			
1	3	1/2	2			
2	3	1/2	3			
3	4					
4	4					
5	4	1/2				
6	4		3		SSW	
7	4		2			
8	4	1/2	3	NE	SW	

According to what has been determined by observation, the completed course sailed was found to be North, corrected.

Distance	81 miles
Difference in Latitude	86′N
Separation	00 —
Latitude by Dead Reckoning	50°21′N
Observed Latitude	50°21′N
Distance from the Meridian	15°14′W
Longitude made	20°14′W
Longitude from the Meridian of San Blas	36°09′W

14th to Friday 15 July 1774

According to the difference that has resulted from yesterday to today, by the observation we have obtained, the completed course steered was found to be running N an angle of 36° East.

Distance	100 miles
Difference in Latitude	81′N
Departure	50′E
Latitude by Dead Reckoning	51°42′N
Observed Latitude	51°42′W

Hr	Mi	½Mi	Br	Courses	Winds	Drift
9	5					
10	5					
11	4		3			
12	4	1/2				

Hr	Mi	½Mi	Br	Courses	Winds	Drift
1	3		1	NE		
2	3		1			
3	3		3			
4	3					
5	3	1/2	2			
6	3	1/2				
7	3	1/2				
8	3	1/2		North		
9	3	1/2	1			
10	3	1/2	1			
11	3	1/2	1			
12	3	1/2	2			
1	3	1/2	3			
2	3					
3	2	1/2	1			
4	2		1	NE		
5	2	1/2	1		SSW	
6	3					
7	3	1/2	1			
8	3	1/2	1			
9	3					
10	3	1/2				
11	3					
12	3					

Hr	Mi	½Mi	Br	Courses	Winds	Drift
1	3			NE	SSW	
2	2	1/2				
3	2		2			
4	2	1/2				
5	2	1/2				
6	2					
7	2					

Distance from the Meridian	14°15′W
Longitude made	18°42′W
Longitude from the Meridian of San Blas	34°37′W

15th to Saturday 16 July 1774

According to the difference in latitude from yesterday to today, as determined by the good observation I obtained today, it was found that the completed course steered was running N an angle of 38° East.

Distance	75 miles
Difference in Latitude	59′N
Separation	46′East
Latitude by Dead Reckoning	52°38′N
Observed Latitude	52°41′N
Distance from the Meridian	13°29′W
Longitude made	17°27′W
Longitude from the Meridian of San Blas	33°22′W

16th to Sunday 17 July 1774

Hr	Mi	½Mi	Br	Courses	Winds	Drift
8	2	1/2				
9	2					
10	2					
11	2					
12	2					
1	2					
2	2					
3	2	1/2				
4	2					
5	2					
6	2					
7	2					
8	2					
9	2					
10	2					
11	2					
12	1	1/2				

Hr	Mi	½Mi	Br	Courses	Winds	[Drift]
1	2			NE	SSW	
2	2					
3	2					
4	1					
5	2					
6	1					
7	1					
8	1					
9	1					
10	1					
11	1					
12	1					
1	1					
2	1			NE1/4E		
3	1					
4	1					
5	1			NE1/4E	SE	
6	1					
7	1				West	
8	1					
[9]						

According to the difference in latitude from yesterday to today, as determined by the good observation I made today, it was found that the completed course sailed was running N an angle of 49° E, a distance of 49 miles

Difference in latitude	32′N
Departure	37′E
Latitude by Dead Reckoning	53°11′N
Observed Latitude	53°13′N
Distance from the Meridian	12°52′W
Longitude made	16°26′W
Longitude from the Meridian of San Blas	32°21′W

17th to Monday 18 July 1774

According to the distance of 27 miles sailed, and being 48 miles from the land, the course was found to be N an angle of 47° E, corrected.

Distance	75 miles
Difference in Latitude	40′N
Departure	55′E
Latitude by Dead Reckoning	54°53′N
Observed Latitude	00 00
Distance from the Meridian	10°15′W
Longitude made	14°48′W

Hr	Mi	½Mi	Br	Courses	Winds	Drift
[10]						
[11]						
[12]						

Hr	Mi	½Mi	Br	Courses	Winds	Drift
1	2		3	SW1/4South	SE1/4South	
2	2		2			
3	2		1			
4	2	1/2				
6	2		3			
7	2		2			
8	2		2			
9	1	1/2	1	SSW5°S	SE1/4E	
10	1	1/2	1			
11	1	1/2	2			
12	1	1/2	3	S6°W	ESE	
1	3		1			
2	2		2			
3	3					
4	3					
5	This distance agrees from 9 at night to 12 noon.					
6						
7						
8						
9						
0						
11						
12						

Hr	Mi	½Mi	Br	Courses	Winds	Drift
1	3			S1/4SW	SE1/4E	2/4
2	2	1/2	2			
3	2	1/2	2			
4	2	1/2	2			
5	2		2			
6	2					
7	2					
8	1	1/2	2	SSE5°S	East	

Longitude from San Blas	31°

At 11:30 we descried the coast to the NE, bearing W, at the nearest distance of 16 leagues.

21st to Friday 22 July 1774

According to the distance of 64 miles that I find myself from the *Cabo de Santa Magdalena*, and the difference of latitude to the S and angle of 45° to the W, corrected

Departure	45′W
Latitude by Dead Reckoning	54°23′N
Observed Latitude	00 00
Distance from the Meridian	12°24′W
Longitude made	16°31′W
Longitude from the Meridian of San Blas	32°26′W

22nd to Saturday 23 July 1774

Hr	Mi	½Mi	Br	Courses	Winds	Drift
9	1			Calm		
10						
11				SSE	W	1/4
12	3					
1	3		2			
2	3		3			
3	3		3			
4	3		1			
5	3		2	ESE	WSW	
6	4	1/2				
7	4	1/2	1			
8	4	1/2	3			
9	4		1	SE1/4S	SSW	
10	4		1			
11	4					
12	4		1			

Hr	Mi	½Mi	Br	Courses	Winds	Drift
1	3			SW1/4W	South1/4SE	2/4
2	3	1/2				
3	3	1/2				
4	3		2	WSW	South	
5	3					
6	3					
7	2	1/2	2			
8	2	1/2	2			
9	2	1/2				
10	2	1/2				
11	2	1/2				
12	2	1/2				
1	2					
2	2			SSE	SW	
3	3	1/2				
4	4				WSW	
5	4					
6	4					
7	4					
8	4	1/2				
9	3	1/2				
10	3	1/2				
11	3	1/2				
12	3	1/2				

According to the observed latitude the completed course sailed was found to be S an angle of 49° East, corrected.

Distance	55 miles
Difference in Latitude	37′South
Departure	29°E
Latitude by Dead Reckoning	53°47′N
Observed Latitude	53°48′N

30th to Sunday 31 July 1774

According to the observed latitude the completed course sailed was found to be 22° W, by correction

Distance	29 miles
Difference in Latitude	27′South
Departure	11′W
Latitude by Dead Reckoning	51°31′N
Observed Latitude	51°35′N
Distance from the Meridian	10°34′W
Longitude made	12°55′W
Longitude from the Meridian of San Blas	28°50′W

Hr	Mi	½Mi	Br	Courses	Winds	Drift
1	2	1/2		SSE	WSW	1/4
2	3	1/2				
3	3	1/2				
4	3	1/2	2			
5	3	1/2	2			
6	3	1/2	1			
7	3	1/2	2		W	
8	3	1/2	2			
9	3	1/2				
10	3	1/2				
11	3	1/2				
12	3	1/2				
1	3	1/2	1			
2	3	1/2	2			
3	3	1/2	1			
4	3	1/2				
5	3	1/2		SE	WNW	
6	3	1/2	1			
7	3		1			
8	3		2			
9	3	1/2	2			
10	3	1/2	2			
11	3		1			
12	3		2			

Hr	Mi	½Mi	Br	Courses	Winds	Drift
1	2	1/2	3	E1/2SE	WNW	
2	2	1/2	1			
3	3		1			
4	3		1			
5	3	1/2				
6	3	1/2				
7	3	1/2		EESE [*sic*]		
8	3	1/2				
9	3	1/2				
10	3	1/2				
11	3	1/2	2			
12	3	1/2	2	SE1/4E		
1	3	1/2	1			
2	3		3			
3	3	1/2	1			
4	3	1/2	2	ESE		

31st to Monday 1 August 1774

According to the latitude observed the completion of the course sailed was found to be South an angle of 28° E, corrected, and for

Distance	85 miles
Difference in Latitude	75′S
Departure	43′E
Latitude by Dead Reckoning	50°20′N
Observed Latitude	50°20′N
Distance from the Meridian	9°54′W
Longitude made	11°46′W
Longitude from San Blas	27°41′W

1st to Tuesday 2 August 1774

According to the latitude observed the completed course sailed was found to be S an angle of 46° East and for a distance 81 miles

Difference in Latitude	56′S
Departure	58′E

Hr	Mi	½Mi	Br	Courses	Winds	Drift
5	3		2			
6	3	1/2	2			
7	3	1/2	2			
8	3	1/2	3		NW	
9	4	1/2				
10	5					
11	4	1/2	1		NNW	
12	4	1/2				

Hr	Mi	½Mi	Br	Courses	Winds	Drift
1	3	1/2				
2	4					
3	3	1/2	2			
4	4					
5	4		1			
6	4	1/2				
7	4	1/2	3			
8	4	1/2	3			
9	3					
10	2	1/2				
11	2		2			
12	2		2			
1	Laid to, prow headed			W1/4SW	NW1/4N	
2						
3						
4				East	North	
5	3	1/2	2			
6	4	1/2				
7	3	1/2	3			
8	3		2	ESE		
9	3		1			
10	3	1/2	3			
11	3		1			
12	3					

Hr	Mi	½Mi	Br	Courses	Winds	Drift
1	3			ESE	NNE	
2	4	1/2		E1/4NE		
3	4	1/2				

Latitude by Dead Reckoning	49°24′N
Observed Latitude	49°24′N
Distance from the Meridian	8°56′W
Longitude made	10°16′W
Longitude from the Meridian of San Blas	26°11′W

2nd to Wednesday 3 August 1774

According to the observed latitude the completed course sailed was found to be South an angle of 64° East, and a distance of 72 miles.

Difference in Latitude	32′S
Departure	65′E
Latitude by Dead Reckoning	48°52′N
Observed Latitude	48°52′N
Distance from the Meridian	7°51′W
Longitude made	8°35′W
Longitude from the Meridian of San Blas	25°30′W

Since I observed 39°43′, which was on July 1, I have had no occasion to learn the compass variation, except today at sunset the variation was found to be 20°34′ from the West by North.

3rd to Thursday 4 August 1774

Hr	Mi	½Mi	Br	Courses	Winds	Drift
4	4	1/2				
5	3	1/2	2			
6	4		2			
7	4		2			
8	4		2			
9	4					
10	4	1/2				
11	4		2	ENE5°E		
12	4		1			
1	3	1/2				
2	3	1/2				
3	3	1/2				
4	3	1/2				
5	3	1/2				
6	3		2			
7	3					
8	3					
9	3	1/2				
10	3					
11	2	1/2				
12	2	1/2				

Hr	Mi	½Mi	Br	Courses	Winds	Drift
1	2			ENE	NNE	With the variation 2/4
2	2					
3	2					
5	2	1/2	2	NE1/4E	N1/4NE	
6	2	1/2	1			
7	2	1/2	2			
8	2					
9	1	1/2	2			
10	1	1/2				
11	1		2			
12	1		2			
1	1	1/2	2	NE	N1/4NW	
2	1	1/2	2			
3	1	1/2	2			
4	2		1			
5	2	1/2				
6	2	1/2	3			

According to the observed latitude the completed course sailed was found to be S an angle of 78° East, corrected.

Distance	89 miles
Difference in Latitude	18′South
Departure	87′East
Latitude by Dead Reckoning	48°35′N
Observed Latitude	48°34′N
Distance from the Meridian	6°24′W
Longitude made	6°28′W
Longitude from the Meridian of San Blas	22°23′W
Variation from West by Northwest	20°34′
Eastern Variation from North by Northwest	22°10′

4th to Friday 5 August 1774

According to the observed latitude and the resulting difference, the completed course sailed was found to be N an angle of 73° East, corrected, and for

Distance	55 miles
Difference in Latitude	16′N
Departure	53′E
Latitude by Dead Reckoning	48°50′N
Observed Latitude	48°50′N

Hr	Mi	½Mi	Br	*Courses*	*Winds*	*Drift*
7	3	1/2				
8	3		2	NE1/4N	NW1/4N	
9	2	1/2	2			
10	2	1/2	2			
11	2	1/2				
12	2	1/2	2			

Distance from the Meridian	5°17′W
Longitude made	5°10′W
Longitude from the Meridian of San Blas	21°05′W
Westerly bearing and variation from West by NW	15°37′

APPENDIX 4

Extract from Joseph Ingraham's Letter
to Esteban José Martínez,
Undated, But Probably Written
Between March and June 1789.[1]

Before I conclude I shall commit to paper agreeable to your desire the account the natives gave us of the First ship that ever came to this [Nootka] sound. I supposed on our arrival here that Captn Cook was the first of any Civiliz'd Nation that ever Visited this sound. Indeed this is the general supposition of most nations, but our stay here enabled us to converse so well with the natives as to put beyond a doubt [that] there was one ship here before him, and this they inadvertantly inform'd us of their own accord. Their account was as follows:

SPANISH STAMP (issued 1967) commemorating Spain's explorations on the Northwest Coast in the late eighteenth century. It depicts the Spanish settlement at Friendly Cove on Nootka Sound (1791).

SPANISH STAMP (issued 1967) commemorating Spain's explorations on the Northwest Coast in the late eighteenth century. It depicts a map of Friendly Cove on Nootka Sound (1791).

About 40 months before Captn Cook's arrival a Ship came into the sound and anchor'd within some rocks on the East side [of] the entrance where she Remain'd 4 Days and Departed.[2] They said she was a larger ship than they had ever seen since; that she was copper'd and had a Copper Head,[3] this I suppose to have been Gilt or painted yellow; that she had a great many guns and men; that the Officers wore Blue lac'd coats;[4] and that most of the men wore Hankerchiefs about their heads. They [the ship's crew] made them presents of Large pearl shells some of which they still have in possession. Besides this they gave them Knives with crooked Blades [and] a black handle. They [the natives] sold them Fish and their Garments, but no furs. When they first saw this ship they said they were exceedingly Terrified and but few of them even ventur'd along side. All the different accounts of this ship agreed in every particular, but one inform'd me he saw from the shore a Small vessel in the offing at a great distance from the Land which had but two masts.[5] From every circumstance I was led to believe at the time this must have been a Spanish ship which immediately account'd to me for the two silver spoons Cap Cook found among the Natives.[6] But your arrival is Key to every thing and clears the conjecture beyond a doubt

SPANISH STAMP (issued 1967) commemorating Spain's explorations on the Northwest Coast in the late eighteenth century. It depicts a 1792 map of the entire west coast of North America, based on survey work initiated by Juan Pérez and carried on by successive Spanish naval officers and seamen.

as you was an officer in the same ship. I have only to add my wish that you bear it on your mind how very sincerely

I am Sir
Your Sincere Friend &
Most Hum[l] Servant
Jos[h] Ingraham

GLOSSARY

BRAZA. Spanish term for fathom. Equivalent to two *varas* (Spanish yards), or five and one-half English feet. An English fathom is six feet.

CODO. Spanish term for cubit. Probably equivalent to one-half *vara*, or about sixteen and one-half English inches.

DEAD RECKONING (*estima*). Determination of a ship's position, without the aid of celestial observation, from the record of courses and distances sailed, allowing for known or estimated drift and leeway when possible.

DEAD-RECKONING LATITUDE (*latitud de estima*). Position north or south of the equator as determined by dead reckoning.

DEPARTURE (*departamento*, or *separación*). Distance due east or west of a meridian (north-south line) coincident with a ship's departure point.

DRIFT (*abatimiento*). Deviation of a ship from its intended course caused by the effects of currents (*abatimiento* also can be used to describe "leeway," or deviation from course caused by winds).

LEAGUE (*legua*). A land measurement in Spanish usage of five thousand *varas*, or about two and two-thirds statute miles. At sea a league (*legua marítima*) equals three nautical miles, or three minutes of latitude. Pérez does not say explicitly which league he intended, but the nautical league (or some approximation thereof) seems most likely.

LEEWAY (*deriva* or *abatimiento*). Deviation of a ship from its intended course caused by winds.

NAUTICAL MILE (*milla marítima*). One minute of latitude, or six thousand and seventy-six English feet.

OBSERVED LATITUDE (*latitud observada*). Position north or south of the equator as determined by a noon observation of the sun's elevation above the horizon.

REEF or REEFING (*rizo*). A part of a sail taken in to reduce, or let out to increase, its size.

STATUTE MILE. Five thousand, two hundred and eighty English feet.

TO HAUL THE WIND (*ceñir el viento*). To sail a ship as close to, or as far into, the wind as its rigging will permit.

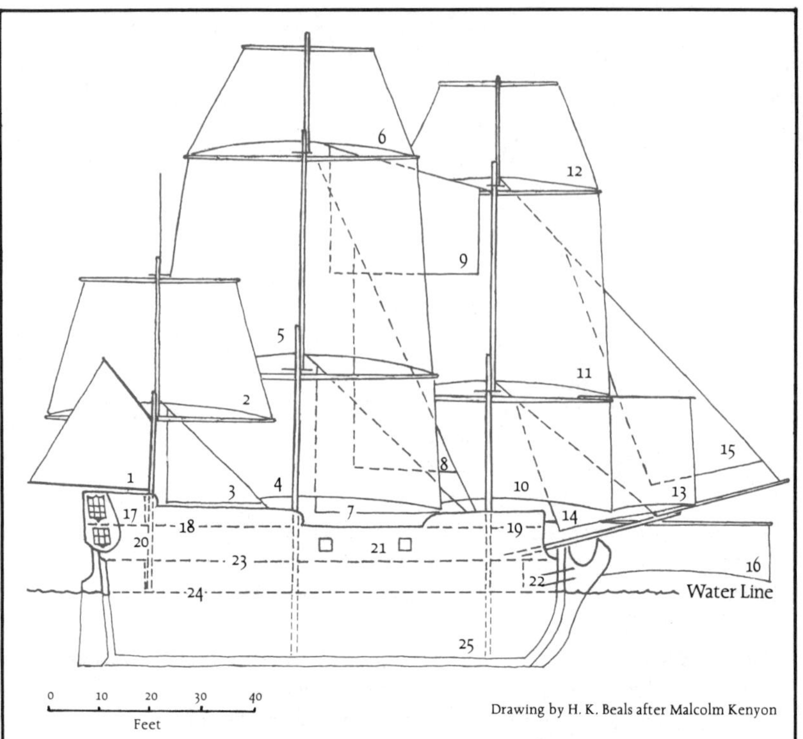

THE FRIGATE SANTIAGO

1. spanker (*mesana*)
2. mizzen topsail (*sobremesana*)
3. mizzen staysail (*vela de estay*)
4. mainsail (*mayor*)
5. main topsail (*gavia*)
6. main-topgallant sail (*juanete mayor*)
7. main staysail (*vela de estay mayor*)
8. main-topmast staysail (*vela de estay de gavia*)
9. flying staysail (*vela de estay volante*)
10. foresail (*trinquete*)
11. fore topsail (*velacho*)
12. fore-topgallant sail (*juanete de proa*)
13. foresail studding sail (*rastrera*)
14. jibsail (*foque*)
15. flying jibsail (*contrafoque*)
16. spritsail (*cebadura*)
17. cabin and topgallant poop
18. quarterdeck
19. forecastle deck
20. berthing
21. waist
22. pantries
23. second deck
24. main deck
25. hold

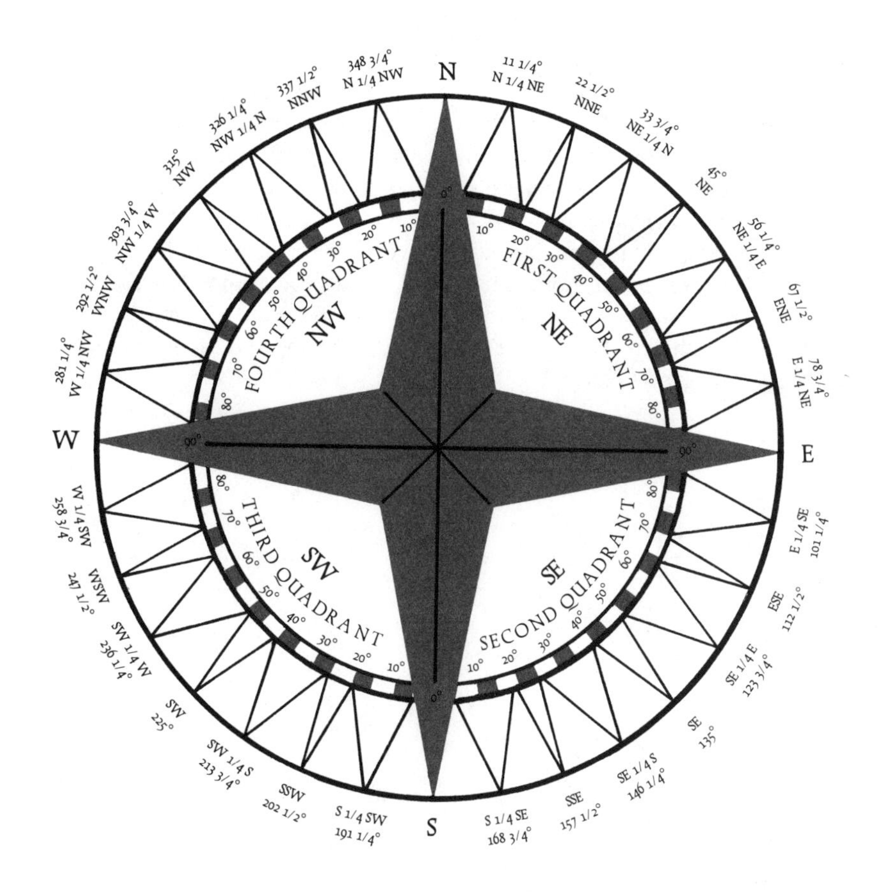

18th CENTURY SPANISH COMPASS DIRECTIONS. Compass bearings and wind directions logged in Pérez's *Diario* and appended Tables are expressed in one of two systems illustrated by this compass rose. One system, stemming from an earlier time before degrees came into use, regarded direction in terms of eight "winds," *los vientos* (N, NE, E, SE, S, SW, W, NW). These were divided into eight "half winds," *los medios vientos* (NNE, ENE, ESE, SSE, SSW, WSW, WNW, NNW): they in turn were divided into sixteen "quarter winds," *las cuartas* (N¼NE, NE¼N, NE¼E, E¼NE, et cetera). The compass rose was thus divided into 32 points, each equivalent to 11 ¼ degrees. A second system (shown in color), of more recent origin and employing degrees, divided the compass rose into four numbered quadrants: First or NE; Second or SE; Third or SW; and Fourth or NW. Each quadrant in turn was divided into 90 degrees, with N and S at zero degrees.

TO LAY TO (*capear* or *hacer capa*). To halt the motion of a ship, usually by turning the bow into the wind and trimming the sails so that they act against each other. Also equivalent to the term "heave to."

TO LIE TO (*pairar* or *estar a la capa*). For a ship to remain comparatively stationary.

TO TACK, VEER, or COME ABOUT (*virar*). To change the course of a ship by either bringing the bow into the wind and falling off to the opposite side (called tacking, *virar para proa*), or by coming about with the stern windward (called veering, *virar para popa*); to sail a zigzag course into the wind is termed beating windward (*virada*).

TO WARP (*espiar*). To move a ship by hauling on a line attached to a fixed object, such as a small anchor (sometimes called a kedge or stream anchor) carried ahead by the ship's boat or launch, and secured on the sea bottom.

VARA. Spanish term for yard. Equivalent to two and three-fourths feet, or thirty-three inches (English).

NOTES

EXPLORING THAT CHILLY, FOG-BOUND COAST

1. Although many direct contacts and much trade between Russians and Alaskan natives occurred before 1774, Aleuts and Eskimos only were involved. *See* Ray, *Eskimos*, pp. 21–38; and Beals, "European and Asian Cultural Materials," pp. 22–57. For Chirikov's encounter, *see* "Exploring" p. 14, this work; and Golder, *Bering's Voyages*, 1:296–97, 315–17, 343–46.

2. For purposes of this discussion, the terms "Pacific Northwest" and "Oregon Country" include British Columbia, Oregon and Washington. Surviving accounts of Drake's voyage off those coasts in 1579 are not only second-hand but often give only sketchy details, and consequently their precise geographical interpretation has been the subject of much controversy. *See*, for example, Hanna, *Lost Harbor*, pp. 4–24; Holmes, "Francis Drake's Course," *The Geographical Bulletin*, 17; Bishop, "Drake's Course in the North Pacific," *British Columbia Historical Quarterly*, 3: 151–82; and Wagner, *Drake's Voyage*, pp. 135–53.

3. This translation is contained in a 1911 master's thesis in the University of California Library entitled "Spanish Exploration of the Pacific Coast by Juan Pérez in 1774," by Margaret Olive Johnson.

4. *See* Cutter, *The California Coast*, pp. 135–278; and Bolton, *Fray Juan Crespi*, pp. 303-66. Copies of Martínez's manuscript account are in Mexico City's Archivo General de la Nación (Historia, 61) and Seville's Archivo General de Indias (V, Guadalajara 516). *See also* Cook, *Flood Tide of Empire*, p. 593.

5. For a more detailed discussion of the Cabrillo-Ferrelo expedition and the search for Quivira, *see* Kelsey, *Juan Rodríguez Cabrillo*, pp. 95–163; Reupsch, ed., *Cabrillo Era*; and Wagner, *Spanish Voyages*, pp. 72–93.

6. The standard work on the Manila–Acapulco trade is Schurz's *Manila Galleon*. For details of the Legazpi expedition and the discovery of the return route from the Philippines to Mexico, *see* Dahlgren, *Discovery of the Hawaiian Islands*, pp. 21–29; Wagner, *Spanish Voyages*, pp. 94–124; and Nowell, "Arellano versus Urdaneta," *Pacific Historical Review*, 31:111–20.

7. Writing in his *Sucesos de las Islas Filipinas* (p. 322), Antonio de Morga, an official in Manila, states that "the galleon crosses . . . as high as a latitude of forty-two degrees north." The evidence stems in part from Asian beeswax and shards of pre-1720 Chinese porcelains (characteristic commodities in the Manila trade) found at Northwest Coast Indian sites. *See*, for example, Beals and Steele, "Chinese Porcelains," *University of Oregon Anthropological Papers*, 23; and Cook, *Flood Tide*, pp. 31-40.

8. *See* Morison, *Admiral of the Ocean Sea*, p. 373; and Reupsch, ed., *Cabrillo Era*, pp. 17-24.

9. The literature on Drake's circumnavigation is far too extensive to cite here. Three useful works covering the entire voyage are: Wagner, *Sir Francis Drake's Voyage Round the World: Its Aims and Achievements*; Wilson, *The World Encompassed: Francis Drake and His Great Voyage*; and Penzer, ed., *The World Encompassed, and Analogous Contemporary Documents Concerning Drake's Circumnavigation of the World*.

10. *See* Hanna, *Lost Harbor*.

11. According to the Gregorian (New Style) calendar, which at that time differed by eleven days from the Julian calendar, the date is 5 April 1579.

12. Penzer, ed., *World Encompassed*, p. 49. This account implies that the "bad bay" was at latitude 48°N. "The Famous Voyage" narrative appearing in Hakluyt's *Principal Navigations*, 8:62–63, fails to mention this bay, and suggests that Drake sailed no higher than latitude 43°N.

13. Penzer, ed., *World Encompassed*, p. 50.

14. For a more detailed discussion of Drake's "bad bay," *see* Aker and von der Porten, *Discovering Portus Novae Albionis*, pp. 6–8; Morison, *European Discovery of America*, pp. 663–69; Bishop, "Drake's Course," *British Columbia Historical Quarterly*, 3:151–82; and Holmes, "Francis Drake's Course."

15. *See* Cook, *Flood Tide*, p. 25.

16. Hakluyt, *Principal Navigations*, 8:242. Ersola made this statement in a letter he tried unsuccessfully to smuggle ashore to warn local Spanish authorities in the Philippines of the English corsair's presence.

17. *See* Gerhard, *Pirates*, p. 94.

18. Details and documents of Unamuno's voyage are in Wagner, *Spanish Voyages*, pp. 139–53. *See also* Beals, *For Honor*, pp. 17–18.

19. Details and documents of Cermeño's voyage are in Wagner, *Spanish Voyages*, pp. 154–67. *See also* Beals, *For Honor*, pp. 19–20.

20. Lok's account of Fuca's claims, as well as correspondence the two men exchanged on the matter, was originally published under the title "A Note Made by Me Michael Lok the Elder, Touching the Strait of Sea, Commonly Called Fretum Anian, in the South Sea, Through the Northwest Passage of Meta Incognito." It appeared in vol. 3 (pp. 849–52) of a four-volume publication issued in London in 1625 by Samuel Purchas called *Hakluytus Posthumus, or Purchas His Pilgrimes: Contayning a History of the World in Sea Voyages and Lands Travells by Englishmen and Others*. Later reprints of this material are also found in Greenhow's *Memoir, Historical and Political*, pp. 207–11, his *History of Oregon and California*, pp. 407–11; and Cook's *Flood Tide*, pp. 539-43.

21. Cook, *Flood Tide*, p. 539.

22. *See*, for example, Mathes, "Apocryphal Tales," *California Historical Quarterly*, 62:1:52–59; Howay, "Early Navigation," *Oregon Historical Quarterly*, 12:2–3; and Bancroft, *History of the Northwest Coast*, 1:43–44.

23. Details and documents of Vizcaíno's voyage are in Wagner, *Spanish Voyages*, pp. 180–272; *See also* Beals, *For Honor*, pp. 20–23.

24. *See* Cook, *Flood Tide*, pp. 34,37,40; Beals, *For Honor*, pp. 25,135 n.69; and Beals and Steele, "Chinese Porcelains," pp. 23–26. Cook places the date of the *Xavier*'s last departure from Manila in January 1707, citing a French source, Jean de Monségur's "Nouveau Mémoires touchant le Mexique ou la Nouvelle Espagne Mémoires," 1707–08. At least two other sources—Dahlgren, *Discovery*, p. 111, and Schurz, *Manila Galleon*, p. 260—say the *Xavier*'s disappearance was in 1705. Dahlgren also points out in a footnote (p. 111 n.2) that Monségur may have been mistaken in identifying the 1707 galleon as the *Xavier*. This possibility is strengthened by the fact that the Manila ships invariably left Manila in midsummer, not in January or midwinter.

25. The *koch* was a single-masted, keeled and decked vessel up to sixty feet in length, twenty feet in width, with a draft of five to six feet. Its single canvas sail was probably square-rigged, limiting its ability to sail into the wind. In other respects, it seems to have been well designed to cope with Arctic navigation. For a detailed description of the *koch*, *see* Fisher, *Voyage of Dezhnev*, pp. 163–67.

26. Details and documents of Dezhnev's voyage are in Fisher, *Voyage of Dezhnev.*

27. The first published account of Dezhnev's voyage appeared in 1742 (almost a century after the fact) in *Notes to the St. Petersburg Gazette.* Although published anonymously, it is known to have been written by Gerhard Friedrich Müller, who was then considered the foremost authority on Siberia. *See* Fisher, *Voyage of Dezhnev*, pp. 5, 23–31. Müller seemed fully confident of the voyage's authenticity, but others have subsequently had their doubts. These stem in large part from the experiences of other navigators who later attempted to sail the same track, only to be turned back by impassable ice. For example, in the summer of 1786, a Russian naval officer and Arctic explorer, Gavriil Sarychev, was unable to penetrate the ice clogging the Arctic waters off the mouth of the Kolyma River. *See* Sarychev, *Voyage of Discovery*, pp. 36–37. But the principal skeptic and detractor of Dezhnev's voyage has been the American historian Frank A. Golder, writing in the early twentieth century. *See* Golder, *Russian Expansion*, pp. 67–95, 267–88. More recently, another American historian, Raymond H. Fisher, has convincingly refuted Golder's position, based substantially on archival research done by Soviet historians since Golder's day. *See* Fisher, *Voyage of Dezhnev*, pp. 277–89.

28. Details and documents of Bering's 1728 voyage are in Golder, *Bering's Voyages*, 1:6–20, and *Russian Expansion*, pp. 133–49.

29. English translations of Peter the Great's orders to Bering are in Golder, *Bering's Voyages*, 1:9–10; and Fisher, *Bering's Voyages*, p. 23.

30. The motives behind the 1728 voyage, as traditionally interpreted, are discussed in Golder, *Russian Expansion*, pp. 133–34 n.296; and Fisher, *Bering's Voyages*, pp. 8-21.

31. *See* Fisher, *Bering's Voyages*, pp. 22–71.

32. Although Bering was unable to catch sight of the Alaskan mainland in 1728, he saw and named St. Lawrence Island, which lies in the midst of the Bering Sea some one hundred and twenty nautical miles south of Bering Strait. *See* Golder, *Bering's Voyages*, 1:18. He also saw one or both of the two Diomede Islands, which lie within the strait midway between Siberia's Cape Dezhneva, the easternmost point of the Chukchi Peninsula, and Alaska's Cape Prince of Wales, the westernmost point of the Seward Peninsula. Four years after Bering's sojourn in those waters, another expedition was organized under cossack leadership to bring the natives of the Chukchi Peninsula under Russian control. Although it was largely unsuccessful in its main mission, one of its ships, the *Sv. Gavriil*, commanded by one Mikhail Gvozdev, visited the Diomede Islands, after which he accidentally discovered another coast to the east. Referred to by the Russians as *Bolshaya Zemlia* (big land), it was almost certainly Alaska's Seward Peninsula. The significance of its discovery was not immediately realized, since it was thought

to be merely one more island and not the North American mainland. Nevertheless, Gvozdev and his men are today credited with being the first Europeans to glimpse the Alaskan mainland. *See* Fisher, *Bering's Voyages*, pp. 168–69; and Golder, *Bering's Voyages*, 1:21–24.

33. Details and documents of the expedition are in Golder's *Russian Expansion*, pp. 165–250, and his *Bering's Voyages*, 1:37–348, and 2:21–249. *See also* Fisher, *Bering's Voyages*, pp. 120–79, concerning the purposes and events of the expedition.

34. These included a French astronomer, Louis Delisle de la Croyère; a German naturalist, Georg Wilhelm Steller; a Russian naturalist, Stepan Krasheninnikov; a German historian-ethnographer, Gerhard Friedrich Müller; and a German botanist, Johan Georg Gmelin. *See* Stejneger, *Steller*, pp. 100–05; and Crownhart-Vaughan, *Explorations of Kamchatka*, pp.xxv–xxxi.

35. As a naturalist whose enthusiasm for observing and collecting was almost boundless, Steller repeatedly quarreled with Bering and his officers about how much of the expedition's time and effort should be devoted to scientific investigation ashore. On one occasion, he claimed, he was told that "I should betake myself on board quickly or they would leave me ashore without waiting for me." *See* Steller's "Journal" in Golder, *Bering's Voyages*, 2:37, 51, 62.

36. This imaginary land mass was named for the Portuguese navigator Juan de Gama, or João da Gama. He supposedly sailed from Macao (a Portuguese-controlled port on the Canton estuary of China's southeast coast) to New Spain by way of the North Pacific in 1589 or 1590. During the voyage, in which he was accompanied by a second ship commanded by one Baltasar Rodríguez, he allegedly encountered land somewhere northeast of Japan. *See* Dahlgren, *Discovery*, pp. 49–50; and Golder, *Bering's Voyages*, 1:3.

37. By his own account, Steller was often at odds with the expedition's officers and crewmen. Had his advice been heeded to continue searching for Gama Land south of the forty-sixth parallel on a course between southeast and east-southeast, the ships might have discovered the Hawaiian Islands after sailing some one thousand, eight hundred nautical miles to the southeast; had they followed a course directly east-southeast, they would have reached Baja California, but not before crossing at least three thousand nautical miles of open ocean. *See* Golder, *Bering's Voyages*, 2:5–6, 22–24.

38. Golder, *Bering's Voyages*, 1:291.

39. *See* Golder, *Bering's Voyages*, 1:292–97, for Chirikov's account. The westward opening of Lisianski Strait, where the tragedy almost certainly occurred, separates Chichagof Island from a much smaller island at its northwest corner named Yakobi Island. The fate of the vanished crewmen remains a mystery. Chirikov

was inclined to think his men had been killed or detained by the natives, but his only supporting evidence was the natives' reluctance to come near the *Sv. Pavel.* It is likely that both boats capsized with the loss of all hands in the treacherous tidal currents near the mouth of Lisianski Strait. *See* Golder, *Bering's Voyages,* 1:311.

40. Golder, *Bering's Voyages,* 1:296. It has been suggested that the words "Agai, Agai" meant "Come here! Come here!" The Tlingit word for this expression is variously spelled "agou" or "hagū." *See* Golder, *Bering's Voyages,* 1:311; Gunther, *Indian Life,* p. 4; Krause, *Tlingit Indians,* p. 241.

41. Esteban José Martínez, second officer and pilot of the *Santiago* in 1774, mistakenly thought that the expedition had reached the vicinity in which Chirikov's fifteen men were lost. He also thought that the fragments of a bayonet and sword held by the Indians at Langara Island were relics from that event thirty-three years earlier. Although Chirikov's men disappeared some two hundred fifty nautical miles to the north of Langara Island, such articles might have been traded over that distance. *See* Pérez, "Diario," p. 78; Martínez, "Extract," p. 102; p. 246 n.5, "Extract," this work.

42. These included Adak, Agattu, Attu, at least one of the Semichi Islands, and the Islands of Four Mountains. *See* Golder, *Bering's Voyages,* 1:302–03, 307.

43. Golder, *Bering's Voyages,* 1:304.

44. Golder, *Bering's Voyages,* 1:348.

45. Golder, *Bering's Voyages,* 2:60.

46. Shumagin's death, apparently from scurvy, was the first among the *Sv. Petr's* crew. *See* Golder, *Bering's Voyages,* 1:142, 336.

47. Golder, *Bering's Voyages,* 1:174–75, 179, 183.

48. Makarova, *Russians,* pp. 37–50.

49. Fisher, *Bering's Voyages,* pp. 144–45.

50. *See* Cook, *Flood Tide,* plates 9 and 10, between pp. 304 and 305.

51. *See* Cook, *Flood Tide,* plate 10, between pp. 304 and 305.

52. *See* Makarova, *Russians,* pp. 146–50.

53. Pérez's biographical details are based on Caster, "Last Days of Don Juan Pérez," *Journal of the West,* 2:15–21; and Thurman, *Naval Department,* pp. 78–79.

54. Cutter, *The California Coast*, pp. 144–45; *see also* p. 240 n.9, this work.

55. The remark is contained in a letter from Serra to Fray Francisco Palóu dated 3 July 1769. *See* Palóu, *Relación histórica*, p. 76.

56. Cutter, *California Coast*, pp. 236, 239.

57. Thurman, *Naval Department*, p. 78. His rank as frigate ensign is qualified here and elsewhere by the Spanish word *graduado*, meaning "brevet" or "acting." *See* Servín, "Instructions," *California Historical Society Quarterly*, 40:238–39; and Pérez, "Diario," p. 58, this work. Palóu (*Relación histórica*, p. 62) also refers to Pérez as a "famous pilot of the Philippines run."

58. Cook, *Flood Tide*, p. 55. But Thurman (*Naval Department*, p. 77) says that few of the pilots serving at San Blas had received formal training in navigation.

59. The newly assigned line officers were Bruno de Hezeta, Manuel Manrique, Fernando Quiros, Juan Manuel de Ayala, Diego Choquet de Yslas, and Juan Francisco de la Bodega y Quadra, all of whom arrived in 1774 and held one of two ranks of lieutenant. Hezeta, Manrique and Quiros were *tenientes de navío*, literally "ship lieutenants," equivalent to senior-grade or first lieutenants; the others were *tenientes de fragata*, "frigate lieutenants," equivalent to junior-grade or second lieutenants. The pilots newly assigned to San Blas were Esteban José Martínez and Francisco Antonio Mourelle, both of whom held the rank of *piloto segundo*, or pilot second class. *See* Thurman, *Naval Department*, pp. 141–43.

60. *See* Cutter, *California Coast*, pp. 143, 211.

61. Caster, "Last Days of Don Juan Pérez," p. 19. Serra wrote a letter to Viceroy Bucareli in Mexico City, dated 9 September 1774, in which he complained of Pérez's change of mind. "Father Palóu and myself," he wrote, "have besought him earnestly that, were it possible, he adhere to his prior determination, in order that the matter of the occupation of San Francisco might be attended to at this time, he has utterly refused to do so, saying that he has various reasons (*varios motivos*) for not delaying and for resolving on a speedy departure." *See* Cutter, *California Coast*, pp. 122–23.

62. *See* Pérez, "Diario . . . 1775," where daily entries are missing for the July dates of 8–9, 9–10, 11–12, 12–13, and 13–14. Pérez began urging a return to Monterey from 19 July until the *Santiago* turned south on 11 August. *See also* Beals, *For Honor*, pp. 79-82.

63. Wagner, "Sierra's Account," *California Historical Quarterly*, 9:239.

64. Bolton, *Fray Juan Crespi*, p.xvii.

65. *See* Vizcaíno's letter to King Philip III of Spain, in Cutter, *California Coast*, pp. 112–17. Wagner (*Spanish Voyages*, pp. 273–82) also discusses the aborted effort to colonize Monterey in the early seventeenth century.

66. Quoted in Thurman, *Naval Department*, p. 53.

67. *See* Thurman, *Naval Department*, pp. 54–55.

68. *See* Thurman, *Naval Department*, pp. 55–56.

69. Details concerning these ships are based on Thurman, *Naval Department*, pp. 57–60, and Kenyon, "Naval Construction," pp. 32, 43, 114–22. Displacement tonnages for the *Concepción* and the *Lauretana* are based on Thurman; similar data for the *Sonora*, *Sinaloa*, *San Carlos*, and *San Antonio* are based on Kenyon.

70. The full names bestowed on these ships by the Jesuits were *La Purísima Concepción de María Santísima* (for the *Concepción*) and *Nuestra Señora de Loreto* (for the *Lauretana*). *See* Palóu, *Historical Memoirs of New California*, 1:17, 20, 21.

71. Details concerning the *San José* are in Thurman, *Naval Department*, pp. 65–66, 95–96, and Kenyon, "Naval Construction," pp. 122–23. According to Kenyon, the vessel had a displacement of about ninety-one tons; he adds that it "was exceptionally broad bottomed—almost rectangular in cross-section."

72. Palóu, *Relación histórica*, p. 58 (author's translation). The third mission was founded in 1771, but named for San Antonio de Padua, not San Buenaventura.

73. Thurman, *Naval Department*, p. 67.

74. Thurman, *Naval Department*, pp. 67–68.

75. The account given here of the launching of the Sacred Expedition's maritime force and Pérez's role in it is based on Palóu, *Relación histórica*, pp. 60–63, and Thurman, *Naval Department*, pp. 67–72.

76. As described by Juan Manuel de Viniegra, a member of Gálvez's inspection party. Quoted in Thurman, *Naval Department*, p. 69.

77. Palóu, *Relación histórica*, p. 61 (author's translation). Thurman (*Naval Department*, p. 71) says that the *San Carlos* left La Paz on 11 January, accompanied by Gálvez; and that together on 14 January the two ships reached Bahía de San Bernabé (presumably the bay at Cabo San Lucas), whence the *San Carlos* departed the next day.

78. Palóu, *Relación historica*, p. 61 (author's translation).

79. Palóu gives a brief account of the voyage in his *Noticias de la Nueva California* (published in English translation under the title *Historical Memoirs of New California*), 2:16–18. Some interpreters (*see*, for example, Caughey, *Pacific Coast*, p. 123) suggest that Pérez sailed too far north because the latitude of San Diego was not accurately known. However, it was not uncommon for mariners approaching anchorages on the California or Northwest coasts to make initial landfall above their destination, so as to have prevailing northwest winds astern when they entered their intended harbor.

80. Palóu says the name was selected because of an incident in which the Indians returned a staff topped with an iron cross that the missionary fathers had forgotten while ashore. *See* Palóu, *Historical Memoirs*, 2:18.

81. Palóu, *Historical Memoirs*, 2:18.

82. Palóu, *Historical Memoirs*, 2:21.

83. That of Fray Juan Crespi. *See* Bolton, *Fray Juan Crespi*, p. 2.

84. Bolton, *Fray Juan Crespi*, p. 2.

85. Smith and Teggart, "Diary of Gaspar de Portolá," *Publications of the Academy of Pacific Coast History*, 1:50–51.

86. Evidently the *San José* had experienced considerable difficulty in getting out of the Gulf of California and onto its northward track to San Diego. Under the command of a pilot named George Storace (or Jorge Estorace), it seems finally to have cleared Cabo San Lucas in mid-June 1770, after which it was never heard from again. Speculation about where the *San José* met its fate has ranged as far north as Nehalem Bay, on the northern Oregon coast. *See* Palóu, *Relación histórica*, p. 63, and *Historical Memoirs*, 2:38–39; Clarke, *Pioneer Days*, 1:175; Thurman, *Naval Department*, pp. 80–81.

87. Palóu, *Historical Memoirs*, 2:276.

88. Cook, *Flood Tide*, p. 62.

89. Palóu, *Historical Memoirs*, 2:277.

90. Caster, "Last Days of Don Juan Pérez," p. 16.

91. Thurman, *Naval Department*, p. 119.

92. According to Kenyon ("Naval Construction," p. 131), the *Santiago* was the largest ship ever built at San Blas. Its capacity of two hundred twenty-five and

one-half tons is expressed in *toneladas de arqueo* ("tons of capacity," which are each equivalent to fifty-three and one-half cubic feet), while in terms of the modern Moorsom ton (one hundred cubic feet) Kenyon calculates the ship's burden at one hundred twenty and one-half tons (p. 131).

93. Thurman, *Naval Department*, p. 120.

94. The full text, in English translation, of Viceroy Bucareli's *Instrucción* (including a model formulary for possession-taking ceremonies) may be found in Servín, "Instructions," pp. 237–48. Article I is on p. 239.

95. Servín, "Instructions," p. 239. Another explanation for this numerical discrepancy may be that the list of officers and crewmen compiled when the *Santiago* left San Blas totals 88 persons. A similar but separate list of passengers (bound for Monterey) fails to mention *padre presidente* Junípero Serra's name among them, although other sources (Palóu, *Relación histórica*, p. 57, for example) confirm his presence aboard the *Santiago*. *See* Appendix 2, "Rosters," pp. 151–57, this work.

96. *See* Appendix 2, "Rosters," pp. 151–57, this work.

97. Servín, "Instructions," p. 239.

98. Servín, "Instructions," p. 242.

99. Servín, "Instructions," pp. 239–40.

100. *See* Thurman, *Naval Department*, pp. 127–32.

101. Servín, "Instructions," p. 240.

102. Servín, "Instructions," p. 240 (Article VIII).

103. An English translation of the formulary is in Servín, "Instructions," pp. 243-46.

104. Servín, "Instructions," p. 241 (Article XIV).

105. Servín, "Instructions," p. 241 (Article XV).

106. Servín, "Instructions," p. 241 (Article XVI).

107. Servín, "Instructions," p. 243 (Article XXX).

108. Servín, "Instructions," p. 241 (Article XVII).

109. Servín, "Instructions," p. 242 (Article XXV).

110. Servín, "Instructions," p. 243 (Article XXXI).

111. *See* Appendix 2, "Rosters," pp. 151–57, this work.

112. Martínez's biographical details are based on Thurman, *Naval Department*, pp. 142–43.

113. For Martínez's role in the 1788 expedition, *see* Wagner, *Cartography*, 1:203; and Thurman, *Naval Department*, pp. 257–76.

114. For Martínez's role in the Nootka Controversy, *see* Cook, *Flood Tide*, pp. 146-79; Thurman, *Naval Department*, pp. 277–300; and Manning, "Nootka Sound Controversy," *American Historical Association, 1904* (1905):279-478.

115. Mugártegui was a 36-year-old Franciscan born at Marquina, in northern Spain. All of his grandparents had Basque names, Mugártegui, Oca, Ormoza and Torrezar, and so there is no doubt that he was Basque. He had accompanied Serra from Mexico City in 1773; if his illness had not prevented him, he was to have remained aboard the *Santiago* throughout its voyage of discovery. Donald Cutter (pers. com., May 1988). *See also* Geiger, *Junípero Serra*, pp. 417–18 n.2, and *Franciscan Missionaries*, pp. 160–61, for brief biographical sketches of Mugártegui.

116. *See* Palóu, *Relación histórica*, p. 159; and Engelhardt, *Mission San Carlos Borromeo*, p. 38.

117. Crespi's biographical details are based on Geiger, *Junípero Serra*, pp. 455–56 n.24, *Franciscan Missionaries in Hispanic California*, pp. 51–55, and Bolton, *Fray Juan Crespi*, pp.xiii-lxiv.

118. Cutter, *California Coast*, pp. 205–07.

119. Peña's biographical details are based on Geiger, *Junípero Serra*, pp. 411–12 n.20, and *Franciscan Missionaries*, pp. 189–91.

120. Cutter, *California Coast*, p. 139.

121. Bolton, *Fray Juan Crespi*. p.xlv.

122. *See* Appendix 2, "Rosters," p. 151, this work.

123. Bancroft, *Northwest Coast*, 1:151.

124. Oak refers to the *Santiago*'s surgeon in 1775 as "Davalos" (Bancroft, *Northwest Coast*, 1: p. 160); Wagner lent his name to this canard by writing (in *Cartography*, 1:p. 175) that "a surgeon by the name of José Davila accompanied the [*Santiago* in 1775]." Hezeta's Diary of the 1775 voyage clearly identifies the ship's surgeon as

Juan Gonzales. *See* Beals, *For Honor*, pp. 76, 79, 143 n.36. For a discussion of Oak's role as Bancroft's expert on Spanish exploration and in the authorship of *History of the Northwest Coast*, *see* Caughey, *Hubert Howe Bancroft*, pp. 104, 261–63.

125. Cutter, *California Coast*, p. 139.

126. Cutter, *California Coast*, p. 141.

127. Pérez, "Diario," p. 99, this work.

128. Pérez, "Diario," p. 99, this work.

129. Pérez, "Diario," p. 82, this work.

130. *See* Cutter, *California Coast*, pp. 167, 245.

131. Pérez, "Diario," p. 62, this work.

132. Pérez, Letter of 3 November 1774, p. 56, this work.

133. Pérez, Letter of 3 November 1774, p. 56, this work. "Leather-jacket" soldiers were so called because of the sleeveless leather-jacket armor they wore to protect them from Indian arrows. *See* Caughey, *History of the Pacific Coast*, p. 120.

134. Greenhow, *History*, p. 116.

135. Wagner, "Fray Benito de la Sierra's Account of the Hezeta Expedition," *California Historical Quarterly*, 9:204.

136. Cook, *Flood Tide*, p. 62.

137. Bancroft, *Northwest Coast*, 1:157. Oak's source for these accusations is to be found in editorial notes that Mourelle appended to his redacted Narrative of the 1774 voyage. Copies of these documents are in The Bancroft Library's collection. For an English translation of his remarks, *see* Mourelle, "Narrative," pp. 116–17, this work. *See also* Hammond, ed., *Manuscript Collections of the Bancroft Library*, 2:72.

138. Bancroft, *Northwest Coast*, 1:157.

139. Thurman, *Naval Department*, p. 139.

140. Quoted from an English translation of Bucareli's letter in Johnson, "Juan Pérez in 1774," pp. 1–4 (translation section).

141. In his letter of 26 November 1774 to Arriaga, Bucareli recommended that Pérez be promoted to lieutenant. However, Pérez died before any action was taken.

142. Pérez, "Diario," p. 73, this work.

143. Pérez, "Letter," p. 52, this work.

144. Pérez, "Diario," p. 79, this work.

145. Pérez, "Diario," pp. 88–89, this work.

146. *See* Wagner, *Cartography*, 1:172–73.

147. Servín, "Instructions," p. 243.

148. Pérez, "Letter," p. 57, this work. *See also* p. 239 n. 11, this work, concerning a recently located map of the expedition's discoveries that appears to have been drawn up soon after the voyage's conclusion.

149. Pérez, "Diario," p. 80, this work.

150. Pérez, "Diario," p. 80, this work.

151. The only indication that Pérez might have seen the Strait of Juan de Fuca is found in comments made by the ship's pilot and second officer, Martínez, long after the fact. Fifteen years later, in 1789, Martínez claimed that he had seen just such an opening there during the 1774 voyage, implying that Pérez had ignored it (*see* Wagner, *Spanish Exploration*, pp. 4–9, which includes a translation of Martínez's claims as they appear in his Diary entry for 5 July 1789; *see also* Greenhow, *History*, p. 116; and Cook, *Flood Tide*, p. 67). Whatever happened, the *Santiago* sailed on, leaving a substantial mystery in its wake as to whether the strait supposedly discovered by Juan de Fuca in 1592 had been found.

152. That the *Santiago* was near the mouth of the Columbia is suggested by the latitude Pérez recorded as he sailed southward along the coast on 13 August 1774. At noon that day, he observed the ship's position at 46°08'N, which is about nine minutes south of Cape Disappointment's latitude. The previous day, Peña had remarked in his diary about noticing "various breaks like bays" (*varias abras como ensenadas*), possibly referring to the entrances of Grays Harbor and Willapa Bay on the coast above the Columbia's mouth (Cutter, *California Coast*, pp. 180–81, 187). But there is no indication that the great river itself was seen.

153. *See* Beals, *For Honor*, pp. 39–43.

154. These two spoons and their purchase by a British seaman from the Nootka natives are described in at least four accounts of James Cook's third voyage. Cook was convinced that the presence of metal articles among the natives was too widespread to be explained by a few direct contacts with Spanish navigators as recently as 1774. He wrote: "I cannot therefore look upon iron as a Mark of the Spaniards having been at this place, and nothing else was seen among them,

except two small silver table Spoons which one of my people purchased of a man who had them hung around his neck as an ornament, there was no mark upon them and the shape was such as I had never seen any like them before" (Beaglehole, ed., *Journals*, 3:321–22; for mention of these spoons by others, *see also* pp. 321 n.1, 1103, 1401). James Burney, a first lieutenant aboard the *Discovery*, thought the spoons were probably Spanish, and it has since come to be generally believed that they were somehow obtained from crewmen of the *Santiago* in 1774. That may well be, but nothing in the voyage's four diaries explicitly mentions spoons' being used in trade. The chaplains do remark, however, that "old clothes" (*trajes viejos*) were traded to the natives, and some spoons may have been left in the pockets of the garments thus exchanged. *See* Pérez, "Diario," pp. 89–90, this work; Martínez, "Viage," Archivo General de la Nación, Ramo: Historia, 61: fojas 458–61; and Cutter, *California Coast*, pp. 176, 181, 254, 259.

155. *See* Bemis, *John Quincy Adams*, pp. 317–40.

156. *See* Pérez, "Diario," pp. 74–75, this work. Elsewhere, in a note that apparently refers to 21 July, Pérez claims to have "observed the sun at midday in latitude N 55 degrees" (p. 81, this work). But his geographic descriptions cast doubt on the likelihood that the *Santiago* actually reached latitude 55°N. The highest latitude recorded in his nautical log is 54°23'N (dead reckoning) for 21–22 July, which is probably closer to the actual northernmost point reached by the expedition.

157. *See* Bemis, *John Quincy Adams*, pp. 523–27.

158. *See* Cutter, *California Coast*, pp. 136–278.

INTRODUCTION TO THE DOCUMENTS

1. Cook (*Flood Tide*, p. 593) cites copies of anonymous accounts at the Museo Naval, Madrid; in the Western Americana Collection of Yale University's Beinecke Rare Book Library, New Haven, Connecticut; and in the Ayer Collection, Newberry Library, Chicago. Listed among The Bancroft Library's H.H. Bancroft Collection is "an anonymous diary on Pérez's voyage, 1774, aboard the *Santiago*, with notes and navigation tables." *See* Hammond, *Manuscript Collections of the Bancroft Library*, 2:72. These so-called "anonymous accounts" are probably versions of two redactions made in 1791 at San Blas by Pilot and Second Lieutenant Francisco Antonio Mourelle, namely a narrative of the entire voyage from San Blas and back; and another document, more or less in the form of a ship's log, referred to as the "Tabla Diaria," also covering the entire voyage from San Blas and back. Both are based mostly, if not wholly, on the Pérez and Martínez *diarios*. For English translations of the Mourelle redactions in The Bancroft Library, *see* pp. 103–33, this work.

2. These inventories are in the Archivo General de la Nación, Mexico City. One, cited and translated by Cutter (*California Coast*, p. 278), is dated 27 December 1774. The other, cited by Gormly, "Early Culture Contact on the Northwest Coast," *Northwest Anthropological Research Notes*, 11:43, is attributed to Francisco Hijosa, San Blas' commissary officer, and dated 3 December 1774.

3. *See* Cutter, *California Coast*, p. 133; and Bolton, *Fray Juan Crespi*, p. 366.

4. Fray Francisco Palóu, a close friend and colleague of Serra, also obtained a copy of Crespi's Diary, which he used in describing the events of the 1774 expedition in his biography of Serra, published at Mexico City in 1787. *See* Palóu, *Relación histórica*, pp. 160–62. Palóu's transcription of Crespi's diary was eventually published in its entirety in *Noticias de la Nueva California* in 1857. *See* Bolton, *Historical Memoirs* 3:147–207, or *Fray Juan Crespi*, pp. 307–66, for an English translation. The most recent (1969) translations (with the Spanish text) of both the Crespi and Peña diaries may be found in Cutter, *California Coast*, pp. 136–278.

5. Johnson, "Spanish Explorations," Introduction, p. 10, notes only that the document she used was "one of the Hearst Transcripts." In her brief bibliography, Introduction p. 1, she cites the "Colección de Documentos Inéditos para la Historia de España," which presumably refers to the source from which her translation was made.

6. Johnson, "Spanish Exploration," p. 9, Introduction.

7. Johnson, "Spanish Exploration," pp. 1–2, Translation.

8. Martínez, Extract from "Diario," p. 101, this work.

9. Martínez, Extract from "Diario," p. 101, this work. *See also* p. 246 n.5, "Extract," this work.

10. Donald Cutter (pers. com., May 1988). *See also* Hammond, *Manuscript Collections*, 2:72.

11. Mourelle's prefatory statement to his compilation of documents (1791) in The Bancroft Library's Hubert Howe Bancroft Collection, M-M403, 3:113 (author's translation).

12. *See* p. 117, this work.

JUAN PÉREZ'S LETTERS TO VICEROY BUCARELI

1. His "Diario" records 33°44'N. *See* p. 171, this work.

2. His "Diario" records 39°54'N. *See* p. 181, this work.

3. His "Diario" records 53°53'N by dead reckoning. *See* p. 197, this work.

4. Based on the detailed descriptions in the *diarios* of Pérez, Martínez, Peña and Crespi, they had arrived at Langara Island, the northernmost of the Queen Charlotte Islands off the coast of what is now British Columbia. *See* pp. 74–75, this work.

5. The Spanish text reads: " . . . *siendo su color blanco, pelo rubio, ojos azules y pardos.*" There is no question that in this context the words *color blanco* refer to the Indians' white complexion. As for the words *pelo rubio*, they can be rendered into English as either "fair hair" or "blond hair." *Ojos azules* can only mean "blue eyes," although the term *pardos* is less precise, variously meaning "brown," "dark," or "colored." Similar mention of white, fair-haired, blue-eyed Indians is also found in Pérez's *Diario* (*see* p. 78, this work), as well as in accounts of the ship's two chaplains, Juan Crespi and Tomás de la Peña. (*See* Cutter, *California Coast*, pp. 161, 237). The veracity of these descriptions has been questioned (*see*, for example, Cutter, *California Coast*, p. 160 n.6), but there are no really compelling reasons to believe that Pérez and the chaplains were mistaken about what they saw and reported. Moreover, their statements are supported in a painting by an artist named Sigismund Bacstrom aboard one of two British fur trading vessels, *Butterworth* or *Three Brothers*, during visits to the Queen Charlotte Islands in September 1792 or spring 1793. In it, a Haida chief named Cunnyha (among other spelling variations) is depicted with blue eyes. *See* Vaughan, *Soft Gold*, pp. 207–08; *see also* Henry, *Early Maritime Artists*, pp. 115–20, and Cole, "Sigismund Bacstrom's Northwest Coast Drawings and as Account of his Curious Career," BC *Studies* 46 (1980), pp. 68–72, for further background concerning Bacstrom's portraits of Cuannyha and other Haidas in the vicinity of Langara Island.

6. The Queen Charlotte Ranges.

7. His Diary records 48°50'N. *See* p. 213, this work.

8. The outer harbor at Nootka Sound, on the west coast of Vancouver Island.

9. The Cape Mendocino of modern charts is in latitude 40°26'N; Pérez was therefore either eighteen minutes too low or he had in mind a different landmark. He may have applied the name "Mendocino" to Punta Gorda (40°15'N), Kings Peak (40°10'N), or Point Delgada (40°02'N). In his Diary (*see* p. 96, this work), he gives the latitude of this cape as 40°09'N, or one minute higher than in this letter. Cabrera Bueno was the author of a navigational handbook published in Manila in 1734, titled *Navegación especulativa y práctica* (Understanding and Practice of Navigation). It was used by pilots of the Manila galleons, who often made landfall on the North American coast at a cape they called Mendocino.

10. His Diary (*see* p. 98, this work) says he anchored temporarily at 4:00 P.M., on Friday, 26 August, "rather far from the regular anchorage"; not until after mass

on the following Sunday (28 August) was the ship actually secured in its customary place.

11. As this work was going to press, information emerged that just such a map had been recently discovered in the U.S. National Archives in Washington, D.C., by James Flatness and John Hebert of the Library of Congress' Geography and Maps Division. Though undated, the map is attributed to Josef Cañizarez, based on the observations and surveys of Juan Pérez in 1774. Preliminary evaluation of the map's authenticity indicates that it was drawn on paper of a kind consistent with the 1770s, and that its cartographic style and handwriting are consistent with other examples of Cañizarez's work. A photographic reproduction of the map appears as the frontis of this work.

PÉREZ'S "DIARIO"

1. *El Príncipe* (also called the *San Antonio*), a supply ship or packetboat launched on the Río Santiago near San Blas, Mexico, in 1768, had arrived three days earlier (on 8 June) with desperately needed supplies for Monterey. Like its sister ship, the *San Carlos* (*El Toisón*), *El Príncipe* was a two-masted vessel of a type called by English-speaking seamen a snow. *See* Kenyon, "Naval Construction," pp. 121–22; and Chapman, "Supply Ships," *Southwestern Historical Quarterly*, 19:190.

2. Punta de Año Nuevo is at the northern extreme of Monterey Bay. Modern charts call it Año Nuevo Point.

3. El Carmelo (called later in the Diary Punta del Carmelo) refers to Carmel Point, on the south side of Carmel Bay.

4. Miguel Costansó (as his name is spelled today) was a royal engineer and cartographer who accompanied the Portolá overland expedition to Monterey, 1769–1770. *See* Bolton, *Fray Juan Crespi*, p. 120; Thurman, *Naval Department*, pp. 56, 62–63; and Fireman, *The Spanish Royal Corps of Engineers*, pp. 93–136.

5. Punta de Pinos marks the south end of Monterey Bay. Today it is called Point Pinos.

6. The correct latitude of Punta de Pinos is 36°38′N.

7. The Sierra de Santa Lucia, a coastal mountain range, stretches southeast of Monterey Bay along the west side of the Salinas Valley. Today it is called the Santa Lucia Range.

8. The two points to which Pérez apparently refers are Punta de Pinos, whose position he gives as latitide 36°30'N, longitude 15°55'W of San Blas, and the ship's own position, at latitude 36°23'N, and longitude 16°39'W of San Blas.

9. Fray Tomás de la Peña and Fray Juan Crespi. Peña's Diary says they also celebrated Pérez's birthday on 24 June. Crespi's account says: " . . . we both celebrated the mass. At the first mass the Captain, the boatswain and two of the sailors, also named Juan, communed." In a footnote to this, Cutter adds that "this was the day of St. John the Baptist, and the birthday—saint's day—of these persons named John [Juan]." *See* Cutter, *California Coast*, pp. 144–45.

10. Probably meaning Drakes Bay.

11. These are some of the signs, or *señas*, by which the Manila galleon pilots knew they were nearing the North American coast. *Aguas malas* refers to a jellyfish-like creature called *Velella velella*, sometimes confused with the Portuguese man-of-war. *See* Ricketts and Calvin, *Pacific Tides*, pp. 226–27; and Schurz, *Manila Galleon*, pp. 238–39.

12. About thc time Pérez recorded his sighting of "ducks and small birds" (*patos y pajaros chicos*), the *Santiago*'s position was logged (noon, 12 July) at latitude 47°32'N and longitude 36°52'W of San Blas. Such a position would have placed it about six hundred fifty nautical miles off the Washington coast. Although Pérez probably overestimated the longitude west, he must have been at least five hundred nautical miles off the coast. The sighting of ducks, or duck-like birds, so far at sea is unusual, although he may have applied the term "duck" to some other type of bird such as the pelagic cormorant (*Phalacrocorax pelagicus*), which is known to feed far offshore at times. *See* Udvardy, *North American Birds*, p. 386.

13. Presumably a reference to Pérez's letter to Viceroy Bucareli accompanying his Diary. *See* "Letter," pp. 50–55, this work.

14. Esteban José Martínez.

15. *Porras* refers to a bulbous-headed, whip-like alga or kelp (*Nereocystis luetkeana*), popularly known as "bull kelp." The sighting of it had long indicated to Manila galleon pilots that land was nearby. *See* Ricketts and Calvin, *Between Pacific Tides*, p. 415; and Schurz, *Manila Galleon*, p. 239.

16. They were in sight of the Queen Charlotte Islands, off the British Columbia coast.

17. *Punta de Santa Margarita* was the name Pérez gave a point of land he discovered at the northernmost end of the Queen Charlotte Islands. Known today as St. Margaret Point, it was one of two on the north side of Langara Island, the other being Langara Point. Both lie at about latitude 54°15½'N, although the former, which is more easterly, is slightly north of the latter.

18. The position Pérez gives for this point is clearly in error, for it is in mid-ocean, some one hundred five nautical miles west of the nearest land (Cape

Augustine, on Dall Island). Other evidence indicates that *Punta de Santa Margarita* was on Langara Island, one hundred twenty-five nautical miles to the southeast. *See* Appendix 1, "Where Pérez Sailed," pp. 141–44, this work.

19. It is difficult to say what these points may have been, except that they were somewhere on the northwestern coast of Graham Island, the largest of the Queen Charlottes, between about 53°40'N and 54°N.

20. Considering that Pérez's vantage was southwest of Langara Island, it is not surprising that he could not be sure of its insularity, since Parry Passage would have been hidden from his view.

21. These were Haida Indians, probably from either (or both) of two villages within Parry Passage called Dadens and Kuista.

22. Presumably the Haidas' customary way of initiating trade.

23. *Farca* evidently refers to a separate piece of wood used to edge or finish the gunwales with splash boards.

24. The "white wool" (*lana blanca*) of which Pérez writes was obtained from small dogs specially bred for the purpose, or from mountain sheep. *See* Drucker, *Indians*, p. 49.

25. The *codo*, or its English equivalent, the cubit, is an ancient form of measurement based on the length of the forearm from the elbow to the tip of the middle finger. Its value has varied, but it seems likely that in Spanish usage it was one-half a *vara*, or about sixteen and one-half English inches. Assuming this value for Pérez's *codo*, the canoe he describes here would have been some thirty-three feet long, and five and one-half feet wide.

26. This "furious current" (*furiosa corriente*) was probably the tidal flow in Dixon Entrance, which is said on modern navagation charts to reach two and one-half knots.

27. The *Santiago* must have been just to the north of Langara Island, in Dixon Entrance.

28. From thirty-four to forty-one feet long, and nearly fourteen feet wide. With these dimensions, the canoe would have been as large, more or less, as the schooner *Sonora*, under the command of Juan Francisco de la Bodega y Quadra in 1775, which measured a little less than thirty-eight feet along its keel and twelve and one-half feet abeam. *See* Kenyon, "Naval Construction," p. 124. The old man who came "representing [himself] to be a king or captain" may have been the same man (or his progenitor) known variously as "Cania," "Cuneah," "Cunnyha," or "Concehaw" to later explorers and fur traders in the vicinity of Langara Island.

See Wagner and Newcombe, "Journal of Don Jacinto Caamaño," *British Columbia Historical Quarterly*, 2:215.

29. *See* Pérez, "Letter," pp. 52, 54, 238 n.5, this work.

30. The presence of iron implements among the Indians was a matter of considerable surprise and interest to the Spanish. *See* Martínez, Extract from "Diario," p. 101; "Exploring," pp. 14, 228 n.41, this work; and Golder, *Bering's Voyages*, 1:293–97, 343–46.

31. Labrets were worn by Haida, Tlingit and Tsimshian women in southeastern Alaska and the Queen Charlotte Islands, and on the mainland coast of British Columbia. Members of the Pérez expedition were the first Europeans to witness and record their use among Northwest Coast Indians. Several theories have been advanced to explain the practice. Anthropologists generally agree that labrets signified their wearers' status in society, but differ as to how they served this purpose. *See* Keddie, "Labrets," *Syesis*, 14:59–80.

32. An inlet (*ensenada*) fitting this description must be on the eastern side of Langara Island. Pérez was probably referring to Explorer Bay, Dibrell Bay, or Egeria Bay; Explorer Bay—the most northerly—seems the most likely.

33. Although Pérez places this point of land (which he named *Santa Margarita*) at latitude 55°N, the description that follows suggests that he was describing Langara Island, the northernmost part of which is no higher than latitude 54° 16′N.

34. This is almost certainly Cloak Bay, on the southwest side of Langara Island. The small island within a cannon shot of the ravine most likely refers to today's Cox Island. The rock described as "about 6 to 8 *varas* high" is probably Harvey Rock, and the "4 or 5 small rocks" with waves breaking over them are probably Swanton Bank, just to the south and southeast.

35. No doubt referring to Langara Rocks, off St. Margaret Point.

36. Cape Knox, on the southwest side of Parry Passage, could be described as "resembling the tongue of a cow."

37. This seems to refer to Gunia Point on the southeast side of Parry Passage, in which case the "two low rocks" would be Douglas and Coneehow rocks.

38. This inlet may have been the easterly entrance to Parry Passage.

39. *Santa María Magdalena* almost certainly refers to Cape Muzon (latitude 54°41'N), the southernmost point of Dall Island on the north side of Dixon En-

trance. Modern charts show a Cape Magdalena at latitude 54°50'N, but this is probably not the cape to which Pérez gave the name.

40. Named *Santa Christina* by Pérez, the island is Forrester Island, which lies about twenty nautical miles west of Dall Island.

41. If true, Pérez's assertion that he had reached latitude 55°N would suggest that the *Santiago* had sailed north through the passage between Dall and Forrester islands. However, his mistaken placement of *Santa Margarita* at latitude 55°N, and his lack of reference to *Santa Christina* (Forrester Island) as bearing south, cast doubt on the likelihood that the *Santiago* had reached a point that far north.

42. Assigning *Cabo de Santa Magdalena* a latitude of 55°24'N would have placed it almost forty-five nautical miles north of Dixon Entrance, which cannot be reconciled with Pérez's visual description of the cape: "said cape makes a mouth with *Punta de Santa Margarita*, forming inside a great enclosure" (*dicho cabo con las punta de Santa Margarita hacen una boca, formando dentro un saco grande*). *See* p. 80, this work. With the sky overcast during most of the *Santiago*'s stay near Dixon Entrance, Pérez was evidently unable to confirm his latitude by observation, and was thus making either estimates or optimistic guesses.

43. These mountains must be those of the Queen Charlotte Ranges, along the west side of Graham Island, for the latitudes Pérez assigns them (54°40' to 53°08'N) are essentially in agreement with this conclusion.

44. Guaynamota appears on a 1768 map of Mexico as a town about forty leagues inland from San Blas, where it is listed as a "Presidio Antigua" (old presidio). On modern maps, the town is apparently that of Huanamota, in the state of Nayarit, some fifty-five miles inland from San Blas. *See* O'Crowly, *New Spain*, with accompanying map, "Nuevo Mapa Geográphico de la America Septentrional, Perteneciente al Virreynato de Mexico."

45. This clearly shows that Pérez's league (*legua*) is equivalent to three miles (*millas*). Although we cannot be certain if he assigned them the same values as modern nautical leagues or miles, the likelihood seems high.

46. The coast and peaks mentioned are on Vancouver Island.

47. Pérez later ("Diario," p. 89, this work) gives the latitude of this locality as 49°30'N, which places it at Nootka Sound on the west coast of Vancouver Island. Although it would be risky to identify *San Lorenzo* as Nootka Sound merely on the strength of the latitude at which he placed it, his description of the anchorage and its surroundings matches Nootka Sound's outer harbor rather well. Moreover, the soundings recorded as the *Santiago* entered the anchorage agree closely with the depths over a submerged rocky ledge extending north-northwesterly

from the Hesquiat Peninsula on the south side of Nootka Sound. *See also* Appendix 1, "Where Pérez Sailed," p. 145, and Appendix 4, "Ingraham Letter," p. 215, this work.

48. Bajo Point, at the north end of Nootka Sound.

49. Pérez's *Punta de Estevan* is probably what modern charts call Estevan Point, at the south end of Nootka Sound. The "inside angle" (*rincón*) probably refers to an indentation on the Hesquiat Peninsula's west coast called Barcaster Bay, lying almost due east of the *Santiago*'s anchorage. When James Cook visited the sound four years later, he named a landmark in the same vicinity as Pérez's *Punta de Estevan* Point Breakers. *See* Beaglehole, *Captain James Cook*, 3:294.

50. This probably refers to the rocks northwest of Estevan Point called on modern charts Pérez Rocks. The breakers Pérez mentions are doubtless the ones that suggested the name Point Breakers to Cook.

51. No doubt these were Nootka Indians, probably from the village of Yuquot at Friendly Cove, on the north side of the channel leading to Nootka's inner harbor, or conceivably from Hesquiat Harbor on the east side of the Hesquiat Peninsula.

52. This is the first mention of the introduction of abalone shells from Monterey among the Northwest Coast Indians. Such shells are described by Robert Heizer as being of the species *Haliotis cracherodii*. *See* Heizer, "Monterey Shells," *Pacific Northwest Quarterly*, 31:399–402.

53. *See* Pérez, "Letter," p. 238 n.5, this work.

54. If Pérez's latitude is correct, this is probably Mount Seghers, on the Hesquiat Peninsula.

55. This latitude places the *Santiago* somewhat south of Cape Flattery (48°23'N). The high snow-covered peak Pérez reported seeing has generally been assumed to be the seventy-nine-hundred foot crest of Mount Olympus.

56. The "island" may have been Cape Flattery and nearby Bahokus Hill, which at a distance sometimes appear to be separated from the mainland. Or Pérez may have perceived the land north of the peak as being separated from it by an arm of the ocean and, thus, part of an island—which in fact it is, namely Vancouver Island. The possibility that it was Tatoosh Island is unlikely, as Pérez seems to have been too far out to have noticed this rather small island off Cape Flattery.

57. In this context it appears that Pérez might be using the name *Santa Rosalía* to refer to the coast in general, but later (in his "Diario" p. 91, this work) he definitely calls it a peak (*cerro*).

58. The hill at San Diego to which Pérez refers is probably Point Loma (Donald Cutter, pers. com., May 1988). The feature he compared it with cannot be identified with certainty, except to say that it was some undefined distance north of 46°08'N, which places it north of the Columbia River estuary, and therefore on the southern Washington coast.

59. Just south of the latitude of Columbia River estuary (Cape Disappointment is at latitude 46°17'N); thus the *Santiago* was then off the Oregon coast.

60. Two nautical miles south of that of Yaquina Bay's mouth, which is at 44°37'N.

61. This point is almost certainly Yaquina Head (latitude 44°41'N), about three nautical miles north of that of Yaquina Bay's mouth, near Newport, Oregon.

62. Pérez was probably heading directly toward Cape Arago.

63. About four and one-half nautical miles south of Port Orford, Oregon, which is at 42°42½'N.

64. This reference to the Chinese is not entirely clear. Presumably Pérez meant that Chinese mariners had found the magnetic variation to be the same on the opposite side of the Pacific as at the latitude of Cape Mendocino.

65. About five and one-half nautical miles south of the Klamath River estuary, on the northern California coast.

66. This latitude is thirty-eight nautical miles south of Cape Mendocino's, which is 40°26'N.

67. Referring, apparently, to his octant.

68. Pérez's observation of Cape Mendocino's latitude was either in error by seventeen minutes, or he applied the name "Cabo Mendocino" to a different landmark. Other possibilities include: Punta Gorda (latitude 40°15'N), Kings Peak (latitude 40°10'N), and Point Delgada (latitude 40°02'N). As for the land or landmark seen in the distance to the southeast, and to which Pérez applied the name San Francisco, it is most likely today's Point Arena (latitude 38°57'N). Whatever the case, it could not have been anywhere near the locality of present-day San Francisco, which would have been at least 90 nautical miles southeasterly of the *Santiago*'s position.

69. The Farallones are islands lying twenty-five to thirty nautical miles west of the Golden Gate.

70. This is probably a reference to Drakes Bay.

EXTRACT FROM MARTÍNEZ'S "DIARIO"

1. This island (whose insularity Martínez doubted) was the one Pérez had named *Punta de Santa Margarita*, now known as Langara.

2. They were then in Dixon Entrance.

3. Labrets. *See* Pérez, "Diario," pp. 79; 242 n.31, this work.

4. *See* Pérez, "Diario," pp. 78, 241 n. 28, this work.

5. Martínez is referring to Aleksei Chirikov, commander of the Russian exploring vessel *Sv. Pavel*, and the loss of two boats and fifteen men from its crew. Chirikov's Journal says that when they made landfall "we were at that time in latitude 55°21'N" (Golder, *Bering's Voyages*, 1:291). The attempted landing to which Martínez refers, however, occurred later when the *Sv. Pavel* was off Lisianski Strait, between Chichagof and Yakobi islands, at latitude 57°50'N. This was nearly two hundred nautical miles north of Dixon Entrance, where the *Santiago* was. *See* Golder, *Bering's Voyages*, 1:290–97, 314–17, 343–45.

MOURELLE'S NARRATIVE

1. The Islas Tres Marías is a chain of four islands, three of which bear the names of biblical Marys, running NW–SE, between sixty and eighty nautical miles southwest of San Blas.

2. On modern charts, the name "Santa Rosa" is applied to the second-most-westerly of the Channel Islands.

3. The island called in this narrative Santa Rosa is today San Miguel; Santa Margarita is Santa Rosa.

4. This small island is evidently what modern charts call the Anacapa Islands (of which there are three).

5. Presumably a hill overlooking the same bay, today called San Pedro at Long Beach, California.

6. The time of this landfall on the west coast of the Queen Charlotte Islands is variously recorded as occurring at 11:00 a.m. and 11:30 a.m. Pérez's narrative statement concerning the events of 17–18 July gives the time as 11:00 a.m. (*see* "Diario," p. 74, this work), while his navigational tables say it was 11:30 a.m. (*see* Appendix 3, p. 203, this work). Mourelle's "Tabla Diaria" also says it was 11:30 a.m. (*see* p. 126, this work).

7. These are apparently Cox Island, Harvey Rock and Swanton Bank, within Cloak Bay on the southwest side of Langara Island, based an the description in Pérez's Diary (*see* "Diario," pp. 79, 242 n.34, this work).

8. Probably Langara Rocks, off St. Margaret Point (*see* "Diario," pp. 79; 242 n.35, this work).

9. Possibly Cape Knox, on the southwest side of Parry Passage (*see* "Diario," pp. 80, 242 n.36, this work).

10. Possibly Gunia Point and Douglas and Coneehow rocks (*see* "Diario," pp. 80, 242 n.37, this work).

11. Cape Muzon, the southernmost point of Dall Island (see "Diario," pp. 80, 242 n.39, this work).

12. This "large gulf" (*crecido seno*) is today called Dixon Entrance.

13. Forrester Island (*see* "Diario," pp. 80, 243 n.40, this work).

14. These were Haida Indians, from villages within Parry Passage (*see* "Diario," pp. 75, 241 n.21, this work).

15. These were labrets (*see* "Diario," pp. 79, 242 n.31, this work).

16. *See* Pérez, "Diario," pp. 78, 241 n. 28, this work.

17. Chirikov's men were actually sent ashore at latitude 57°50'N, nearly two hundred nautical miles north of the place where the bayonet and sword fragments were seen. *See* Pérez, "Diario," pp. 78, 242 n.30, Martínez, "Extract," pp. 102, 246 n.5, this work.

18. The Queen Charlotte Ranges, on the west side of Graham Island.

19. They were in the outer harbor of Nootka Sound.

20. Bajo Point, at the northern extreme of Nootka Sound. Pérez, however, gives the distance to this point as only four leagues (*see* "Diario," p. 88, this work).

21. A point at the southern extreme of Nootka Sound, near or at present-day Estevan Point. Pérez's Diary also mentions an "inside angle" (*rincón*) lying one league eastward of the *Santiago*'s anchorage (*see* "Diario," pp. 88, 244 n.49, this work).

22. *See* Pérez, "Letter," pp. 52, 238 n.5, this work.

23. For this "high mountain covered with snow," *see* Pérez, "Diario," pp. 91, 244 n.55, this work.

24. *See* Pérez, "Diario," pp. 96, 245 n.68, 238 n.9, this work.

25. This apparently should read "9th," not "29th," because a few lines later the former date is given as the time of departure. The "Tabla Diaria" (*see* p. 131, this work) also states that the *Santiago* left Monterey for San Blas on 9 October.

26. This no doubt refers to what modern charts call Punta Eugenia, on the central west coast of Baja California, northwest of which lie two islands, Natividad (or Navidad) and Cedros.

27. Written by Francisco Antonio Mourelle, whose name and the date, 15 February 1791, appear on the prefatory page of the documents that include this Narrative and the "Tabla Diaria."

28. "Entrada de Bucareli" refers to a passage between Baker and Suemez islands (latitude 55°17'N), in the archipelago west of Prince of Wales Island. It was discovered in 1775 by Juan Francisco de la Bodega y Quadra, commander of the schooner *Sonora* (*see* Mourelle, *Voyage of the Sonora*, pp. 48–49).

29. The phrase "they were doing no work" (*no trabajaban*) probably refers to the shipboard procedure called a "day's work," by which the data and events at the end of each nautical day (noon to noon) were transcribed into the individual *diarios* kept by the ship's officers. *See* Hayes, *Log of the Union*, p. 135; or Bowditch, *Practical Navigator*, pp. 260–61, 264–65.

30. For an English translation of the "Tabla Diaria," *see* pp. 118–33, this work.

"TABLA DIARIA"

1 .A point on the north side of Langara Island, probably the St. Margaret Point on modern charts.

2. Cape Muzon, at the south end of Dall Island.

3. Forrester Island, west of Dall Island.

4. This "large gulf" (*crecido seno*) is today called Dixon Entrance.

5. These mountains are probably the Queen Charlotte Ranges, on the west side of Graham Island.

6. For an explanation of the phrase "They did no work," *see* p. 248 n.29, this work.

7. The depths given here of the *Santiago*'s anchorage at *San Lorenzo* (Nootka Sound) are mistakenly stated in *varas* instead of *brazas*. *See* "Diario," p. 88, this work.

WHERE PÉREZ SAILED

1. Wagner, *Cartography*, 1:147.

2. *See* Appendix 3, Navigation Tables, p. 163, this work; and Cutter, *California Coast*, pp. 143, 211.

3. *See* Appendix 3, Navigation Tables, p. 203, this work; and "Diario," p. 74, this work.

4. *See* Cutter, *California Coast*, pp. 154–55, 222–23.

5. The entry in Martínez's Diary for 20–21 July (*see* pp. 100–02, this work) agrees with the captain's that the first contact with natives was made on 19 July and not the following day.

6. *See* "Diario," p. 98, this work.

7. Misjudging the effects of currents can be particularly deceiving for the mariner relying on dead reckoning (*see* Glossary). Pérez had no other means but his dead-reckoning estimates by which to fix his longitude, expressed in this case in degrees and minutes west of San Blas. For a discussion of Bruno de Hezeta's difficulties with dead reckoning and longitude in 1775, *see* Beals, *For Honor*, pp. 103, 109, 112.

8. Pérez, "Diario," p. 75, this work.

9. Pérez, "Diario." p. 75, this work.

10. Pérez, "Diario," p. 79, this work.

11. *See* Martínez, Extract, p. 100, this work.

12. *See* Cutter, *California Coast*, pp. 156–57, 224–25.

13. In a note Pérez entered (possibly later) between his standard entry for 17–18 July and the one for 18–19 July, he says "the said point [*Santa Margarita*] was found to be in latitude 55°N and longitude 14°08' West of Monterey" (p. 74, this work); in another, following the standard entry for 20–21 July, he remarks that "A hill was found in latitude 55 degrees with a fairly high, steep point of land, which juts out seaward from the coast for about three leagues, forming a semicircle with the coast" (p. 79, this work), and, "I observed the sun at midday

[presumably 21 July] in latitude N 55 degrees, the sighted land bearing S, as before" (p. 81, this work).

14. Pérez, "Diario," p. 74, this work.

15. *See* p. 242, ns. 32–38, this work, for the details of Pérez's description, which so closely matches Langara Island and adjacent terrain on Graham Island.

16. Gunther (*Indian Life*, pp. 8–9) places the encounter with natives in twenty-one canoes, which occurred on the afternoon of 20 July, somewhere on Dall Island (which extends north of Dixon Entrance and is roughly bisected by the fifty-fifth parallel). She remarks that the natives were "a segment of these people [Haida] who had migrated across Dixon Entrance." Gormly ("Early Culture Contact," p. 7) believes this encounter was even farther north, at Bucareli Bay, near Cape Bartolome (latitude 55°14'N).

17. Pérez, "Diario," p. 80, this work.

18. Gormly ("Early Culture Contact," p. 7) asserts that "some trading was done near Forrester Island," and Gunther (*Indian Life*, p. 9) makes similar claims for Dall Island, as noted in n.16, above.

19. Pérez, "Diario," p. 87, this work. Both Crespi and Peña say this occurred at 11:00 a.m. on 6 August (*see* Cutter, *California Coast*, pp. 177, 253).

20. Pérez, "Diario," p. 88, this work.

21. Pérez, "Diario," p. 88, this work.

22. Pérez, "Diario," p. 88, this work.

23. *See* Pérez, "Diario," pp. 89, 243, 244 ns.46, 47, this work.

24. Pérez, "Diario," p. 88, this work.

25. Ingraham to Martínez, Ramo: Historia, 65: fojas 52–65, Archivo General de la Nación, Mexico City. Robert Haswell, second officer on the *Lady Washington*, also recorded essentially the same information in a somewhat more abbreviated form in his log of the voyage. *See* Howay, *Voyages of the "Columbia,"* pp. 58–59; and Appendix 4, Extract from Ingraham's Letter to Martínez, p. 215, this work.

26. Wilson [Engstrand] ed. and trans., *Noticias de Nutka*, pp. 65–66.

27. *See* Pérez, "Diario," p. 215, this work.

28. *See* Wagner, *Cartography*, 1:173; and Bancroft, *Northwest Coast*, 1:155–56. Henry Oak, Bancroft's expert on Spanish exploration of the Northwest Coast, wrote the description of Pérez's 1774 voyage in Bancroft's *History of the Northwest Coast* (*see* Caughey, *Hubert Howe Bancroft*, pp. 104, 262–63).

29. *See* Pérez, "Diario," p. 89, this work. I am indebted to Gregory Foster of Galiano Island, British Columbia, for calling to my attention the inference that Pérez's intention may have been to seek an anchorage in or near Hesquiat Harbor for protection from west or northwest winds.

30. Wagner, *Spanish Explorations*, p. 5. *See also* Howay, "Early Navigation," *Oregon Historical Quarterly*, 12:3–5.

31. Pérez, "Diario," p. 90, this work.

32. Pérez, "Diario," p. 90, this work.

33. Pérez, "Diario," p. 93, this work.

EXTRACT FROM INGRAHAM'S LETTER TO MARTÍNEZ

1. The original English-language text and its Spanish translation are in the Archivo General de la Nación, Mexico City, Ramo: Historia, 65: fojas 52–65. Microfilm copies of both documents are also in the manuscript collection of the Oregon Historical Society.

2. James Cook's ships, the *Resolution* and *Discovery*, anchored within Nootka Sound's inner harbor on 31 March 1778. Forty months before their arrival would place the date of the earlier ship's visit some time late in November 1774. Pérez and the *Santiago* were actually there between 7 and 9 August of that same year, or some forty-four months earlier than Cook's visit.

3. While it is not certain that the *Santiago* was coppered, British ships are known to have been copper-sheathed as early as 1764, as in the case of the frigate *Dolphin*, commanded by John Byron. *See* Beaglehole, *Exploration*, p. 195.

4. "Lac'd," a contraction of laced, meaning ornamented with gold braid.

5. This may be a reference to the two-masted schooner *Sonora*, which was off Vancouver Island's west coast in September 1775. *See* Mourelle, *Voyage of the Sonora*, p. 53.

6. Concerning the two spoons, *see* "Exploring," pp. 40; 235 n.154, this work.

BIBLIOGRAPHY

BOOKS

Aker, Raymond, and Edward von der Porten. *Discovering Portus Novae Albionis: Francis Drake's California Harbor*. Palo Alto: Drake Navigators Guild, 1979.

Bancroft, Hubert Howe [Henry L. Oak and Frances F. Victor]. *History of the Northwest Coast*. 2 vols. San Francisco: A.L. Bancroft and Co., 1884.

Bancroft, Hubert Howe [Alfred Bates and Ivan Petroff]. *History of Alaska, 1730–1885*, San Francisco: A.L. Bancroft and Co., 1886.

Beaglehole, J.C. *The Exploration of the Pacific*. 3rd ed. Stanford: Stanford University Press, 1968.

Beaglehole, J.C., ed. *The Journals of Captain James Cook on his Voyages of Discovery*. 3 vols. Cambridge: Hakluyt Society, 1967.

Beals, Herbert K., ed. and trans. *For Honor and Country: The Diary of Bruno de Hezeta*. Portland: Western Imprints, The Press of the Oregon Historical Society, 1985.

Bemis, Samuel Flagg. *John Quincy Adams and the Foundations of American Foreign Policy*. New York: Alfred A. Knopf, 1950.

Bolton, Herbert Eugene. *Fray Juan Crespi, Missionary Explorer on the Pacific Coast, 1769–1774*. New York: AMS Press, 1971.

Bowditch, Nathaniel, *The New American Practical Navigator*, 13th ed. New York: E. & G. Blunt, 1842.

Caughey, John Walton. *History of the Pacific Coast*. Los Angeles: privately published, 1933.

———. *Hubert Howe Bancroft: Historian of the West*. Berkeley and Los Angeles: University of California Press, 1946.

Chapman, Charles Edward. *The Founding of Spanish California: the Northward Expansion of New Spain, 1687–1783*. New York: Macmillan Co., 1916.

Clarke, S.A. *Pioneer Days of Oregon History*, 2 vols. Portland: J.K. Gill Co., 1905.

Cook, Warren L. *Flood Tide of Empire: Spain and the Pacific Northwest, 1543–1819*. New Haven and London: Yale University Press, 1973.

Crownhart-Vaughan, E.A.P., ed. and trans. *Explorations of Kamchatka, North Pacific Scimitar*. Portland: Western Imprints, The Press of the Oregon Historical Society, 1972.

Cutter, Donald C., and George Butler Griffin, eds. and trans. *The California Coast: A Bilingual Edition of Documents from the Sutro Collection*. Norman: University of Oklahoma Press, 1969.

Dahlgren, E.W. *The Discovery of the Hawaiian Islands*. 1916. Reprint. New York: AMS Press, 1977.

Drucker, Philip. *Indians of the Northwest Coast*. Anthropological Handbook 10. New York: American Museum of Natural History and McGraw-Hill Book Co., 1955.

Engelhardt, Fr. Zephyrin, O.F.M. *Mission San Carlos Borromeo (Carmelo), the Father of the Missions*. Ramona, Calif.: Bellena Press, 1973.

Fireman, Janet R. *The Spanish Royal Corps of Engineers in the Western Borderlands, . . . 1764 to 1815*. Glendale, California: The Arthur H. Clark Co., 1977.

Fisher, Raymond H. *Bering's Voyages: Whither and Why*. Seattle and London: University of Washington Press, 1977.

Fisher, Raymond H., ed. *The Voyage of Semen Dezhnev in 1648: Bering's Precursor*. London: Hakluyt Society, 1981.

Gabrielson, Ira N., and Stanley G. Jewett. *Birds of the Pacific Northwest*. New York: Dover Publications, 1970.

Geiger, Maynard J., O.F.M., ed. and trans. *Palóu's Life of Fray Junípero Serra*. Washington, D.C.: Academy of American Franciscan History, 1960.

———. *Franciscan Missionaries in Hispanic California, 1769–1848, A Biographical Dicitionary*. San Marino, Calif.: The Huntington Library, 1969.

Gerhard, Peter. *Pirates on the West Coast of New Spain, 1575–1742*. Glendale: Arthur Clark Co., 1960.

Golder, Frank A. *Bering's Voyages: An Account of the Efforts of the Russians to Determine the Relation of Asia and America*. 2 vols. New York: Octagon Books, 1968.

———. *Russian Expansion on the Pacific, 1641–1850*. 1914. Reprint. Gloucester, Mass.: Peter Smith, 1960.

Greenhow, Robert. *Memoir, Historical and Political, on the Northwest Coast of America, and the Adjacent Territories*. Washington, D.C.: Blair and Rives, Printers, 1840.

———. *History of Oregon and California*. 4th ed. Boston: Freeman and Bolles, 1847.

Gunther, Erna. *Indian Life on the Northwest Coast of North America as seen by the Early Explorers and Fur Traders During the Last Decades of the Eighteenth Century*. Chicago and London: University of Chicago Press, 1972.

Hakluyt, Richard. *The Principal Navigations, Voyages, Traffiques and Discoveries of the English Nation*. 8 vols. London: J.M. Dent and Co., 1910.

Hammond, George P., ed. *A Guide to the Manuscript Collections of the Bancroft Library*. Berkeley and Los Angeles: University of California Press, 1972.

Hanna, Warren L. *Lost Harbor: The Controversy over Drake's California Anchorage*. Berkeley, Los Angeles, and London: University of California Press, 1979.

Hayes, Edmund, ed. *The Log of the Union: John Boit's Remarkable Voyage to the Northwest Coast and Around the World, 1794–1796*. Portland: Western Imprints, The Press of the Oregon Historical Society, 1981.

Henry, John Frazier. *Early Maritime Artists of the Pacific Northwest Coast, 1741–1841.* Seattle and London: University of Washington Press, 1984.

Heizer, Robert F. and John E. Mills. *The Four Ages of Tsurai: A Documentary History of the Indian Village on Trinidad Bay.* Translation of Spanish documents by Donald C. Cutter. Berkeley and Los Angeles: University of California Press, 1952.

Howay, Frederic W., ed. *Voyages of the "Columbia" to the Northwest Coast, 1787–1790 and 1790–1793.* Cambridge, Mass.: Harvard University Press, 1941.

Jane, Cecil, ed. and trans. *A Spanish Voyage to Vancouver and the North-West Coast of America.* 1930. Reprint. New York: Da Capo Press, 1971.

Kelsey, Harry. *Juan Rodríguez Cabrillo.* San Marino, Calif.: Huntington Library, 1986.

Krause, Aurel. *The Tlingit Indians.* Translated by Erna Gunther. Seattle and London: University of Washington Press, 1956.

La Pérouse, Jean François Galaup de. *A Voyage Round the World Performed in the Years 1785, 1786, 1787, 1788 by the "Boussole" and "Astrolabe".* Translated from the French. 2 vols. London: Robinson, Robinson, Edwards, and Payne, 1799.

Makarova, Raisa V. *Russians on the Pacific, 1743–1799.* Edited and translated by Richard A. Pierce and Alton S. Connelly. Kingston. Ontario: Limestone Press, 1975.

Meares, John. *Voyages Made in the Years 1788 and 1789 from China to the North West Coast of America, 1790.* Reprint. New York: Da Capo Press, 1967.

Morga, Antonio de. *Sucesos de las Islas Filipinas.* Edited and translated by J.S. Cummins. Cambridge: Hakluyt Society, 1971.

Morison, Samuel Eliot. *Admiral of the Ocean Sea: A Life of Christopher Columbus.* Boston: Little, Brown and Co., 1942.

———. The European Discovery of America: *The Southern Voyages, 1492–1616.* New York: Oxford University Press, 1974.

Mourelle, Francisco Antonio. *Voyage of the "Sonora" in the Second Bucareli Expedition.* Edited by Thomas C. Russell. Translated by Daines Barrington. San Francisco: Thomas Russell, 1920.

O'Crowley, Pedro Alonso. *A Description of the Kingdom of New Spain.* Edited and translated by Sean Galvin. San Francisco: John Howell Books, 1972.

O'Scanlan, Timoteo. *Diccionario Marítimo Español.* Madrid: La Imprenta Real, 1831. (Reprint: Madrid, Isabel Méndez, 1974).

Palóu, Fray Francisco. *Historical Memoirs of New California.* 4 vols. Edited and translated by Herbert E. Bolton. New York: Russel and Russel, 1966.

———. *Relación historica de la vida y apostólica tareas del venerable padre fray Junípero Serra.* 1787. (Readex Microfilm reprint, 1966).

Penzer, N.M., ed. *The World Encompassed and Analogous Contemporary Documents Concerning Sir Francis Drake's Circumnavigation of the World.* New York: Cooper Square Publishers, 1969.

Ray, Dorothy Jean. *The Eskimos of Bering Strait, 1650–1898.* Seattle and London: University of Washington Press, 1975.

Reupsch, Carl F., ed. *The Cabrillo Era and His Voyage of Discovery.* San Diego: Cabrillo Historical Association, 1982.

Ricketts, Edward F., and Jack Calvin. *Between Pacific Tides.* 4th ed., revised by Joel W. Hedgepeth. Stanford: Stanford University Press, 1969.

Sarychev, Gavril A. *Account of a Voyage of Discovery to the North-east of Siberia, the Frozen Ocean and the North-east Sea.* 1806. Reprint. New York: Da Capo Press, 1969.

Schurz, William Lytle. *The Manila Galleon.* New York: E.P. Dutton & Co., 1959.

Smith, Frances Rand. *The Architectural History of Mission San Carlos Borromeo, California.* Berkeley: California Historical Survey Commission, 1921.

Stejneger, Leonhard. *Georg Wilhelm Steller, the Pioneer of Alaskan Natural History.* Cambridge, Mass.: Harvard University Press, 1936.

Thurman, Michael E. *The Naval Department of San Blas, New Spain's Bastion for Alta California and Nootka, 1767–1798.* Glendale: Arthur H. Clark Co., 1967.

Townsend, John Kirk. *Narrative of a Journey Across the Rocky Mountains to the Columbia River.* Lincoln: University of Nebraska Press, 1978.

Turanzas, José Porrúa, ed. *Relación del viage hecho por las goletas Sutil y Mexicana en el año de 1792 para reconocer el Estrecho de Fuca.* Madrid: Artes Gráficos Minerva, 1958.

Udvardy, Miklos D.F. *The Audubon Society Field Guide to North American Birds, Western Region.* New York: Alfred A. Knopf, 1977.

Vaughan, Thomas, and Bill Holm. *Soft Gold, The Fur Trade and Cultural Exchange on the Northwest Coast of America.* Portland: Press of the Oregon Historical Society, 1982.

Wagner, Henry R. *Sir Francis Drake's Voyage Around the World: Its Aims and Achievements.* San Francisco: John Howell, 1926.

———. *Spanish Voyages to the Northwest Coast of America in the Sixteenth Century.* 1929. Reprint. N. Israel, 1966.

———. *Cartography of the Northwest Coast of America to the Year 1800.* 2 vols. 1937. Reprint. N. Israel, 1968.

———. *Spanish Explorations in the Strait of Juan de Fuca.* 1933. Reprint. New York: AMS Press, 1971.

Wilson, Derek. *The World Encompassed: Francis Drake and His Great Voyage.* New York and London: Harper & Row, 1977.

Wilson [Engstrand], Iris Higbie, ed. and trans. *Noticias de Nutka: An Account of Nootka Sound in 1792 by José Mariano Moziño.* Seattle and London: University of Washington Press, 1970.

ARTICLES

Beals, Herbert K., and Harvey Steele. "Chinese Porcelains from Site 35–TI–1, Netarts Sand Spit, Tillamook County, Oregon." *University of Oregon Anthropological Papers, No. 23*: 1981.

Bishop, R.P. "Drake's Course in the North Pacific." *British Columbia Historical Quarterly* 3 (1963): 151–82.

Caster, James. "The Last Days of Don Juan Pérez, the Mallorcan Mariner." *Journal of the West* 2 (1963): 15–21.

Chapman, Charles E. "The Alta California Supply Ships, 1773–76." *Southwestern Historical Quarterly* 19 (1915): 184–94.

Cole, Douglas. "Sigismund Bacstrom's Northwest Coast Drawings and an Account of his Curious Career." *BC Studies* 46 (1980): 61–86.

Cutter, Donald C. "California Training Ground for Spanish Naval Heroes." *California Historical Quarterly* 40 (1961): 109–22.

———. "Spain and the Oregon Coast." In *The Western Shore: Oregon Country Essays Honoring the American Revolution*. Edited by Thomas Vaughan. Portland: Oregon Historical Society, 1975.

Gormly, Mary. "Early Culture Contact on the Northwest Coast, 1774–1795: Analysis of Spanish Source Material." *Northwest Anthropological Research Notes* 11 (1977): 1–80.

Heizer, Robert F. "The Introduction of Monterey Shells to the Indians of the Northwest Coast." *Pacific Northwest Quarterly* 31 (1940): 399–402.

Holmes, Kenneth L. "Francis Drake's Course in the North Pacific, 1579." *The Geographical Bulletin* 17 (1979).

Howay, Frederic W. "Early Navigators of the Straits of Fuca." *Oregon Historical Quarterly* 12 (1911): 1–32.

Keddie, Grant R. "The Use and Distribution of Labrets on the North Pacific Rim." *Syesis* 14 (1981): 58–80.

MacDonald, George F. "Haida Burial Practices: Three Archaeological Examples: The Gust Island Burial Shelter; The Skungo Cave, North Island; Mass Burials from Tanu." *Mercury Series, Archaeological Survey of Canada*, No. 9, March 1973. National Museum of Man, National Museums of Canada, Ottawa.

Majors, Harry M. "The Hezeta and Bodega Voyage of 1775." *Northwest Discovery* 1 (1980): 208–52.

Manning, William Ray. "The Nootka Sound Controversy." *American Historical Association Annual Report for the Year 1904* (1905): 279–478.

Mathes, W. Michael. "Apocryphal Tales of the Island of California and Straits of Anian." *California Historical Quarterly* 62:1 (1983): 52–59.

Nowell, Charles E. "Arellano versus Urdaneta." *Pacific Historical Review* 31 (1962): 111–20.

Rickard, T.A. "The Use of Iron and Copper by the Indians of British Columbia." *British Columbia Historical Quarterly* 3 (1939): 25–50.

Servín, Manuel P., ed. and trans. "The Instructions of Viceroy Bucareli to Ensign Juan Pérez." *California Historical Quarterly* 40 (1961): 237–48.

Smith, Donald Eugene, and Frederick J. Teggart, eds. and trans. "Diary of Gaspar de Portolá During the California Expedition of 1769–1770." *Publications of the Academy of Pacific Coast History* 1 (1909): 3–59.

Wagner, Henry R. "Creation of Rights of Sovereignty Through Symbolic Acts." *Pacific Historical Review* 7 (1938): 297–326.

Wagner, Henry R., ed. "Fray Benito de la Sierra's Account of the Hezeta Expedition to the Northwest Coast in 1775." *California Historical Society Quarterly* 9 (1930): 201–42.

Wagner, Henry R., and W.A. Newcombe, eds."The Journal of Don Jacinto Caamaño." Translated by Harold Grenfeld. *British Columbia Historical Quarterly* 2 (1938): 189–222, 265–301.

UNPUBLISHED SOURCES

Beals, Herbert K. "The Introduction of European and Asian Cultural Materials on the Alaskan and Northwest Coasts before 1800." Master's thesis, Portland State University, 1983.

Hijosa, Francisco, and Joseph Faustino Ruíz. "Lista de los oficiales, artilleros, marineros, grumetes, cosineros, y pages que tripulan la Fragata de Su Mag. Nombrada Santiago Alias la Nueva Galicia en el presente viage que va hacer al Puerto de Monterrey. . . . San Blas, veinte y ocho de Enero de mil setecientos setenta y quatro." Mexico City. Archivo General de la Nación. Ramo: Historia, 61: fojas 226–28. Microfilm copy in the manuscript collection of the Oregon Historical Society, Portland.

———. "Lista de las Familias que pasan a Monterrey en la Frag[a]ta nombrada Santiago alias la Nueva Galicia al el Alférez de Fragata de la Real Armada Don Juan Pérez. . . . Puerto San Blas a 23 de Enero de 1774." Mexico City. Archivo General de la Nación. Ramo: Historia, 61: fojas 225–26. Microfilm copy in the manuscript collection of the Oregon Historical Society, Portland.

Ingraham, Joseph, to "Don Estephan Joseph Martínez, Commander of His most Catholic Majesties Ship Princessa." English-language text and Spanish translation, n.d., Mexico City. Archivo General de la Nación. Ramo: Historia, 65: fojas 52–65. Microfilm copy in the manuscript collection of the Oregon Historical Society, Portland.

Johnson, Margaret Olive. "Spanish Exploration of the Pacific Coast by Juan Pérez in 1774." Master's thesis, University of California, 1911.

Kenyon, Malcolm H. "Naval Construction and Repair at San Blas, Mexico, 1767–1797." Master's thesis, University of New Mexico, 1965.

Martínez, Esteban José. Extract from "Diario," entry for 20–21 July 1774: "Copia de lo que el segundo Piloto de Departamento de San Blas, Dn Estevan José Martínez, espresa en su diario de Navegación a descubrimientos desde Monte Rey, en las ocurrencias del veinte a el veinte y uno de Julio de este año." Seville. Archivo General de Indias. Estado 38A–3. Microfilm copy in the manuscript collection of the Oregon Historical Society, Portland.

———. "Viage executado por el Piloto Estevan Josef Martínez en la Fragata Sant[iag]o alias la Nueva Galicia propio de S.M., y por orden del Exmo. S[eñ]or Baylio Fr. dn Antonio María Bucareli y Ursúa Virrey Gover[n]or y Capitan G[ene]ral de los Reynas de N[ueva] E[spaña] a los Puertos de Sn. Diego: y Monterrey y desde este a la Altura de 55 Grados Norte según y como en el se expresa Haviendo Salido del Puerto de Sn. Blas (que se halla en 21 grados 21 min[uto]s de latitud Norte) en 24 días del Mes de Henero de 1774." Mexico City. Ramo: Historia 61: fojas 385–474. Archivo General de la Nación. Microfilm copy in the manuscript collection of the Oregon Historical Society, Portland.

Mourelle, Francisco Antonio, ed, "Viage del Puerto de S. Blas a Monterrey y costa septentrional de California por el Alférez de Fragata D. Juan Pérez," 15 February 1791. A redacted narrative of the *Santiago*'s voyage, 25 January–5 November 1774. Berkeley. The Bancroft Library. H.H. Bancroft Collection. M–M401.5.

———. "Tablas de las latitudes, longitudes, variaciones y vientros observados en dicha viage," 15 February 1791. A redacted log of the *Santiago*'s voyage, 25 January–5 November 1774. Also called "Tabla Diaria." Berkeley. The Bancroft Library. H.H. Bancroft Collection. M–M401.5.

Pérez, Juan. "Continuación del Diario que formó el Alférez graduado de Fragata Don Juan Pérez, Primer Piloto del Departamento de San Blas, con la titulada Santiago, alias la Nueva Galicia de su mando, que comprehende su salida de Monterrey a explorar la Costa Septentrional, y su regreso a esta propio Puerto en 26 de Agosto de este año de 1774." Seville. Archivo General de Indias. Estado 38A–3. Microfilm copy in the manuscript collection of the Oregon Historical Society, Portland.

———, to Bucareli, 31 August and 3 November 1774. Seville. Archivo General de Indias. Estado 38A–3. Microfilm copies in the manuscript collection of the Oregon Historical Society, Portland.

———. "Diario de la Navegación, que con el favor de Dios comprehende hacer el Alférez de Fragata de la R[ea]l Armada, y primer Piloto de la Fragata de S.M. nombrada Santiago, alias la Nueva Galicia, en el tercero Descubrimiento, y sexto Viage en la Costa Occidental de la California, comprehendido en el Mar del Sur Septentrional de este nuebo Reyno en el Año de 1775." Mexico City. Historia, tomo 324: numero 6. Archivo General de la Nación. Microfilm copy in the manuscript collection, Oregon Historical Society, Portland.

INDEX

North Pacific Studies Series

No. 1 *Explorations of Kamchatka: North Pacific Scimitar* [*Opisanie zemli Kamchatki*].
By Stepan P. Krasheninnikov.
Translated and edited by E. A. P. Crownhart-Vaughan.
1972

No. 2 *Colonial Russian America: Kyrill T. Khlebnikov's Reports, 1817–1832.*
Translated and edited by Basil Dmytryshyn
and E. A. P. Crownhart-Vaughan.
1976

No. 3 *Voyages of Enlightenment: Malaspina on the Northwest Coast, 1791/1792.*
By Thomas Vaughan, E. A. P. Crownhart-Vaughan and
Mercedes Palau de Iglesias.
1977

No. 4 *The End of Russian America: Captain P. N. Golovin's Last Report, 1862.*
Translated with introduction and notes by Basil Dmytryshyn and
E. A. P. Crownhart-Vaughan.
1979

No. 5 *Civil and Savage Encounters: The Worldly Travel Letters of an Imperial Russian Navy Officer, 1860–61.*
By Pavel N. Golovin.
Translated and annotated by Basil Dmytryshyn and
E. A. P. Crownhart-Vaughan, introduction by Thomas Vaughan.
1983

No. 6 *Log of the* Union: *John Boit's Remarkable Voyage to the Northwest Coast and Around the World, 1794–1796.*
Edited by Edmund Hayes, foreword by Thomas Vaughan.
1981

No. 7 *For Honor and Country: The Diary of Bruno de Hezeta.*
Translated and edited by Herbert K. Beals,
foreword by Thomas Vaughan.
1985

No. 8 *The Wreck of the Sv.* Nikolai: *Two Narratives of the First Russian Expedition to the Oregon Country, 1808–1810.*
Edited with introduction and notes by Kenneth N. Owens.
Translated by Alton S. Donnelly.
1985

No. 9 *Russia's Conquest of Siberia, 1558–1700:* A *Documentary Record.*
Edited and translated by Basil Dmytryshyn, E. A. P. Crownhart-Vaughan and Thomas Vaughan.
To Siberia and Russian America: Three Centuries of Russian Eastward Expansion, 1558–1867. Volume one.
1985

No. 10 *Russian Penetration of the* North *Pacific Ocean, 1700–1797:* A *Documentary Record.*
Edited and translated by Basil Dmytryshyn, E. A. P. Crownhart-Vaughan and Thomas Vaughan.
To Siberia and Russian America: Three Centuries of Russian Eastward Expansion, 1558–1867. Volume two.
1988

No. 11 *The Russian American Colonies, 1798–1867:* A *Documentary Record.*
Edited and translated by Basil Dmytryshyn, E. A. P. Crownhart-Vaughan and Thomas Vaughan.
To Siberia and Russian America: Three Centuries of Russian Eastward Expansion, 1558–1867. Volume three.
1989

COLOPHON

The text and display headings of *Juan Pérez on the Northwest Coast* were set in Cartier, a face originally designed by Carl Dair. Cartier shares design associations of both Geralde and Transitional type faces. Its many special characteristics include an absence of italic capitals and a capital Q with a detached lower stroke.

The typesetting was done by Graphic Composition, Inc., Athens, Georgia.

This volume is printed on sixty-pound Glatfelter B-16, an acid-free paper.

Printing (black and PMS 199 as the second color) was done by Malloy Lithographing, Inc., Ann Arbor, Michigan. John H. Dekker & Sons, also of Ann Arbor, bound the books.

The ornamental borders used throughout are Monotype 280 (18 points), supplied by Harold Berliner's Type Foundry, Nevada City, California.

Christine Rains prepared the two-color maps.

Juan Pérez on the Northwest Coast was designed and produced by the Oregon Historical Society Press.

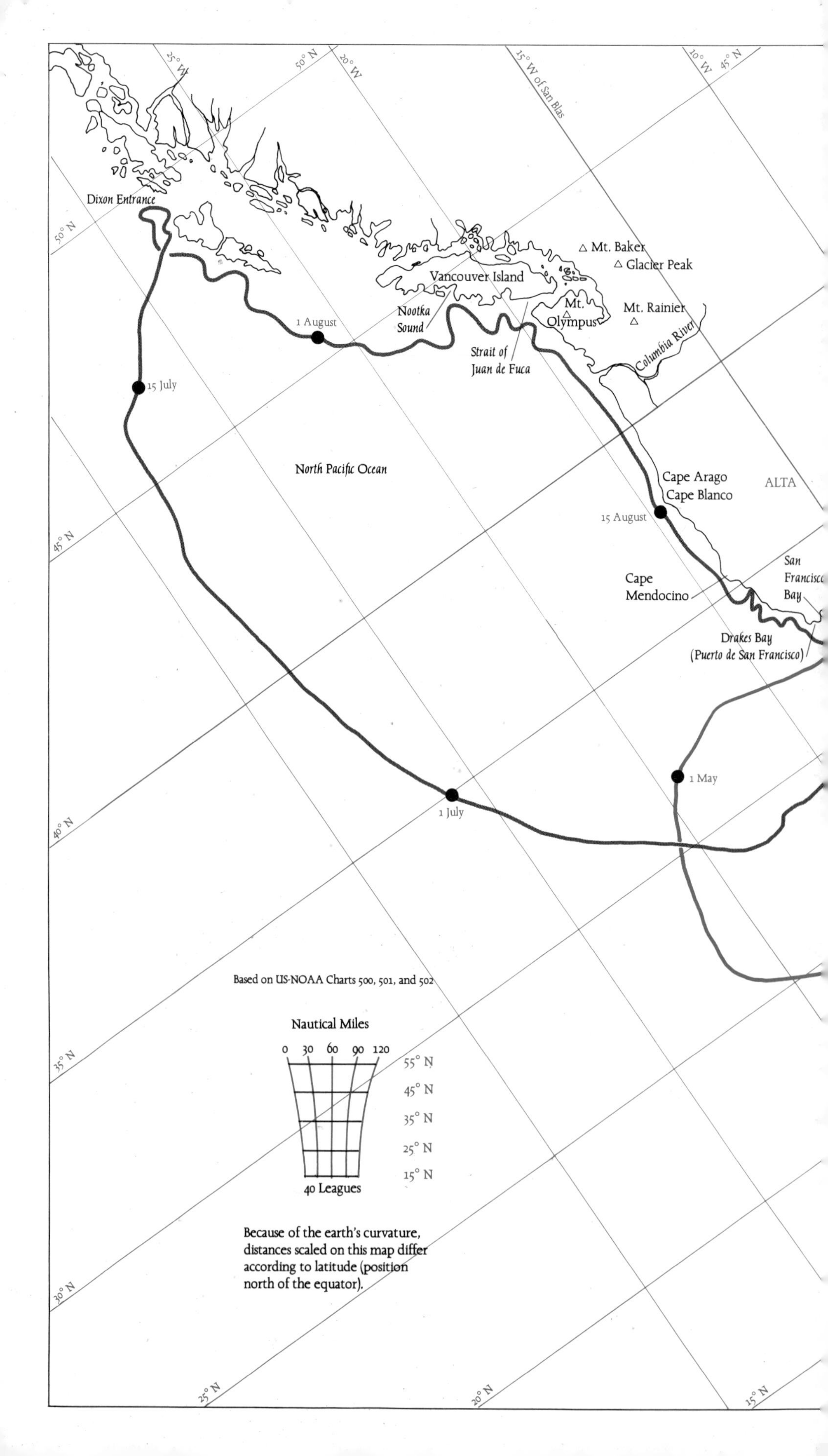

25° W
50° N
20° W
15° W of San Blas
10° W
45° N
Dixon Entrance
50° N
Mt. Baker
Glacier Peak
Vancouver Island
Nootka Sound
1 August
Mt. Olympus
Mt. Rainier
Strait of Juan de Fuca
Columbia River
15 July
North Pacific Ocean
Cape Arago
Cape Blanco
ALTA
15 August
45° N
Cape Mendocino
San Francisco Bay
Drakes Bay (Puerto de San Francisco)
1 May
1 July
40° N
Based on US-NOAA Charts 500, 501, and 502
Nautical Miles
0 30 60 90 120
55° N
45° N
35° N
25° N
15° N
40 Leagues
35° N
Because of the earth's curvature, distances scaled on this map differ according to latitude (position north of the equator).
30° N
25° N
20° N
15° N